THE LANDLORD'S LEGAL GUIDE

IN ILLINOIS

Diana Brodman Summers
Mark Warda
Attorneys at Law

SPHINX® PUBLISHING
AN IMPRINT OF SOURCEBOOKS, INC.®
NAPERVILLE, ILLINOIS
www.SphinxLegal.com

First Edition, 2002

Published by: **Sphinx® Publishing, An Imprint of Sourcebooks, Inc.®**

<u>Naperville Office</u>
P.O. Box 4410
Naperville, Illinois 60567-4410
630-961-3900
Fax: 630-961-2168
www.sourcebooks.com
www.SphinxLegal.com

This publication is designed to provide accurate and authoritative information in regard to the subject matter covered. It is sold with the understanding that the publisher is not engaged in rendering legal, accounting, or other professional service. If legal advice or other expert assistance is required, the services of a competent professional person should be sought.

From a Declaration of Principles Jointly Adopted by a Committee of the American Bar Association and a Committee of Publishers and Associations

This product is not a substitute for legal advice.

Disclaimer required by Texas statutes.

Library of Congress Cataloging-in-Publication Data
Summers, Diana Brodman.
    The landlord's legal guide in Illinois / by Diana Brodman Summers and Mark Warda.-- 1st ed.
        p. cm.
Includes index.
    ISBN 1-57248-252-4
    1. Landlord and tenant--Illinois--Popular works. 2. Leases--Illinois--Popular works. I. Warda, Mark. II. Title.
    KFI1317.Z9 S86 2002
    346.77304'34--dc21
                                                            2002012179

CONTENTS

USING SELF-HELP LAW BOOKS

Before using a self-help law book, you should realize the advantages and disadvantages of doing your own legal work and understand the challenges and diligence that this requires.

THE GROWING TREND

Rest assured that you won't be the first or only person handling your own legal matter. For example, in some states, more than seventy-five percent of divorces and other cases have at least one party representing him or herself. Because of the high cost of legal services, this is a major trend and many courts are struggling to make it easier for people to represent themselves. However, some courts are not happy with people who do not use attorneys and refuse to help them in any way. For some, the attitude is, "Go to the law library and figure it out for yourself."

We at Sphinx write and publish self-help law books to give people an alternative to the often complicated and confusing legal books found in most law libraries. We have made the explanations of the law as simple and easy to understand as possible. Of course, unlike an attorney advising an individual client, we cannot cover every conceivable possibility.

COST/VALUE ANALYSIS

Whenever you shop for a product or service, you are faced with various levels of quality and price. In deciding what product or service to buy, you make a cost/value analysis on the basis of your willingness to pay and the quality you desire.

When buying a car, you decide whether you want transportation, comfort, status, or sex appeal. Accordingly, you decide among such choices as a Neon, a Lincoln, a Rolls Royce, or a Porsche. Before making a decision, you usually weigh the merits of each option against the cost.

When you get a headache, you can take a pain reliever (such as aspirin) or visit a medical specialist for a neurological examination. Given this choice, most people, of course, take a pain reliever, since it costs only pennies; whereas a medical examination costs hundreds of dollars and takes a lot of time. This is usually a logical choice because it is rare to need anything more than a pain reliever for a headache. But in some cases, a headache may indicate a brain tumor and failing to see a specialist right away can result in complications. Should everyone with a headache go to a specialist? Of course not, but people treating their own illnesses must realize that they are betting on the basis of their cost/value analysis of the situation. They are taking the most logical option.

The same cost/value analysis must be made when deciding to do one's own legal work. Many legal situations are very straight forward, requiring a simple form and no complicated analysis. Anyone with a little intelligence and a book of instructions can handle the matter without outside help.

But there is always the chance that complications are involved that only an attorney would notice. To simplify the law into a book like this, several legal cases often must be condensed into a single sentence or paragraph. Otherwise, the book would be several hundred pages long and too complicated for most people. However, this simplification necessarily leaves out many details and nuances that would apply to special or unusual situations. Also, there are many ways to interpret most legal questions. Your case may come before a judge who disagrees with the analysis of our authors.

Therefore, in deciding to use a self-help law book and to do your own legal work, you must realize that you are making a cost/value analysis. You have decided that the money you will save in doing it yourself outweighs the chance that your case will not turn out to your satisfaction. Most people handling their own simple legal matters never have a problem, but occasionally people find that it ended up costing them more to have an attorney straighten out the situation than it would have if they had hired an attorney in the beginning. Keep this in mind if you decide to handle your own case, and be sure to consult an attorney if you feel you might need further guidance.

LOCAL RULES   The next thing to remember is that a book that covers the law for the entire nation, or even for an entire state, cannot possibly include every procedural difference of every county court. Whenever possible, we provide the exact form needed; however, in some areas, each county, or even each judge, may require unique forms and procedures. In our *state* books, our forms usually cover the majority of counties in the state, or provide examples of the type of form that will be required. In our *national* books, our forms are sometimes even more general in nature but are designed to give a good idea of the type of form that will be needed in most locations. Nonetheless, keep in mind that your *state*, county, or judge may have a requirement, or use a form, that is not included in this book.

You should not necessarily expect to be able to get all of the information and resources you need solely from within the pages of this book. This book will serve as your guide, giving you specific information whenever possible and helping you to find out what else you will need to know. This is just like if you decided to build your own backyard deck. You might purchase a book on how to build decks. However, such a book would not include the building codes and permit requirements of every city, town, county, and township in the nation; nor would it include the lumber, nails, saws, hammers, and other materials and tools you would need to actually build the deck. You would use the book as your guide, and then do some work and research involving such matters as whether you need a permit of some kind, what type and grade of wood are available in your area, whether to use hand tools or power tools, and how to use those tools.

Before using the forms in a book like this, you should check with your court clerk to see if there are any local rules of which you should be aware, or local forms you will need to use. Often, such forms will require the same information as the forms in the book but are merely laid out differently, use slightly different language, or use different color paper so the clerks can easily find them. They will sometimes require additional information.

CHANGES IN THE LAW

Besides being subject to state and local rules and practices, the law is subject to change at any time. The courts and the legislatures of all fifty states are constantly revising the laws. It is possible that while you are reading this book, some aspect of the law is being changed or a court is interpreting a law in a different way. You should always check the most recent statutes, rules and regulations to see what, if any changes have been made.

In most cases, the change will be of minimal significance. A form will be redesigned, additional information will be required, or a waiting period will be extended. As a result, you might need to revise a form, file an extra form, or wait out a longer time period; these types of changes will not usually affect the outcome of your case. On the other hand, sometimes a major part of the law is changed, the entire law in a particular area is rewritten, or a case that was the basis of a central legal point is overruled. In such instances, your entire ability to pursue your case may be impaired.

To help you with local requirements and changes in the law, be sure to read the section in Chapter 2 on "Research."

Again, you should weigh the value of your case against the cost of an attorney and make a decision as to what you believe is in your best interest.

INTRODUCTION

An Illinois landlord who does not know landlord/tenant laws, or ignores them, can lose thousands of dollars in lost rent, penalties, and attorney's fees. However, a landlord who knows the law can simplify life and save money. Knowing the laws governing rentals gives landlords the power to protect his or her rights and to deal with problems effectively.

Laws are written to be precise, not to be easily readable. This book explains the law in simple language so Illinois landlords can know their rights and what is required of them under the law. If you would like more detail about a law, you can check the statutes in Appendix A or research the court cases as explained in the section on "Further Assistance for Landlords" in Chapter 1.

No book of this type is able to cover every situation that may arise. Laws change and different judges have different interpretations of what the laws mean. Only a lawyer, reviewing the unique characteristics of a particular situation, can give a professional opinion of how the laws apply to a specific case. This book gives the legal framework necessary to avoid costly mistakes.

When following the procedures in this book it should be kept in mind that different counties may have special customs, and some judges have their own way of doing things, so the requirements in your area may differ from those outlined in this book. Clerks and judge's assistants cannot give legal advice, but they can often explain what they require in order to proceed with a case. Before filing any forms, ask if the court provides its own forms or has any special requirements.

Chapter 1 provides general information on laws that cover residential rental property. Chapter 2 lists assistance for landlords, including how to find an attorney and how to save money. Chapter 3 goes from interviewing potential tenants to the details of creating a landlord tenant legal relationship. Chapter 4 addresses pets in rental property. Chapter 5 explains the legal requirements of obtaining security deposits. Chapter 6 covers maintenance and who is responsible for repairs. Chapter 7 lists potential liabilities of a landlord and how to avoid them.

Chapter 8 explains how to change the terms of a tenancy, and Chapter 9 lists major problems that can occur during the tenancy. Chapter 10 covers problems at the end of a tenancy. Chapter 12 and Chapter 11 cover how to terminate the tenancy and the eviction process. Chapter 13 expands on the eviction process in dealing with damages and back rent. Chapter 14 discusses self-service storage space rentals and Chapter 15 mobile home parks. Chapter 16 is a brief overview of the most important aspects in commercial renting. Chapter 17 reviews section 8 and low cost housing. The final chapter looks at renting from the perspective of a tenant.

This book contains definitions that will help in understanding those legal terms used both in this book and in speaking with an attorney. These are located in the back of this book in the glossary. In the back of the book are also charts and forms which will be of assistance.

THIS BOOK IS A GUIDE

No book can provide all the information and resources needed for a subject as broad or as important as divorce. This book will serve as a guide, giving specific information, and pointing you to other resources. This is just like if you decided to build your own backyard deck. You might purchase a book on how to build decks. However, such a book would not include the building codes and permit requirements of every city, town, county, and township in the nation; nor would it include the lumber, nails, saws, hammers, and other materials and tools needed to build the deck. You would use the book as a guide, and then do some work and research involving such matters as whether you need a permit of some kind, what type and grade of wood are available in your area, whether to use hand tools or power tools, and how to use those tools.

Laws that Govern Rental Property

1

Today's landlords are required to adhere to many laws. From Federal, to State, to local *statutes*, the landlord must keep his/her property within the confines of all these regulations. Landlords that do not follow this mix of regulations can find themselves in an expensive legal battle. The easiest way of looking at all these laws is like a tree. The top is the federal laws, those primarily are concerned with people's broad civil rights. Underneath federal laws are Illinois state laws, these statutes are directed at a more detailed level and carve out laws for particular types of property such as mobile homes. Lower than federal and state laws are the laws enacted for a particular county, city/town and community within that town. Your rental property can be subject to all of those laws. At minimum, all rental property in the state of Illinois is subject to *both* federal and state laws.

Illinois Landlord/Tenant Law

Illinois landlord/tenant law consists of statutes passed by the Illinois legislature, various municipal ordinances, and legal opinions written by judges. The statutes and ordinances usually address specific issues that have come up repeatedly in landlord/tenant relations. The court opinions interpret the statutes and ordinances, and decide what the law is in areas not specifically and clearly covered by statutes and ordinances.

Unfortunately, since the statutes were written at different times by different legislators, they sometimes conflict. There are also state and local regulations that conflict with those statutes, and judges do not always interpret them in the same way. So a landlord can be caught in a difficult situation, where even an experienced lawyer cannot find an easy solution.

Fortunately, these situations are rare. If it does occur, two choices exist: fight the issue in a higher court (through an appeal) or give in and do what is demanded. Most small landlords cannot afford a long court battle, so the only practical solution is to relent. For this reason, it is usually better to work out a settlement with a tenant than to let an issue go to a building inspector or before a judge. This will be explained in more detail later in this book.

Illinois landlord/tenant laws have changed tremendously since the 1970s, and are constantly changing, even today. Prior to the 1970s, the law favored the landlord because the courts put an emphasis on the actual ownership of the property. Recognizing tenants' rights began in the 1970s; significantly changing the status of residential tenants. The current legal restrictions on a landlord terminating lease rejects this. The landlord's absolute right to terminate has been limited because a residential tenant has an expectation that their tenancy will continue for the full term listed in the lease. In some instances, this expectation has been found to outweigh a landlord's traditional rights.

The other significant influence in Illinois landlord/tenant laws is the adoption of local ordinances that specifically protect residential tenants. Many cities, towns, and counties in Illinois have adopted their own landlord/tenant ordinances, but the most extensive is in force in the city of Chicago.

ILLINOIS STATE LAWS

Unlike many other states, which have only one landlord/tenant law, Illinois has many state laws that affect the landlord/tenant relationship. The following is a list of the significant Illinois laws that may affect the landlord/tenant relationship (other laws may also apply):

- Chapter 305/Act 5/Article 5—Illinois Public Aid Code

- Chapter 310/Act 65—Illinois Affordable Housing Act

- Chapter 310/Act 70—Homelessness Protection Act

- Chapter 745/Act 75.1—Snow and Ice Removal Act

- Chapter 735/Act 5 / Article VI—Ejectment

- Chapter 735/Act 5 / Article IX—Forcible Entry and Detainer

- Chapter 765/Act 100—Illinois Real Estate Time-Share Act

- Chapter 765/Act 605—Condominium Property Act

- Chapter 765/Act 705—Landlord and Tenant Act

- Chapter 765/Act 710—Security Deposit Return Act

- Chapter 765/Act 715—Security Deposit Interest Act

- Chapter 765/Act 720—Retaliatory Eviction Act

- Chapter 765/Act 725—Property Taxes of Alien Landlords Act

- Chapter 765/Act 730—Rent Concession Act

- Chapter 765/Act 735—Rental Property Utility Service Act

- Chapter 765/Act 740—Tenant Utility Payment Disclosure Act

- Chapter 765/Act 745—Mobile Home Landlord and Tenant Act

- Chapter 775/Act 5/Article 3—Illinois Human Rights Act

Along with these laws, basic contract law is used when a lease is involved.

ILLINOIS DISCRIMINATION LAWS

CONSTITUTION
OF THE STATE
OF ILLINOIS

The Illinois Constitution prohibits discrimination in the sale or rental of property on the basis of race, color, creed, national ancestry, sex, or physical or mental handicap. (Illinois Constitution, Article 1, Sections 17, 18, 19, 20.)

ILLINOIS
HUMAN RIGHTS
ACT

The *Illinois Human Rights Act* (775 ILCS 5) addresses in detail the prohibitions against discrimination. Article 3 specifically deals with real estate transactions, both rentals and sales. Discrimination based on handicap, race, color, religion, national origin, ancestry, age, sex, marital status, or familial status is prohibited within this statute.

Under this statute, a civil rights violation occurs when an owner, real estate broker or salesperson, or any other person engaging in a real estate transaction (sale or rental) does any of the following acts because of the above discriminatory criteria:

- refuses to engage in a real estate transaction;

- alters the terms, conditions, or privileges of a real estate transaction;

- alters furnishings, facilities, or services of the real estate;

- refuses to receive or transmit a bona fide offer to the owner;

- refuses to negotiate for a transaction;

- misrepresents that a property is not available for inspection, sale, rental, or lease by failing to bring the property listing to a person's attention or by refusing permission to inspect;

- uses print material, advertisements, signs, or rental applications; or makes any oral or written statements which express an intent (either directly or indirectly) to engage in unlawful discrimination;

- offers, solicits, accepts, uses, or retails a listing of a property with knowledge that unlawful discrimination is intended;

- refuses to permit, at the expense of the handicapped person, reasonable modifications of the premises;

- refuses to make reasonable accommodations in rules, policies, practices, or services, when these accommodations are necessary to afford a person equal opportunity to use and enjoy a dwelling;

- solicits property for sale or lease on the grounds of loss of property value due to a particular type of person moving into the vicinity—commonly known as *blockbusting* ;

- refuses to sell or rent because a person has a guide, hearing, or support dog; or,

- enters into a restrictive covenant (either in a sale document or a lease) which forbids or restricts on the basis of discriminatory criteria.

Violation complaints concerning both real estate sales and rentals, are heard before a hearing officer, or a three-member panel, of the *Human Rights Commission*.

Penalty: Possible penalties include cease and desist orders; payment of actual damages suffered by the *complainant*; fines up to $10,000 for a first offense, up to $25,000 for a second offense, and up to $50,000 for third and subsequent offenses; and payment of attorney fees and costs. (See 755 ILCS 5/8B-104.)

Exemptions: The Illinois Human Rights Act does *not* affect:

- rentals of apartments in a building with less than five independent units, if the owner or a member of the owner's family lives in one of the units;

- rentals of rooms in a private home, if the owner or a member of the owner's family also resides there;

- rentals or rooms in a private home, in the absence of the owner or a member of the owner's family, if the absence is less than twelve months and if the owner or member of the owner's family intends to return to the private home;

- rentals of rooms with the restriction to people of the same sex;

- refusal to rent to persons convicted of drug-related offenses; and,

- housing accommodations restricted to specified older persons, if the accommodations provided under a state or federal program that is designed and operated to assist elderly persons, or if the housing or community complies with rules adopted on restrictions for elderly persons.

LOCAL LAWS

In addition to the various state laws covering this topic; many cities, towns, and counties have their own ordinances which govern landlord and tenant relations. The reason for this mix of state and local laws can be traced back to the Constitution of the State of Illinois, in Article VII on "Local Government." This Article gives municipalities (cities, towns, and counties), based on population numbers or referendum, the power of *home rule*. Home rule allows municipalities to issue their own regulations in addition to state law, which are usually stricter than the state law and impose additional requirements, often upon the landlord. Some municipalities require that the landlord supply the tenant with either a copy or a summary of the local landlord/tenant ordinances.

Some cities have created an extensive series of laws that cover every aspect of the landlord/tenant relationship. The CITY OF CHICAGO RESIDENTIAL LANDLORD AND TENANT ORDINANCE is an example of such an all-encompassing law. Several cities have similar significant local ordinances that govern the landlord/tenant relationship within that city, although they are not as complex as the Chicago ordinance.

Another approach is to have local ordinances cover only certain aspects of the landlord/tenant relationship (such as eviction, security deposits, etc.), and rely on the state laws to cover the rest. Even cities that appear not to have any interest in governing the landlord/tenant relationship may have laws specifically aimed at the landlord within their building code. Be sure to check with both your city and county governments for any local laws, and be careful to make sure it apples to you. For example, the Chicago ordinance does not apply to owner-occupied buildings of six or less.

LOCAL LAWS ON DISCRIMINATION

You should check your city and county ordinances before adopting a discriminatory policy—even a policy that merely limits tenants to elderly persons. Municipalities with home rule may have their own laws that cover discriminatory policies or limits on tenants by age, race, familial designation, sex, etc. Local ordinances that cover aspects of the landlord/tenant relationship usually grant greater protections against housing discrimination than the Illinois Human Rights Act or other state laws.

The following cases are samples of the types of discriminatory action that is prohibited by law.

- A tenant who is mentally ill is considered handicapped. Therefore, discrimination against the tenant is prohibited under the law. (*Anast v. Commonwealth Apartments*, 956 F.Supp. 792 (N.D. Ill. 1997).)

- A village was not required to grant a zoning variance to a developer to tear down a single family home and build an apartment building with special first floor access for the handicapped. This was not a "reasonable accommodation" since the single family home could have easily been remodeled to accommodate the handicapped. (*Brandt v. Village of Chebanse*, Ill., 82 F.3d 172 (C.A.7 Ill. 1996).)

📖 A court found that a qualified black prospective tenant was discriminated against when a landlord refused to rent to her. The landlord claimed that delinquent student loans made her unqualified, yet the credit report in the landlord's possession contained no adverse credit information. (*Atkins v. City of Chicago Commission on Human Relations*, 667 N.E.2d 664 (Ill.App. 1 Dist. 1996).)

📖 Where the landlord maintained an oral policy restricting children, the landlord was found to have violated a prospective tenant's civil rights by refusing to lease to him because he had a child under the age of fourteen. (*Rackow v. Illinois Human Rights Commission* 504 N.E.2d 1344 (App. 2 Dist. 1987).)

📖 Jury awarded $3,000 in damages to prospective tenants because the landlord refused to rent to a "mixed couple" (one black and one white). (*Thronson v. Meisels*, 800 F.2d 136 (C.A. 7 Ill. 1986).)

📖 Under the Fair Housing Act (part of the Civil Rights Acts), discrimination in refusing to rent because of the prospective tenant's race, color, religion, sex, or national origin can be proved by the prospective tenant by showing all of the following: (1) that the tenant belongs to a minority group; (2) that the landlord was aware of that fact; (3) that the prospective tenant was ready, willing, and able to accept the landlord's offer to rent; and, (4) that the landlord refused to deal with the prospective tenant. (*Hamilton v. Svatik* 779 F.2d 383, (CA. 7 Ill. 1985).)

LOCAL DISCRIMINATION LAWS— AN EXAMPLE

In February 2002, the Naperville City Council passed laws which required access for those with disabilities to all newly built private homes. Naperville was the only town in Illinois to attempt to address the accessibility requirements for private homes. Most communities require this of commercial buildings and publicly funded buildings only.

The Naperville law required that doorways accommodate wheelchairs, bathroom walls be reinforced to allow for installation of grab-bars, light switches and electrical outlets be at wheelchair accessible height, and that the entrance be "no-step". In May 2002, Naperville eliminated the "no-step" portion of this ordinance due to excessive expense to builders. As of the publication of this book, the rest of this ordinance remains in effect.

FEDERAL LAWS

Besides state laws and local laws, landlords must also be concerned with the federal laws that cover the landlord/tenant relationship. Federal laws that apply to the rental of real estate include discrimination laws such as the *Civil Rights Act* and the *Americans with Disabilities Act*. Landlords may also need to consult the laws of the *Environmental Protection Agency* in regards to lead-based paint and radon.

For public housing, the United States Department of Housing and Urban Development (HUD) has a handbook that explains the rules applicable to public housing and other HUD programs. (See Chapter 17 "Section 8 and Public Housing" for more information.)

FEDERAL DISCRIMINATION LAWS

Since the United States Congress passed the Civil Rights Act of 1968, it has been a federal crime for a landlord to discriminate in the rental or sale of property on the basis of race, religion, sex, or national origin. With the Civil Rights Act of 1982, Congress increased penalties in certain types of cases.

In 1988, Congress passed an amendment to the original Civil Rights Act that bans *discrimination* against both people with disabilities and families with children. Except for apartment complexes that fall into certain special exceptions, all rentals must now allow children in all units.

CIVIL RIGHTS
ACT OF 1968

Under the Civil Rights Act of 1968 (42 USC 3601-17), a policy that has a discriminatory effect is illegal.

Penalty. A victim of discrimination can file a civil suit, a HUD complaint, or request the U.S. Attorney General to prosecute. Damages can include actual losses and *punitive damages* of up to $1,000. Failure to attend a hearing or failure to produce records can subject you to up to a year in prison or $1,000 fine.

Limitation. The complaint must be brought within 180 days.

Exemptions. This law does not apply to single-family homes if the owner owns three or less; if there is no more than one sale within twenty-four months; if the person does not own any interest in more than three at one time; and, if no real estate agent or discriminatory advertisement is used. It also does not apply to a property in which the owner resides if it has four or less units.

Coercion or Intimidation. Where coercion or intimidation is used to effectuate discrimination, there is no limit to when the action can be brought or the amount of damages.

   📖 A real estate agent was fired for renting to African-Americans. (*Wilkey v. Pyramid Construction Co.,* 619 F.Supp. 1453 (D. Conn. 1983).)

CIVIL RIGHTS
ACT SECTION
1982

The Civil Rights Act Section 1982 (42 USC 1982) is similar to the 1968 Act. However, where the 1968 Act applies to any policy that has a discriminatory effect, Section 1982 applies only where it can be proven that the person had an intent to discriminate.

Penalty. Actual damages plus unlimited punitive damages.

> Example: In 1992, a jury in Washington, D.C. awarded civil rights groups $850,000 damages against a developer who only used white models in rental advertising. *The Washington Post* now requires that twenty-five percent of the models in ads that it accepts be black to reflect the percentage of blacks in the Washington area.

Limitation. None.

Exemptions. None.

CIVIL RIGHTS
ACT 1988
AMENDMENT

The 1988 Amendment to the Civil Rights Act (42 USC 3601) bans discrimination against the handicapped and families with children. Unless a property falls into one of the exemptions, under this law it is illegal to refuse to rent to people who have a disability or who have children. While landlords may be justified in feeling that children cause damage to their property, Congress has ruled that the right of families to find housing is more important than the rights of landlords to safeguard the condition of their property.

Regarding people with disabilities—the law allows them to remodel the unit to suit their needs as long as they return it to the original condition upon leaving. It also requires new buildings of four units or more to have electrical facilities and common areas accessible to the disabled.

Penalty. These can range from $10,000 for first offense; $25,000 for the second violation within five years; and up to $50,000 for three or more violations within seven years. Unlimited punitive damages in private actions.

Limitation. Complaint can be brought within two years for private actions.

Exemptions. This law does not apply to single-family homes if the owner owns three or less units; if there is no more than one sale within twenty-four months; if the person does not own any interest in more than three at one time; and, no real estate agent or discriminatory advertisement is used. (A condominium unit is not a single-family home, so it is not exempt.) The law also does not apply to a property that the owner lives in if it has four or less units.

There are also exemptions for dwellings in state and federal programs for the elderly, for complexes that are solely used by persons sixty-two or older, and for complexes where at least eighty percent of the units are rented to persons fifty-five or older.

AMERICANS
WITH
DISABILITIES
ACT

The Americans with Disabilities Act (*ADA*) requires that "reasonable accommodations" be made to provide people with disabilities access to commercial premises, and forbids discrimination against them. People with disabilities must be able to get to, enter, and use the facilities in commercial premises. It requires that if access is not readily achievable without undue burden or undue hardship, changes must be made to the property to make it accessible. Under the ADA, any newly constructed or remodeled commercial premises must include modifications that make the premises accessible.

NOTE: *The ADA does not apply to residential rental property.*

What qualifies for reasonable accommodations under the law will usually depend upon the size of the business. Small businesses will not have to make major alterations to their premises if the expense would be an undue hardship. Even large businesses would not need shelving low enough for people in wheelchairs to reach, as long as an employee was readily available to assist the person.

However, there are tax credits for businesses of less than thirty employees and less than one million dollars in sales that make modifications to comply with the ADA. (For more information on these credits, obtain IRS forms 8826 and 3800 and their instructions from the IRS website: **www.irs.gov**.)

Some of the changes that must be made to property to make it more accessible to the disabled are:

- installing ramps;
- widening doorways;
- making curb cuts in sidewalks;
- repositioning shelves;
- repositioning telephones;
- removing high pile, low density carpeting; and,
- installing a full-length bathroom mirror.

Both the landlord and the tenant can be liable if the changes are not made to the commercial rental property. Most likely, the landlord would be liable for common areas, and the tenant for the area under his or her control. However, since previous leases did not address this new statute either party could conceivably be held liable.

Penalty. Can range from injunctions and fines of $50,000 for the first offense; and $100,000 for subsequent offenses.

Exemptions. Private clubs and religious organizations are exempt from this law. And remember, the ADA does not apply to residential rental property.

FAIR HOUSING ACT & FAIR HOUSING AMENDMENTS ACT

The *Fair Housing Act* and *Fair Housing Amendments Act* prohibit housing discrimination against people who have a mental or physical disability which limits one or more life actions, those who have a have a history of disability, and/or those who are regarded by others as having a disability. Disabilities mentioned are hearing loss, loss of mobility, visual impairments, mental illness, AIDS, HIV, and mental retardation. However, this law is not limited to these specific disabilities.

Landlords are required to evaluate a disabled potential tenant on the SAME financial stability and history criteria that is used to evaluate all other prospective tenants. (This presents yet another good reason for landlords to keep very detailed records on potential tenant evaluations.) Landlords cannot question the severity of a disability or require a disabled person to produce his/her medical records.

Landlords must accommodate the "reasonable" needs of disabled tenants at the landlord's expense (42 USC Section 3604 (f)(3)(B)). Accommodations include handicapped parking, a large parking space for wheelchair access, or other reasonably easy changes. Landlords are not required to go into major expenses such as installing an elevator in a building. However, some courts have found that installing an inexpensive concrete ramp for access to an entrance door is reasonable.

Disabled tenants must be allowed to make "reasonable" modifications to their own living units or common areas at the tenant's expense if the modification is necessary for the tenant to live comfortably and safely (42 USC Section 3604 (f)(3)(A)). These modifications must be: 1) reasonable; 2) needed for the comfort/safety of the tenant; and, 3) items that will not make the unit unacceptable for the next tenant or that will be restored to the original condition.

Landlords should require written descriptions of the modifications and proof that the work will be done in a safe, legal manner and will adhere to all local building code ordinances. The landlord should also request proof that the modification will address the disabled tenant's needs.

If the modifications proposed are such that the landlord will require the tenant to restore the premises, the landlord can require that the tenant put funds into an interest-bearing escrow account in an amount which will pay for the restoration. The cost of the modification is legally the responsibility of the tenant, however if the modification is something that will remain after the disabled tenant leaves, most landlords will assume a portion of the cost.

Nursing Homes and Related Facilities

Nursing homes and related facilities are not covered by the landlord/tenant statutes, and are beyond the scope of this book. Illinois has special statutes regulating "Nursing Homes, Long-Term Care Facilities, Home Health Care Facilities, and Supportive Living Facilities." These are found in the *Nursing Home Care Act* (210 ILCS 45). This act details resident's rights, licensing of the facilities, and sets up definitions to determine which facilities are covered by this statute.

Hotels and Motels

Hotels and motels are not covered by the landlord/tenant statutes. The *Innkeeper Protection Act*, (740 ILCS 90) regulates hotels, motels, apartment hotels, residential hotels, motor courts, inns, and boarding and lodging houses where twenty-five or more rooms are used for lodging travelers and guests. This act details liability of the proprietor for guests' valuables, baggage, and other losses. It also covers the duties of the guest, obtaining lodging without paying, and the removal of hotel property.

This is not the only statute that pertains to hotel or motel business. Like all other businesses, a hotel must adhere to local laws and codes, state laws, and federal laws such as the Civil Rights Act, the Americans with Disabilities Act, and the Environmental Protection Agency ordinances.

ASSISTANCE FOR LANDLORDS 2

The wealth of laws listed in Chapter 1 can be overwhelming, but there are things a landlord/property owner can do to help himself or herself understand and comply with these laws. The first step is to find out which laws effect your property. Once you know which laws you need to adhere to then the next step is to gather some understanding of these laws. This can be accomplished by doing research into federal, state, and specific community laws. The research can include both library and internet usage. Ultimately the landlord may decide to turn to someone who is knowledgeable in this area of law, an attorney who concentrates in landlord/tenant law.

RESEARCH

You may want to research your predicament further by reading the entire state or local laws that apply, or by looking up court cases. You can find local laws at a public library, law library, or the government office of a particular city. For example, the City of Evanston sells copies of its current "Residential Landlord and Tenant Ordinance" at its City Clerk's office for a nominal fee. A copy of the CHICAGO RESIDENTIAL LANDLORD AND TENANT ORDINANCE SUMMARY is included in Appendix C, but since it can be amended at any time, you should occasionally get an update from the city clerk's office at:

Office of the City Clerk
City Hall, Room 107
121 N. LaSalle Street
Chicago, Illinois 60602

LIBRARIES

Many local libraries have the current Illinois statutes in printed format. Your local library will probably have a copy of your city/town's laws, if they do not you can usually obtain a copy from your city hall. Because your property must adhere to the local laws, it is imperative that you review your local laws.

Your city/town laws may not be easy to read. Many times the laws that effect landlords are not in a neat section called landlord/tenant law. Most commonly these important laws are been found in sections such as "public housing," "land use," "zoning," "building codes," "residential housing." Those administrative personnel who work in your city/town hall can be helpful in directing you to the area of law you need to look at and would be a good place to start.

There are also law libraries that the public can use, especially in reviewing the federal and state laws. These law libraries are located in law schools and at the majority of circuit court buildings. Librarians, especially those in law libraries, are usually extremely helpful to the public. Besides the actual printed laws there are also books that will assist you in understanding the laws.

State laws are found in a set of books called *West's Smith-Hurd Illinois Compiled Statutes Annotated* (abbreviated *ILCS* for *Illinois Compiled Statutes*). Laws are easy to look up by topic in the index, or by the chapter number. For example, the abbreviation "765 ILCS 710" is a reference to Chapter 765, Act 710, of the Illinois Compiled Statutes.

If you decide to represent yourself in an eviction, you will need to look in the section of Illinois Civil Law for the *Forcible Entry and Detainer* law, which governs evictions. Then look at the *Rules of Practice* for the circuit court where the eviction case will be filed. Your library may have other books that contain the same information.

It is more difficult to look up court cases. Court cases in this book are identified by the book symbol: 📖. Case citations give the name of the case, the name of the set of books (the *reporter*), the volume and page of the reporter.

Example: A case listed as *J.B.Stein & Co. v. Sandberg*, 419 N.E.2d 652, would be found in volume 419 of the *Northeastern Reporter, Second Series*, on page 652.

When using court cases, it is important to know if the case is binding on the court where your case is being heard (if a case is *binding*, your judge is legally required to follow it). *Illinois Supreme Court* opinions are binding on all courts in Illinois. *Appellate courts* are divided into geographic areas, and their opinions only apply to the district that they cover. Similarly, *circuit* or *trial courts* only cover certain geographical areas, and their opinions are only binding in the circuit they cover. If the court that issued a particular opinion does not cover your area, that opinion is not binding on the judge hearing your case. However, even though a court opinion may not be binding in a particular district or circuit, a judge can still decide to agree with and follow that outside opinion.

Another problem with using court cases is determining whether a particular case is still valid. For example, you may find an Appellate Court case that helps your position, only to find out in court that it was appealed to the Illinois Supreme Court and overturned. Or, the seemingly helpful case you found was decided in 1997, but the same court changed its mind in a completely different case in 1998. Legal research can be complex, and you may want to refer to a book specifically on the subject of legal research before you enter the law library.

INTERNET

Another place for research on landlord/tenant laws, and to find assistance for landlords, is the Internet. By typing "landlord" into a search engine, you will find several entries that may be of interest:

- law firms that offer assistance and information;

- law libraries that have the state laws;

- city websites that have included their local laws; and,

- organizations that provide information for landlords and tenants.

An example of this type of organization is the Center for Renters' Rights (**www.renters-rights.com**), which is mostly for Chicago and Cook County. Although the information is directed to the renter, it is still useful to landlords. This site also provides names and addresses for government agencies that are involved with renters' rights.

> *Warning:* Although many internet sites provide accurate and complete information, that is not true of all internet information. Websites on landlord/tenant law may not be updated with the latest laws, or may even provide incorrect information.

The following are some other sites you may want to check out:

- Chicago Department of Housing:
  http://www.cityofchicago.org/housing

- Evanston Public Library ("Renter's Guide"):
  http://www.evanston.lib.il.us/city/renter.html

- Illinois Bar Association:
  http://illinoisbar.org/

- Metropolitan Tenants Organization (for Chicago):
  http://www.cnt.org/

- St. Clair County ("Guide for Litigants to Forcible Entry and Detainer"):
  http://sheriff.co.st-clair.il.us/

- Illinois Statutes:
  http://www.legis.state.il.us/ilcs/chapterlist.html

- Chicago Eviction Information:
  http://www.illinois-attorney.com

There are many other sites, which are directed at generally increasing the public's knowledge of the law and legal documents. Many of the bar associations provide helpful information, links to other information sites, and a place for the public to obtain the names of member attorneys. The following Internet sites have been around for some time and should be reliable places to begin general research.

American Bar Association:

> www.abanet.org

DuPage County Bar Association:

> www.dcba.org

Illinois State Bar Association:

> www.isba.org

Legal Research:

> www.SphinxLegal.com
> www.findlaw.com
> www.lawguru.com
> www.law.com
> www.nolo.com

State of Illinois: www.state.il.us.gov

Cook County Clerk of Court (includes forms):

> www.cookcountyclerkofcourt.org

DuPage County Clerk of Court (includes forms):

> www.dupageco.org/courtclerk/

WORKING WITH ATTORNEYS

In Illinois, landlord/tenant law can be complex, especially when the landlord has to deal with local ordinances and building codes. For that reason, many landlords turn to attorneys for assistance. Sometimes a landlord can get into a situation which will require a court appearance. It can be in conjunction with removal of a tenant or in a suit against a former tenant. Landlords/property owners can also find themselves in court responding to not complying with certain laws or as a third party who is brought in because of an incident at the rental property. As our laws become more complex it is becoming more common place for landlords/property owners to hire an attorney to draw up legal documents and to advise the landlord/property owner on how to comply with the law.

As a rental property owner, it is almost a guarantee that you will need an attorney to assist you regarding your rental property at some point. It may be your first experience with the legal system, a system which is complex, slow, and at times may *seem* unfair. This area of law is listed as landlord/tenant or maybe even real estate law. While Illinois does not license specialties in this area, as is done for patent attorneys, some attorneys and law firms do limit their practice to this particular area of law.

When You Need an Attorney

A rule of thumb for those are attempting to handle their own legal work is that you hire an attorney when: 1) the other side hires an attorney; 2) when you are being brought into court for not complying with civil rights laws; 3) when you are the third party in a suit brought due to an incident between a tenant and another party; 4) if you lost at a preliminary hearing in front of city/town authorities on this same matter; 5) when the amount you are being sued for will cause you to go into bankruptcy; and/or, 6) when you feel that you are overwhelmed with the legal procedure.

Costs

The biggest concern with hiring an attorney is how much it will cost. There are some things that you can do to keep attorney expenses down and because there are a number of attorneys licensed in Illinois you are likely to get someone who is in your price range if you look.

The first step, of course, is to shop around for an attorney who meets your legal and financial criteria. This may require calls to several law firms inquiring about their services, their experience in this area of law and their costs. Attorneys are usually not able to give you precise costs over the phone. They usually need to look at the case and determine how much time it may take.

Most law firms will require a *retainer* which is an amount of money given in advance that the firm will apply to the bills on a particular schedule. Many firms will bill all the work done on a case against the retainer on a monthly basis. If the amount of work done exceeds the amount provided for in the retainer, the firm will require additional funds.

Some firms will charge a *flat amount* (or fixed fee), which is also paid in advance. However, even those who charge a flat amount usually have a provision for additional charges or expenses in association with the case.

For firms that either use the retainer system or those that charge flat amounts, the charges are calculated by the number of hours spent by the attorney, paralegal, law clerk, or other staff times the hourly rate for that person. Other charges are expenses such as court filing fees, charges for having paperwork served, and different expenses in association with the case.

The amount of retainer and hourly rates should be spelled out in an attorney client contract, usually called the *client-attorney representation agreement*. No matter what it is called, it should list how costs are calculated, if there is a retainer or flat charge. It should be signed and dated by both the client and the attorney. If a law firm is reluctant to give you a copy of this agreement to look over before you sign—find another law firm.

FREE LEGAL HELP

Many bar associations and legal aid associations help people who need legal assistance but cannot afford to pay. In general, only those who qualify under the "Federal Poverty Guidelines" will qualify for these programs. Some circuit courts allow a person to file as indigent with proof that they qualify under these guidelines. (Contact the clerk of the circuit court in your county.)

Many of these programs are specifically for the elderly, disabled, military, or people in special circumstances (such as in the case of a natural disaster, those with breast cancer, victims of domestic violence). Since the War on Terrorism has begun, several bar associations and agencies are providing legal help for those in the military. Many of these programs are free to the service person and are run by volunteer attorneys.

If you think you may qualify for free or reduced legal services, it is up to you to do some research and be prepared to prove that you qualify. If your income is below the "Federal Poverty Guidelines" and you are getting state or local assistance, check with the office that is providing you this assistance for legal referrals. Others should begin with their local community. Many community-based programs offer limited services to residents.

Start with your city/town/suburb, then go on to the county services, then to the state services. Look in phone books, local directories, state program directories, federal program directories, for "lawyer referral services," "legal aid," "free legal hotlines," and/or "pro bono legal services or directories." Some local law schools also provide low cost services done by the "about to be graduated" students which are supervised by licensed attorneys. Local and national bar associations may also provide referrals to low cost attorneys who are members of their association.

The largest bar association in the country is the American Bar Association. There are state associations like the Illinois Bar Association; local city associations such as the Chicago Bar Association; county associations such as DuPage County and Will County Bar Associations; and, numerous others. Almost every county in Illinois has its own bar association. Many of the organizations and bar associations maintain websites on the Internet. One notable site is the one provided by the American Bar Association—**www.abanet.org.** It has a section on obtaining free legal help.

CHOOSING AN ATTORNEY

Choosing an attorney can be confusing. Many people rely on referrals from family, friends, or business associates such as your investment broker, insurance broker, or bank. You can also obtain referrals from local, county or state bar associations as discussed in the previous section, "Free Legal Help." There are some attorneys who limit their practice to working for just tenants or just landlords.

Keeping Legal Costs Down

At your first meeting with an attorney, you should be honest about your ability to pay and the limits of your budget. Let the attorney know the extent that you are willing to assist in keeping the costs down. Some attorneys will welcome a client who is willing to perform some of the legwork, others have a tight system which is efficient as it stands. All attorneys will welcome a client who is honest about finances and will not waste the attorney's time.

A good way to keep costs down is to be prepared for all meetings with your attorney. Don't wait until the last minute to gather information, copies of documents, or a list of questions for your meetings with your attorney. A client who comes prepared to meetings with information and promptly provides documents when asked to do so, conveys the message that they will not pay for wasted time.

Answering questions can take up a large amount of time by an attorney and cause the client to be billed a large sum. Some questions can be answered by the paralegal or law clerk or secretary and do not have to go to the attorney. It is in your financial interest to limit your calls to your attorney to important matters. Before calling, gather together all issues and questions. You may wish to write everything down you want to discuss with your attorney so that you can efficiently use the time allotted to you.

What to Bring to Your First Meeting with an Attorney

When you set up an initial meeting with an attorney, you may be asked to bring certain documents, information, and possibly a check for the initial *consultation fee*. Make sure that you know what documents and information you are being asked for and that what you provide is both current and accurate. If you agree to meet with an attorney who requires an initial consultation fee, please remember to bring the check with you. By bringing all that you were asked for, you are sending a message that you will cooperate with the attorney to move the case along.

Your attorney will need to see any documents regarding the reason he/she is being hired. Depending on your case, you may also need to provide ownership papers to the property, a copy of a signed lease, standard lease and rider forms used, and/or any other business documents. Many attorneys will want you to leave these documents with the attorney so he or she can review them.

NOTE: *For your own protection, it is best that you make copies of all documents that you intend to leave with your attorney and keep your originals in your own safekeeping.*

Your attorney will ask you specific financial information. Respond honestly. Information given to your attorney is held in confidence by law. Discuss your objectives with your attorney. Cover all your concerns with your attorney. Do not make him or her pull the information out or try to be a mind reader. Insist on clarification of any legal issues that you do not understand. It is also a very good idea to take notes at every meeting and phone conversation with your attorney, especially the initial consultation.

Above all—if you hire an attorney, FOLLOW YOUR ATTORNEY'S ADVICE. Clients who ask their attorney for advice and then do not follow it are wasting both their money and their attorney's time. There is nothing more frustrating and more detrimental to a good attorney-client relationship than a client who ignores or acts against his or her attorney's direction.

PROBLEMS WITH YOUR ATTORNEY

If it seems that the court is taking too long in your case or if the court rules against you, your first inclination may be to blame the attorney. In reality, many problems can be due to a court that has so many cases or a judge who has an over-booked calendar. The judge himself or herself can be very thorough, reviewing every document, making sure everything submitted to the court withstands rigorous examination to prevent his or her decision from being overturned. Judges may rule against you on motions or at hearings. These things and others are beyond the control of any attorney. The financial truth is that attorneys want their cases to be fairly and quickly decided so that they can work on the next case.

Contact your attorney. Some problems are misunderstandings that can be quickly resolved. An example would be a ruling that went against you in court due to an obscure law. If the problem is that your attorney will not return your calls, send a certified letter requesting that he or she call you. If your attorney works in a large law firm he or she may be working under a senior attorney or partner who may be able to assist you. If the problem is that you are unhappy with the decision made by the court, ask to meet with your attorney so that he or she can explain the decision and advise you of any future options. Set up this meeting as a professional appointment, and offer to pay for your attorney's time.

Filing a Complaint. If you still believe that you have serious problems with your attorney, you can consider filing a complaint against him or her or firing the attorney and retaining another.

NOTE: *If you do fire your attorney, you will still be legally liable for all legal fees incurred up to that point. Some attorneys will not take a case that has been started by another attorney, those who do may require an additional fee for reviewing a prior attorney's work.*

Unfortunately, as with every occupation, there are a few attorneys who do act fraudulently. These few should be reported to the Attorney Registration and Disciplinary Commission of the Supreme Court of Illinois.

CREATING THE LANDLORD/TENANT RELATIONSHIP

3

The most important thing a landlord can do to protect his or her property is to thoroughly screen each prospective tenant who applies to live in the rental property. It is no longer sufficient to just rely on a cursory name, address, and employer form. Landlords must review pertinent information including credit reports, criminal history, and financial records for each potential tenant in order to protect their property and the property of the other tenants.

SCREENING PROSPECTIVE TENANTS

The first step in avoiding legal problems with tenants is to carefully choose your tenant. As long as you do not discriminate based on such categories as race, sex, and age (see pages 4–14), you can be selective in to whom you rent your property. A tenant who has had the same apartment and job for the last five years will probably be a better risk than one who has been evicted several times.

TENANT APPLICATION

You should get a written TENANT APPLICATION from all prospective tenants. (see form 1, p.237.) Besides allowing you to check his or her past record as a tenant, the information can be helpful in tracking down the tenant if he or she disappears owing you rent or damages.

NOTE: *If you choose not to use the TENANT AGREEMENT in this book on p.237, be sure that the form you do use does not ask illegal questions regarding nationality, race, sex, age, etc.*

BACKGROUND
INVESTIGATION

You may wish to check if the prospective tenant has been a *defendant* (been sued) or a *plaintiff* (sued someone) in your county or the last county where the tenant lived. Although each suit is different, a landlord may be reluctant to rent to someone who has recently or repeatedly been sued for nonpayment of bills. Also, a person who has a history of initiating many frivolous lawsuits may not be the type that a landlord would want for a tenant.

You should check with a prior landlord to see if he or she would rent to them again. Do not rely on a positive reference from their present landlord, who may lie just to get rid of them. Be sure the people you talk to are really former landlords. Some tenants use friends to lie and claim to be the landlord.

There are some companies that, for a fee, will investigate tenants, including employment, previous landlords, court cases, and the company's own files of "bad tenants." Landlords may require a non-refundable application fee to cover such an investigation.

CREDIT
REPORTS

There is nothing in Illinois state or federal law that prohibits the landlord from charging for obtaining credit reports on prospective tenants as long as credit reports are required for all prospective tenants, and the same amount is charged for each tenant. Landlords should check for any local laws which address this issue.

A landlord may also wish to obtain a credit report on a prospective tenant. By law the tenant must be informed of the potential of a credit check and give permission for a credit report. Once given permission, contact a local credit bureau such as Equifax, TRW, or Trans Union in order to obtain pertinent credit information. You may also contact a company that runs credit checks such as American Tenant Screen (800-888-1287) or Rent Grow (800-736-8476, ext. 286).

INFORMATION
FROM TENANT

Additional information that you should obtain is the prospective tenant's checking and savings account numbers, social security number, and credit card information. You may also wish to see a pay stub, last year's W-2 or 1099 tax form or income tax return. Call the prospective tenant's employer and verify the salary and length of time on the job.

NOTE: *Be mindful that when getting employers' names and other references, some deceitful tenants may give the number of a friend who poses as a reference.*

Courts allow Illinois landlords to legally ask each prospective tenant the following: names, past addresses, employment history, current income, and if the tenant is of legal majority age. These questions may be asked of ALL the prospective tenants who intend to live in the rental unit.

Landlords can ask the relationship between multiple people who are attempting to rent one unit ONLY in cities where a local law regulates the number of non-related people living together. (As of this publication, Evanston and Waukegan are examples of this type of law.)

Courts have also determined that it is not illegal for the landlord to ask prospective tenants the following; *however*, the prospective tenant *can refuse to answer:*

- social security number;
- bank account information;
- drivers license number;
- release to do a credit check;
- release to do an employment check;
- criminal history;
- character references; and,
- number of anticipated visitors.

A landlord is under no obligation to rent to prospective tenants who refuse to answer these questions as long as these questions are part of the screening process that *all* prospective tenants go through.

Whatever is done for tenant checking, it must be objective and done for all prospective tenants. The *Fair Housing Laws* prohibit landlords from doing extensive prospective tenant checks on just one person or one type of person. The steps used in screening prospective tenants should be on a checklist that is filled out for each prospective tenant and kept on file.

NOTE: *The screening process should be objective. The same things should be done regarding every prospective tenant.*

Making prospective tenants of one particular race pay for extensive credit reports, or fill out a more expansive tenant application, may be considered by a court as an act of discrimination in housing. Simply, require all tenants to submit to the same extensive credit reports and expansive application.

Neither state nor federal laws impose any specific record keeping requirements of prospective tenants on landlords. However, if a discrimination suit is brought, a landlord may be required to prove to a court that all prospective tenants were treated in the same manner. Therefore, it is wise to keep good records regarding the standard procedures used for screening prospective tenants.

Maintain a list of all prospective tenants; the date they applied; what procedures were used in evaluating the prospective tenant (credit reports, calls to former landlords, etc.); and, the outcome of the evaluation. Due to the various fair housing laws (federal, state, and municipal), these records of prospective tenants may need to be retained for several years.

AVOIDING DISCRIMINATION LAWSUITS

Landlords should review specific laws against discrimination, especially the local fair housing law in your particular city. In general, all fair housing laws say it is illegal to refuse to rent to someone because of their race, religion, ethnic origin, sex, age, because of children (except in senior housing), or due to a disability. Some cities also include discrimination on a prospective tenant's marital status, and sexual orientation.

Landlords can legally select tenants based on sound business reasons such as insufficient income, very poor credit history, and past behavior in rental property (such as damaging rental units, evictions, complaints). A landlord can also create a valid rule as to the number of people living in a single unit as long as that rule can be clearly justified on the basis of health and safety.

BROKERS AND AGENTS   One way to screen potential tenants is to hire a licensed real estate broker or agent who handles rentals to represent you. These brokers offer such services as advertising, interviewing potential tenants, providing tenant information forms, ordering credit reports, contacting the potential tenant's employer, etc. Some brokers will also offer full services as rental or managing agents of the landlord's entire rental building.

These brokers and agents are governed by specific laws. If they issue false or misleading advertising about the rental, they violate the *Federal Consumer Fraud and Deceptive Practices Act*. Under the Federal Fair Housing Act, brokers cannot use race, color, religion, sex, or national origin as a basis to deny a person access to a real estate broker's service, to deny a person access to a residential real estate facility, to refuse to show a prospective tenant the property, or as a preference in advertising the rental. Illinois also has state laws that prohibit discrimination by real estate brokers or salespeople.

📖 Because the obligation to obey the law cannot be delegated to another person, a landlord's agent's discriminatory conduct can legally affect the landlord. (*Oliver v. Shelly*, 538 F.Supp. 600 (1982, SD Tex.).)

AGREEMENTS TO LEASE

An *agreement to lease* is a document occasionally used in a residential situation. This document might be useful if the units to be leased are under construction, occupied by another tenant, or if an apartment complex is being sold and the new owner wants assurances of tenants. An agreement to lease locks in the terms of the future lease, so that there will be no negotiation when the final lease is signed.

📖 An agreement to lease does not create the landlord tenant relationship, but is a contract to formally execute a lease at a future time. As such, this agreement is governed by contract law rather than landlord tenant or real estate law. (*Feeley v. Michigan Ave. National Bank*, 490 N.E.2d 15 (1st Dist. 1986).)

In the case of a disagreement, it may be important whether the landlord and tenant entered into a *lease* or an *agreement to lease*. The rights and liabilities of parties to an agreement to lease are different from those of a lease, and these documents are judged on different bodies of law. To determine if there is a lease or just an agreement to lease, courts will look at the document in question, the negotiations leading up to the agreement, and the intention of the parties.

As a practical matter, it will probably not be worth the time and expense to sue someone for breaching an oral agreement to lease. Whether a landlord could keep a deposit after a prospective tenant changed his or her mind would depend upon the facts of the case and the understanding between parties. Writing "non-refundable" on the deposit receipt would work in the landlord's favor.

LEASES AND RENTAL AGREEMENTS

There are basically two types of contracts for the rental of property:

1. A *rental agreement*, which is an open-ended agreement with no definite ending point.

2. A *lease* is an agreement for a set term. It can be as short as a few days, or for as long as several years.

RENTAL AGREEMENTS VS. LEASES

There are different opinions as to whether a landlord should use a lease or a rental agreement. Some argue that they would rather not have a lease, so they can get rid of a tenant at any time. The disadvantage to this is that the tenant can also leave at any time, which means the unit may be vacant during the slow season.

In all cases (even month-to-month tenancies), there should be a written agreement between the parties. If the landlord does not want to tie up the property for a long period of time, he or she can use a rental agreement which states that the tenancy is month-to-month. That agreement also includes rules and regulations that protect the landlord. (see form 8, p.246.)

LEASE CLAUSES

REQUIRED
CLAUSES

Under Illinois law, a *lease* is primarily a *contract*. A lease must contain all the elements of a valid contract, including:

- a meeting of the minds between the landlord and tenant as to the contents of the lease;

- all essential terms;

- an obligation on the part of both landlord and tenant; and,

- a delivery and acceptance of the lease.

📖 The essential terms of a lease are: the extent/bounds/description of the property, the time period of the lease, the amount of rent, the time and manner of payment. (*Ceres Illinois Inc. v. Illinois Scrap Processing, Inc.*, 500 NE2d 1, (Illinois 2d, 1986).)

📖 According to another case (*Daehler v. Oggoian*, 390 N.E.2d 417 (1st Dist. 1979)), an Illinois lease should contain at least the following:

- the name of the landlord (lessor, trustee of the land trust) or agent;

- the name of the tenant (lessee);

- a description of the premises, sufficiently identifying it;

- the amount of rent; and,

- the starting date of the lease, and the term of lease.

As with other portions of landlord/tenant law, municipalities with home rule laws (such as Chicago, Evanston, and Oak Park) may impose additional requirements on what must be contained within the written lease. A lease must comply with both the state laws and the applicable local ordinances in order to be a valid lease.

LEAD-BASED
PAINT
DISCLOSURE

In 1996, the Environmental Protection Agency (EPA) and the Department of Housing and Urban Development (HUD) issued regulations requiring notices to be given to tenants of rental housing built before 1978 that there may be lead-based paint present, and that it could pose a health hazard to children. This applies to all housing except housing for the elderly or zero-bedroom units (efficiencies, studio apartments, etc.) It also requires that a pamphlet about lead-based paint, titled *Protect Your Family From Lead in Your Home* be given to prospective tenants. The recommended disclosure form is included in this book as form 5, p.241.

The rule is contained in the *Federal Register*, Vol. 61, No. 45, March 6, 1996, pages 9064-9088. More information, as well as copies of the pamphlet, can be obtained from the National Lead Information Clearinghouse at 800-424-5323. The information can also be obtained at: http://www.nsc.org/nsc/ehc/ehc.html

SUGGESTED
CLAUSES

The following types of clauses are not required by any law, but are suggested by the authors to avoid potential problems during the tenancy.

- security or damage deposit;

- last month's rent payable at the beginning of the lease term;

- limiting use of the property (*Residential rentals:* this is typically a provision that the property may only be used for residential purposes, and that no illegal activity will be allowed. *Commercial property:* This can be a provision as to the type of business conducted by the tenant, and a prohibition against any illegal activity.);

- maintenance clause (spelling out who is responsible for which maintenance);

- limitation on landlord's liability within the law;

- limitation on assignment or subletting of the lease by tenant;

- clause granting attorney's fees for enforcement of the lease;

- clause putting duty on tenant for own insurance;

- late fee and fee for bounced checks;

- limitation on number of persons living in the unit;

- in a condominium, a clause stating that the tenant must comply with all rules and regulations of the condominium association;

- requirement that if locks are changed by the tenant, the landlord must be given a key (Forbidding tenants to change the locks may subject the landlord to liability for a break-in.);

- limitation on pets;

- limitation on where cars may be parked (not on the lawn, etc.);

- limitation on storage of boats, etc., on the property;

- in commercial leases there should be clauses regarding the fixtures, insurance, signs, renewal, eminent domain, and other factors related to the business use of the premises;

- identification of trustee, date and trust number if property is in a land trust;

- rent concessions, if any;

- landlord's access to premises;

- payment of utilities;

- maintenance and repair of leased property;

- ownership of improvements or alterations in the property;

- furnishings, if any;

- smoke detectors; carbon dioxide detectors;

- tenant's use of storage, laundry, and recreational facilities;

- garage or parking space(s);

- *holding-over* policy;

- eminent domain and the effect of condemnation;

- purchase options, if any; and,

- landlord reserves the right to enter rented property for inspections or to show prospective tenants the premises.

Oral Leases

The *Statute of Frauds* requires that a lease for a term of more than one year must be in writing in order to be enforceable. So, a lease for less than one year can be oral and still comply with the law. The Statute of Frauds does not prohibit parties from making a lease any way they want, nor does it make an oral lease illegal. (*Shugan v. Colonial View Manor*, 437 N.E.2d 731 (1st Dist. 1982).)

An *oral lease* (or an unsigned lease) cannot be enforced by either the landlord or tenant for more than one year. If that oral or unsigned lease is followed by both parties for the term of the lease, neither party can force the other side to return or pay the rent after the term is over.

Without a formal lease, a court may find a written agreement by looking at any written memorandum between the two parties that is signed by the party against whom enforcement is sought and contains the essential elements of a lease: parties names, description of property, amount of rent, term of lease. Also the doctrine of *part performance* may be invoked to avoid the Statute of Frauds. Part performance is usually looked at as possession of property, payment of rent, and making improvements to the property in reliance on the oral lease.

NOTE: *To avoid legal problems, all leases should be in writing.*

Problem Clauses

Residential lease forms are available on the Internet at **www.SphinxLegal.com**, from office supply stores, or real estate agents. These general leases rarely contain clauses that are blatantly unconscionable or unfair to tenants. The leases are designed to adhere to the law of the state and the law of the municipality. Forms created for some landlord or real estate investment seminars, however, may be designed to avoid the requirements of the law. Generally, if the lease follows the requirements of the state and local laws, it should not be considered unfair to the tenant.

RESIDENTIAL
LEASES

A *residential lease* cannot limit or negate tenant's rights or landlord's duties that are required by state law or local ordinance. If a landlord intends to write a lease that will favor the landlord, he or she should first consult the local ordinances to see exactly what is required of the the landlord.

The following terms are implied in an Illinois residential lease and cannot be diminished or negated by the lease.

   📖 A covenant of quiet enjoyment. (*64 East Walton Inc. v. Chicago Title & Trust Co.*, 387 N.E.2d 751 (1st Dist. 1979).)

   📖 The warranty of habitability (residential only). (*Glasoe v. Trinkle*, 479 N.E.2d 915 (1985).)

   📖 Performance in good faith. (*Dasenbrock v. Interstate Restaurant Corp.*, 287 N.E.2d 151 (5th Dist. 1972).)

The following types of clauses would be prohibited and unenforceable in a residential lease:

- tenant's waiver of a jury trial;

- waiver of venue in the county where the tenant resides or the transaction occurred;

- discrimination against occupants in violation of the civil rights laws, the Illinois Human Rights laws, or other statutes prohibiting discrimination; and,

- landlord exempting self from liability from the landlord's own negligence in the operation or maintenance of the premises by the landlord, or by agents, servants, or employees of the landlord.

COMMERCIAL
LEASES

Commercial leases are legal agreements for renting business, office, or manufacturing property. This type of lease has few standard clauses and is usually drafted only after negotiations between the parties. Most commercial leases are very detailed in listing the rights and obligations of the parties. Illinois laws that affect commercial leases can be extensive, depending upon factors such as the type of business, the location, etc.

NOTE: *Due to the complexity of commercial lease law, this area will not be covered in depth.*

OPTIONS

OPTIONS TO
RENEW

Both residential and nonresidential leases may contain clauses granting the tenant an option to extend the lease for another term or several terms. These options often provide for an increase in rent during the renewal periods.

OPTIONS TO
PURCHASE

If a lease contains an *option to purchase*, it will usually be enforceable exactly according to its terms.

FORMS

Illinois has no statute requiring that any particular lease format be used. The lease must comply with all applicable state and local laws (such as local landlord/tenant ordinances). Some landlords employ an attorney who is experienced in landlord/tenant issues to draft a lease. This is routinely done for large apartment complexes, or those rentals managed by an outside corporation.

A landlord can also purchase printed lease forms off the Internet at **www.SphinxLegal.com** or from a local stationery or business supply store. If the landlord decides to purchase one of these lease forms, he or she must be careful to select a lease that will comply with the local ordinances of the city where the rental property is located. Some local ordinances require that certain clauses be included in every residential lease. For example, when renting a property located in Chicago, some landlords must use a lease form that complies with the Chicago Landlord and Tenant Ordinance. Also, only leases approved by the Department of Housing and Urban Development (HUD) can be used with federally subsidized housing rentals. If the form does not comply with the local municipal ordinances, you will have to modify the form.

Not only should the lease form be for the correct municipal area, the lease must be the proper type for the property leased. There are different leases for apartments, single-family houses, unfurnished and furnished rentals, garages, HUD leases, etc. These forms vary as to the type of premises and the types of provisions included. Standard lease forms include blank areas for variable information. Before either party signs the lease, all blanks should be either filled in with information, "n/a" (for "not applicable"), "xxxxx," or lined out.

The landlord may make modifications to a lease form at the tenant's request, or to cover a specific situation with the particular tenant or property. Sometimes it is necessary to add a provision to cover items that are not in the standard lease, such as renting an additional parking space, a storage area, or a pet provision. If the lease form has to be modified, any crossed out or added provisions should be dated and initialed by both the landlord and the tenant. For additional security, you might wish to add a *rider* at the end of the lease that lists the provisions crossed out or added. The rider can also be signed and dated by both parties.

Any ambiguous provision in the lease will be construed in court against the party who drew up or selected the lease. This means that a landlord must be very careful when selecting or creating a lease form.

This book contains three general lease and rental agreement forms that can be used for many situations. (see form 6, p.242, form 7, p.244, and form 8, p.246.) If local laws require additional clauses in your lease, an ADDENDUM is provided so you can incorporate these requests. (see form 38, p.280.) For property in Chicago, use form 9 on page 248 as an ADDENDUM TO LEASE.

SIGNATURES

If you do not have the proper signatures on the lease, you could have problems enforcing it, or evicting the tenants.

LANDLORD   The lease must be signed by the property owner(s)/landlord(s). If the owners employ an agent, such as an attorney or managing company, to handle the leases the attorney or managing agent must sign "as the agent of the principal." If the title to the property is held in a land trust, the land trustee or the beneficiaries may sign as landlord.

TENANT   In most cases, it is best to have all adult occupants sign the lease so that more people will be liable for the rent. Each adult should sign in order to impose liability on each person.

INITIALS   Some landlords have places on the lease for the tenant to place their initials. This is usually done next to clauses that are unusual or very strongly pro-landlord. It might be helpful to draw attention to clauses because in one case a judge refused to enforce a clause that was "buried" on page two of the lease, even though the judge admitted it was highlighted. However, even initials might not help if a judge really does not like a clause.

WITNESSES   No witnesses are required for a lease to be valid.

NOTARY   A lease does not need to be notarized to be valid.

BACKING OUT OF A LEASE

RESCISSION   Contrary to the beliefs of some tenants, there is no law allowing a - *rescission period* for a lease. Once a lease has been signed by both parties, it is legally binding on them. All the tests used to determine if a contract is valid can be used to determine if a lease is valid, because a lease is a form of contract.

FRAUD   If one party fraudulently misrepresents a material fact concerning the lease then the lease may be unenforceable. The *Illinois Consumer Fraud and Deceptive Practices Act* prohibits the use of unfair or deceptive acts or practices in obtaining a contract. These include:

- deception;
- fraud;
- false pretense;
- false promise;
- misrepresentation of a material fact; and,
- concealment of a material fact.

For example, if a landlord fraudulently gets a tenant to enter into a lease, the tenant will be able to sue under this act. Landlords must guard against making misrepresentations about the premises or suppressing any information that could be regarded as material to a tenant.

IMPOSSIBILITY   The lease may not be enforceable if it states that the premises are rented for a certain purpose and it is impossible to use the premises for that purpose.

ILLEGALITY   If a lease is entered into for an illegal purpose, it is void and unenforceable by either party.

PETS 4

The issue of pets in rentals is important to both the landlord and the tenant. Conventional wisdom is that pets and landlords don't mix. For the tenant, a pet or companion animal can be their only friend—a part of their family. For the landlord, a pet can bring damages to their property, can annoy other tenants, and, at worst, cause a lawsuit that involves the landlord. However, landlords in Illinois cannot just bar all pets. The public perception and laws about companion animals are in the process of change and it is only a matter of time until Illinois landlords are affected.

LAWS ABOUT COMPANION ANIMALS

FEDERAL LAWS   The National Housing Act (12 USC 1701) and the Federal Regulations on Housing and Urban Development [HUD (24 CFR 5.300)] address the issue of pet ownership in "federally assisted rental housing" that is specifically for the elderly or handicapped. These laws allow the elderly or handicapped to "own common household pets" in housing that (1) has been properly designated by HUD as for the elderly or handicapped and (2) receives federal money for rent subsidy for these people. In addition, the National Housing Act has given the Secretary for Housing and Urban Development the power to enact very specific guidelines regarding these common household pets in the housing for the elderly or handicapped. These HUD guidelines direct that the owner or manager of any federally assisted rental housing for the elderly or handicapped set up reasonable rules regarding pets for their individual rental property. These rules are required to conform with the HUD guidelines. The site-specific rules are to address such issues as:

- density of tenants to pets;

- pet size;

- types of pets;

- potential financial obligations of tenants for their pets; and,

- standards of pet care. [See 12 USC 1701r-1(b)(2).]

Allowing the owners and managers to enact their own rules regarding pets for the elderly or handicapped in federally assisted housing is why rules on pets can differ by building.

ILLINOIS LAWS   At this time, Illinois has few laws or cases concerning the keeping of companion animals in rental property. The *Illinois Human Rights Act*, Article 3-104.1, makes it a civil rights violation to refuse to rent to a person because that person has "a guide, hearing, or support dog." There are, of course, laws against animal abuse and procedures about liability when there is a dog bite. Municipalities may have local ordinances that:

- restrict the number of animals in a rental property;

- allow a tenant to keep an animal that has been with the tenant for a period of time; or,

- prohibit a landlord from changing a lease to "no pets" without a specified notice.

Continuous, loud dog barking may also violate a local noise ordinance.

Illinois legislature is planning to review a law that will allow pets in Chicago Housing Authority (CHA) property. If Illinois follows other states and municipalities in the country, CHA residents may soon be able to keep a certain number and size of pets in their rental units.

Although the following cases did not occur in Illinois, they may be indicators of things to come. In some western states, if a person can prove a "special need" for a companion animal, the no pets clause in a lease can successfully be challenged in court. Those tenants who have won court cases on this theory have been able to prove that their companion animal is necessary because of a physical or an emotional condition; the animal is required for their health and well-being; and, that they would suffer if they were forced to give up their animals. This argument is backed up by testimony from the tenants' doctors and experts in the field of companion animals who cite studies that show companion animals will lower blood pressure, improve self esteem, and generally improve the animal owner's overall health.

The medical studies on animals' effects on humans are becoming more convincing, and the public's perception of the need for companion animals is increasing daily. Even the National Institutes of Health, a prestigious scientific agency, has found evidence to support the findings that pets are medically beneficial to some people's health.

Other cases have been won when the tenant asserted that the animal was needed as security in a rental property where there is a history of break-ins.

Pet Owners as Tenants

In a survey done by the San Francisco SPCA, landlords that permitting pet owners allowed for:

- more stable tenants;

- lower vacancy rates;

- a larger pool of prospective tenants;

- more happy and satisfied tenants; and,

- tenants who take the responsibility to properly care for pets are more responsible in taking care of the rental property.

Responsible pet owners do take care to clean up after their animals and repair damages that their animals cause; but the question for landlords is: How do you find pet owners that are responsible?

INTERVIEW FOR TENANT PET OWNERS

The first step comes in the interview of the potential tenant. (Once a property is advertised as "pets OK," there should be no shortage of people who wish to be a tenant.) In the interview, the landlord should ask the following:

- How long have you had the pet?

- Have there been any complaints about your pets at your current address? How did you resolve these complaints?

- Did your pet cause any damage at your current address? If so, did you pay your current landlord for the damage?

- May we contact your current landlord to discuss your pets further?

- Who will care for your pets when you are away on vacation or business?

- Would you object to my periodically checking on your pet to note any damage to the unit and to see how the pet is adjusting?

- Has your dog or cat been spayed or neutered?

- Does your cat use a litter box?

- Do you have a regular veterinarian?

- Is your pet up to date on his or her shots? License?

- Does your animal have any medical or behavior problems? If so, what treatment or training is it receiving?

- How does your pet get along with other animals and people?

- How much time will your animal spend alone each day?

- Would you bring the pet by so I can see it? (This can give you some idea of the pet's behavior, as well as how well the owner cares for the pet. If the pet does not appear clean and well-groomed, you may be dealing with an irresponsible owner.)

WRITING PET RULES

The purpose in having rules for pet owners is to keep property damage to a minimum and to allow all tenants the "quiet enjoyment" of the property as required by law. Be realistic in making rules. Both cats and dogs can cause damage, so all pet owners should be on notice that any damage done by their pets will be charged to them.

For cats, tenants must provide a sufficient number of litter boxes so that the cat uses the box, (usually one box per cat). Cats that are spayed and neutered usually do not spray urine, and cats that are kept indoors do not have the opportunity to leave urine marks on lawns. It is a myth that cats must be free to roam. Domestic cats adapt very well to being kept indoors, and often live longer and healthier lives as a result.

Dog owners must clean up after their dogs as soon as the dog messes. Some municipal ordinances require that all dog walkers carry and use a "pooper scooper." Building owners may wish to designate a portion of their property for dog walking or even establish a dog run. Dogs should also be spayed or neutered. Female dogs in heat can attract noisy and persistent suitors.

Determine how big of a dog to allow in a rental unit. Many large dogs such as *great danes* and *mastiffs* are laid-back, easygoing types that can live quite happily in an apartment as long as they are given daily exercise. On the other hand, more active breeds such as *border collies* and some *spaniels* may require more exercise than can be given in one or two daily walks. It also depends on the individual dog, which is one reason for the landlord to ask questions about the dog and perhaps even meet with the dog prior to renting.

The age of the pet is also a factor. A young puppy is an unstable element. It may cry during the night for feedings—just like a human baby does. Older dogs and older cats tend to be less active, but they also can be crabby and set in their ways.

Finding a home for an older animal can be a problem if the landlord decides to set up a no pets rule in a building where pets were previously permitted. Older animals have almost no chance to be adopted from humane shelters where the tenants may surrender their animal.

Some pets suffer from separation anxiety or become bored and destructive when left alone for periods of time, like the typical ten hours a day when their owner goes to work. Cats typically sleep sixteen hours a day or more, but dogs may bark, chew, or destroy things. For a prospective tenant that has had the animal for a period of time, this separation anxiety should be known and they should have some solutions for this problem. Sometimes such an animal needs additional exercise, professional training, or the addition of another animal for company.

As for repairing animal damage, it would be best if any damage can be spotted before it becomes extensive. This may mean periodic inspections of a rental unit, enforcing a rule on litter boxes, or even making materials for cleaning up pet messes available to pet owners. Illinois has many chain pet stores that stock such items as professional animal odor neutralizers, pooper scoopers, and other items to clean up after an animal.

The landlord should set up rules specifically for pet owners. These should be shown to the prospective tenant during the interview so that the prospective tenant clearly understands what is expected. These rules should then be incorporated into the lease. Rules and requirements for pet owners include such matters as:

- limit pet ownership to one particular animal by name;

- cats and dogs should be spayed or neutered;

- for cats there should be one litter box for each cat;

- cats must be kept indoors, going out only in carriers or harnesses;

- cats must not be allowed on balconies or in windows without screens;

- dogs must be kept on a leash when outside;

- dog owners must clean up after their dog;

- pets should have annual vaccinations and proof of vaccinations must be presented to landlord for lease renewal;

- tenants with pets must carry insurance to indemnify the landlord in case of damage or injury;

- prospective tenants must provide landlord with references from former property owners, former neighbors, and their veterinarian;

- pet owner must provide landlord or rental property office with name and address of current veterinarian;

- when they move out, the tenant will pay for professional steam cleaning of the unit;

- the tenant agrees to reimburse the landlord for any damage that the animal has done over and above any security deposit; and,

- the tenant agrees to resolve complaints from other tenants and will participate and pay for mediation to settle disputes.

In addition, the landlord may wish to restrict the number of pets, the type of pets, or the size of pets. Landlords can also require that a pet owner pay an additional security deposit to repair pet damages, or even pay a monthly fee in addition to the rent. The pet security deposit is still subject to the same Illinois laws as other security deposits—see the section on "Security Deposits" in Chapter 5.

The regulations for pet owner tenants should be in writing and given to all prospective and current tenants. Both landlord and tenant should follow these rules. See the sample forms for a PET REFERENCE (form 3, p.239) and PET AGREEMENT (form 4, p.240) in Appendix D.

LANDLORD LIABILITY FOR TENANT'S DOG

One of the reasons that landlords want a "no pets" clause is the fear that in some circumstances the landlord may be financially responsible for damage or injury caused by a tenant's dog to a third party. Most Illinois courts are not eager to extend liability beyond the owner of the offensive dog, but it can happen. Leasing the premises to a tenant, however, usually is not enough to make the landlord liable. Most courts hold the landlord liable if the landlord:

- knew the dog was dangerous and could have had the dog removed; and

- harbored or kept the tenant's dog (that is, cared for or had control over the dog).

NOTE: *To avoid liability as a landlord, require that the dog owner have liability insurance.*

It must be proven in court that the landlord knew the dog was dangerous and had the legal power to make the tenant get rid of the dog. Dogs are not presumed to be vicious, however, if a dog was particularly threatening or had caused problems in the past, it may be inferred that the landlord had such knowledge. As for the power to remove a dog, if the landlord buys a building that has current leases, the landlord may not be able to legally evict the tenant (depending upon the lease and how it handles pets). Harboring or keeping a tenant's dog is having some control over the dog. Some courts have held that if a landlord allows a dog the run of the property, he does have some control over the animal.

📖 Both landlord and tenant were held liable for a dog bite. The landlord rented half the building to the tenant and lived in the other half. The landlord allowed the dog to roam around the entire building as security. (*Edelstein v. Costelli*, 229 N.E.2d 557 (1967).)

ENFORCING "NO PETS" CLAUSES

The majority of form leases include a no pets clause, and a landlord can legally decide to restrict his property to no pets. Some cities have restricted the practice of no pets when that clause was added to existing leases merely to get rid of a tenant. The landlord in such a case would have to prove that the change was not aimed at a particular tenant and was "reasonable" for that property.

Another problem with a no pets lease comes when the landlord has not enforced this restriction. Most courts require that the landlord enforce this provision. If the landlord knows of a pet, he must take immediate steps to inform the tenant that the animal violates the terms of the lease and give the tenant time to get rid of the animal. In the case of a landlord who knowingly permits the animal to stay for a long period of time, some courts have decided that the landlord has lost his right to object to that pet.

If a landlord wishes to allow a particular tenant to have a pet, the landlord should strike out the "no pets" clause in that particular lease. In no situation should the landlord allow a tenant to sign a lease that contains a "no pets" clause if the landlord knows that the tenant intends to have a pet. A landlord who allows this, and later sells his property, may be included in a lawsuit if the new owner wants to enforce this term of the lease.

RECENT PROBLEMS WITH TENANT'S DOG

On March 21, 2002, Marjorie Knoller, the owner of two dogs, was found guilty of the murder of her neighbor Diane Whipple. To those who don't remember the San Francisco case, Ms. Knoller and her husband lived in an rental unit down the hall from Ms. Whipple. Ms. Whipple was mauled to death by Ms. Knoller's dogs. In court proceedings it was brought out that these dogs had been the subject of complaints (some to the landlord), due to prior aggressive problems.

Even before this criminal case began, wrongful death suits against the landlord and the apartment management company were filed. This has become the most visible dog-attack liability suit ever filed against a landlord—a suit that up to now was a rare occurrence. In order to win in such a lawsuit it must be shown that the dogs had a history of being vicious; the landlord knew about that history; the landlord had an opportunity to resolve the problem; and, that the landlord's failure to resolve the problem caused the attack.

Since this case many insurance providers have imposed additional restrictions on landlords and property owners who rent to dog-owner tenants. In some cases the insurance company is requiring additional premiums for liability coverage of rental property that allows dogs. A few insurance companies are completely dropping dog-attack liability coverage for rental property.

There are some things that a landlord can do to limit dog-attack liability. The primary thing is have and strictly enforce pet rules. In the above San Francisco case the apartment was small, yet the large dogs (about 120 pounds each) were allowed to stay in the cramped area. Also, several of the neighbors complained to the landlord about vicious incidents with these dogs prior to the death.

A landlord who allows dogs should restrict weight, size, and the number of dogs for each rental unit. Dogs should be required to be securely leashed when outside of the unit and never left unattended. Landlords should vigorously investigate each complaint about dogs owned by tenants that is made by other tenants and guests. Dogs that exhibit vicious natures should be required to pass obedience training, at the cost of the dog owners, or be permanently removed from the unit. Landlords should also consider requiring tenants with dogs to carry a certain amount of liability insurance to protect the landlord and property owner from any dog-attack liability.

RESIDENTIAL SECURITY DEPOSITS 5

Illinois state law addresses rental security deposits with the *Security Deposit Return Act* (765 ILCS 710); and the *Security Deposit Interest Act* (765 ILCS 715). Both of these statutes are short and provide a limited amount of information. Disputes over security deposits continue to end up in court because of the limitations of the Illinois statutues.

The majority of the municipalities that exercise *home rule* have more specific laws regarding security deposits. This chapter will discuss what the state laws provide, what certain courts have decided, and two of the most prominent municipalities' (Chicago and Evanston) security deposit laws. (Not all municipalities will follow either Chicago or Evanston laws, so be sure to check your local laws.)

REQUIREMENTS

The state Security Deposit Return Act applies to residential property containing five or more units. The Security Deposit Interest Act applies to residential property containing twenty-five or more units in either a single-building or a complex of buildings on a contiguous piece of land. The Chicago Landlord and Tenant Ordinance applies to all residential rental units except those where the owner lives in the building that contains six or less units. (The Chicago law also contains other exemptions which are similar to the state laws). The Evanston statute follows the state law.

A landlord who lived in a building that contained an additional seven units was subject to the landlord and tenant ordinance that excluded owner occupied buildings with six or fewer dwelling units, even though only three of the seven units were occupied at the time the lease was signed. (*Meyer v. Cohen*, 260 Ill.App.3d 351 (Ill.App. 1 Dist. 1993).)

AMOUNT

The state law and the Chicago ordinance (5-12-080) do not restrict the amount of security deposit that a landlord may require. The Evanston ordinance (5-3-5) limits the amount of security deposit to one and one-half times the monthly rent.

BANK ACCOUNT

Neither the state law nor the Evanston ordinance specify the type of bank account that must be used for renters' security deposits. The Chicago ordinance requires that all security deposits be held in "a federally insured interest-bearing account in a bank, savings and loan association or other financial institution located in the State of Illinois."

The Chicago ordinance also specifies that both the security deposit and the interest on the security deposit are the property of the tenant, even though the monies are held by the landlord. In addition, this deposit may not be commingled (mixed) with any money of the landlord, nor be used to pay any of the debts of the landlord.

This rule against commingling and non-usage by the landlord requires that Chicago landlords set up a separate interest bearing bank account strictly for security deposits and their interest. This bank account cannot contain any of the landlord's money. The landlord must keep excellent records of the tenant, the amount of security deposit, the interest on that security deposit, and the dates that the security deposit was put in and returned to the tenant.

A tenant was entitled to damages of two times her security deposit plus five percent interest for landlord's violation of Chicago Residential Tenant Ordinance's prohibition against commingling tenant's security deposits. (*Plambeck v. Greystone Management & Columbia National Trust Company*, 281 Ill.App.3d 260 (Ill.App. 1 Dist. 1996).)

RECEIPT FOR SECURITY DEPOSIT

Illinois law does not require that a receipt be given for a security deposit, however, it is good practice for all landlords to give a receipt for every payment from the tenants. With a receipt, it is less likely a tenant will lie about having paid.

The Chicago Residential Landlord and Tenant Ordinance requires the landlord to give the tenant a written receipt for the security deposit. The receipt must contain the owner's name, the date the security deposit was received, and a description of the rental unit. The receipt must be signed by the person accepting the security deposit and by the person giving the security deposit. The penalty for not complying with this statute is that the tenant is entitled to immediate return of the security deposit. Many stationery and office supply stores offer books of blank rent receipts that contain areas on the face of the receipt for all of the required information.

INTEREST

ILLINOIS LAW   Illinois law requires that all security deposits for residential properties of twenty-five units or more accrue interest. The rate of interest by law is "a rate equal to the interest paid by the largest commercial bank, as measured by total assets, having its main banking premises in this state on minimum deposit passbook savings accounts as of December 31." Interest is to be computed on any deposits held for more than six months. At the end of each twelve month period, the amount of interest is paid to the tenant, either in cash or as a rent reduction, unless the tenant is in default on rent. The amount must be paid to the tenant within thirty days after the end of each twelve month rental period. Failure to pay the interest required by this law makes the landlord liable for an amount equal to the security deposit plus court costs and reasonable attorney's fees.

   📖 Lease provision which stated that "security deposit is net of security deposit interest, if any" was intended to circumvent the Security Deposit Interest Act. The landlord who failed to pay interest was liable to tenants for the full penalty of costs, attorney fees, and an amount equal to the amount of the security deposit. (*Gittleman v. Create, Inc.*, 545 N.E.2d 237 (App. 1 Dist. 1989).)

EVANSTON
ORDINANCE

The Evanston Residential Landlord and Tenant Ordinance specifies the interest rate that must be paid on security deposits. The rate changes, so check with the City of Evanston for the current rate. Evanston agrees with the state law on the period the interest is calculated (twelve months), that within thirty days of that twelve month rental period the tenant receives cash or credit on rent (if not in default on rent), and that the landlord is liable for the amount of security deposit plus costs and attorney's fees if interest is not paid to the tenant.

The Chicago ordinance on security deposit interest is a bit more complicated (see 5-12-080 through 082).

NOTE: *Most of the Chicago ordinance, including the provisions on security deposit interest, does not apply to owner-occupied buildings with six or fewer units.*

CHICAGO
ORDINANCE

Like the state law, Chicago landlords must pay security deposit interest to tenants within thirty days after the end of each twelve month rental period. The interest is paid either in cash or a credit that is applied to the rent due. As with the state law, the interest is calculated for any security deposits held by the landlord for more than six months. The first six months are not interest free. Rather, if a tenant leaves prior to six months, the tenant is not entitled to any interest on the security deposit.

The interest rate required is "an interest rate set by the City Comptroller." On the first business day of each year, the Chicago City Comptroller announces the security deposit interest rate for that year. The rate is based on the average interest rates of passbook savings accounts, insured money market accounts, and six-month certificates of deposit from a commercial bank having its main branch located in the city and having the largest asset value.

If a Chicago landlord fails to comply with the security deposit interest ordinance, the tenant can be awarded damages of two times the amount of the security deposit plus interest. Also, the tenant may be eligible for other damage amounts including court costs and attorney fees.

📖 A tenant sued a landlord claiming that the landlord did not pay the tenant due interest on the security deposit. Cook County court found that the landlord's failure to pay interest was "not willful" and therefore did not subject the landlord to the penalty of double damages, interest and attorney fees. The tenant appealed. The appellate court sided with the tenant. The landlord appealed. The Illinois Supreme Court held that the fact that the landlord's failure to pay security deposit interest was not willful did not matter and awarded the tenant double the amount of deposit, interest, court cost, and attorney fees. (197 Ill.2d 1, 754 N.E.2d 334, 257 Ill. Dec. 676, (July 26, 2001).)

RETURNING THE SECURITY DEPOSIT OR DEDUCTING FOR DAMAGES

Generally, when a tenant comes to the end of the lease and vacates the rental unit, he or she is entitled to the return of the security deposit minus documented repairs to the unit for damages done by the tenant.

State law requires that within thirty days of the tenant vacating the unit, the landlord must provide to the tenant—either by mail or in person—an itemized statement of the damage allegedly caused to the unit, and written estimates or actual receipts for the repairs. If estimated costs are given, copies of paid receipts must be furnished to the tenant withing thirty days from the date of the itemized statement. If no such itemized statement or receipts are furnished to the tenant, the security deposit plus and interest accrued must be returned to the tenant within forty-five days from the date the tenant vacated the unit.

NOTE: *If the landlord refuses to supply an itemized statement of damages with receipts, supplies a fraudulent statement in bad faith, or fails to return the security deposit within the time limits provided, the landlord will be liable for twice the amount of the security deposit due (which would include interest), plus court costs and attorney's fees.*

If the landlord wishes to do the repairs himself, he may deduct the responsible value of his labor. This should be backed up by estimates. It is helpful to get a written estimate before doing the work yourself.

Both the Evanston and the Chicago ordinances contain the same requirements as the state law, but the Chicago ordinance is more detailed regarding the receipts for actual repairs (see 5-12-080(d)(2).)

 📖 When the landlord withheld the security deposit beyond the forty-five day limit, the landlord had the burden to come forward with evidence of a good-faith dispute regarding damages. The residential tenant is entitled to double the amount of the deposit, plus costs, if the landlord refuses to supply an itemized statement of damages complete with receipts, or has done so in bad faith, and has failed to return the security deposit within the time provided. (*Mallah v. Barkauskas*, 130 Ill.App.3d 815 (Ill.App. 2 Dist. 1985).)

 📖 A landlord may deduct $40 for cleaning a stove and refrigerator himself, as the court found that this amount was fair when comparing the rate to that of professional cleaners, and what was charged by the employees of the landlord, for the same type of cleaning. (*Evans v. International Village Apts.*, 520 N.E.2d 919 (Ill.App. 1988).)

The damages that may be deducted from the tenant's security deposit do not include what is considered *normal wear and tear*, or items that are broken or defective prior to the tenant's occupation. The tenant should not have to pay for normal wear and tear on the rental unit. Normal wear and tear would be items like a rug that shows two years of normal wear after a tenant has lived in the unit for two years; or a fifteen-year-old dishwasher that breaks down through normal usage. Things that are not normal wear and tear are the unusual usage of the item, such as the rug with a grease stain because the tenant rebuilt an engine on it, or the dishwasher that breaks down because the tenant washed car hubcaps in it.

    📖 Evidence showed that the landlord was aware of nail holes in the wall before the tenant vacated and had advised the tenant that there was no damage in the rental unit and the tenant would receive the entire security deposit. The repair of these nail holes should not have been deducted against the tenant's security deposit because they constituted normal wear and tear. (*Tobin v. McClure*, 144 Ill.App.3d 33 (Ill.App. 3 Dist. 1986).)

Usually, the landlord and prospective tenant will do an inspection of the rental unit prior to the tenant moving in to record the condition of the unit and the furnishings or appliances at the time of the rental. When the tenant vacates the unit, this record of the unit's condition will assist the landlord in proving that the security deposit is used to repair "unusual wear and tear" or damages. This INSPECTION REPORT should be done by both tenant and landlord, and signed by both parties as an indication that they both agree to what is written on the report. (see form 2, p.238.)

APPLYING THE SECURITY DEPOSIT AGAINST RENT

A practice in some communities is for the security deposit to be used as the payment of rent for the last month before a lease expires. While this may be true in some cases, the security deposit is primarily for damages; not for rent. One way to handle this conflict is to require the last month's rent plus a security deposit when the tenant begins a lease. Other landlords have addressed this problem by inserting a clause within their lease that states that the security deposit may not be used by the tenant as rent. However, standard lease forms usually contain a clause that allows the security deposit to be applied to unpaid rent. For the landlord who uses these forms, he or she must be careful when adding a clause to a form lease that prohibits use of the security deposit for rent.

 📕 A typewritten clause in an addendum to the lease which stated that the security deposit could never be used as rent took precedence over a clause that was printed in a standard lease form that said that the owner had the right, but not the obligation, to apply the security deposit to unpaid rent. (*Pyramid Enterprises, Inc. v. Amadeo57*, 10 Ill.App.3d 575 (Ill. App. 1 Dist. 1973).)

Illinois state law does not address the use of security deposits against unpaid or last month's rent. The Security Deposit Interest Act, however, does allow interest on the security deposit to be used for rent due. The Chicago ordinance does allow the landlord to deduct "any unpaid rent" from the security deposit or from the security deposit interest.

SECURITY DEPOSITS AND SALE OF THE RENTAL PROPERTY

When a landlord, who has received security deposits or prepaid rent from tenants, sells, leases, transfers, or disposes of the residential property to another landlord, the new owner becomes liable for the security deposits, prepaid rent, and security deposit interest, just as the original landlord was. In addition, the original landlord remains jointly and severally liable with the new landlord for the security deposits, prepaid rent, and interest. The Security Deposit Return Act was enacted to prevent a landlord from taking the security deposits when he or she sells the rental property.

In addition to the above, the Chicago Ordinance requires that the new landlord must notify the tenants who have made security deposits within ten days of the transfer or sale of the rental property. By delivering or mailing the notice to the tenant's last known address, it is sent by the new landlord to any tenant with security deposits. The written notice informs the tenant that the new landlord is holding the security deposit, and includes the new landlord's name, business address, and business telephone number; as well as the business telephone number of the new landlord's agents (if any). If the new landlord fails to comply with this law, he or she is liable for an amount equal to twice the security deposit plus interest, and may also be liable for other damages.

HOME RULES

This chapter has just briefly touched on the topic of security deposits under the Illinois state law, the Chicago ordinance, and the Evanston ordinance. Any municipality using home rule can create its own laws as to security deposits and security deposit interest. Home rules are usually stricter than the state law. Landlords should check with their own municipality and county to find out if there are any such rules, and not just rely on the state laws. If there are such home rules, obtain a copy and be sure to read them carefully. If you do not understand the rules, ask for an explanation from the government agency that monitors or enforces the rules, or consult an attorney.

RESPONSIBILITY FOR MAINTENANCE **6**

The responsibility for maintenance on a rental building is a vague area of law. The classic common law principal was that the landlord owes the tenant no duty to maintain the premises. However, during the last three decades the courts and local municipalities have established the legal concept of the *implied warranty of habitability*, which places a duty on the landlord to put and to maintain the rental property in a condition that meets the standards of state and municipal housing codes, sanitary regulations, and building codes.

    📖 A tenant was allowed to use a breach of the warranty of habitability as a defense to the landlord's action of eviction. (*Javins v. First National Realty Corp.*, 428 F.2d 1071 (D.C. Cir. 1970).) (The warranty of habitability will be covered in depth later in this chapter on page 65.)

Technically, Illinois state landlord/tenant law does not state that the landlord is responsible for maintenance. This means that a landlord could put into his rental agreement that the maintenance is the responsibility of the tenant, or the property could be rented "as is." However, landlords should keep in mind that a tenant's failure to do some small maintenance like a plumbing leak could lead to thousands of dollars damage to the property.

Some municipalities have very specific laws that detail the maintenance responsibility of the landlord. The Chicago's Landlord and Tenant Ordinance 5-12-070 requires that the landlord "maintain the premises in compliance with all applicable provisions of the municipal code and shall promptly make all repairs necessary to fulfill this obligation." This allows Chicago to add requirements to the landlord and tenant ordinance, to building codes, and to other local laws that the landlord must follow.

NOTE: *This law does not apply to landlords who live in their building of six units or less.*

Several years ago, Chicago added a requirement that there be smoke detectors in all rental units. Failure to install smoke detectors could result in serious liability for a landlord in the event of a death or injury to a tenant.

The Chicago Landlord and Tenant Ordinance 5-12-110 gives the tenant remedies if the landlord fails to maintain the rental unit. Some of the items that specifically must be maintained are:

- structural integrity of the building;

- exits, stairways, and fire escapes;

- smoke detectors, sprinkler systems, standpipe systems, fire alarm systems, fire detectors, fire extinguishers;

- elevators;

- plumbing, flush water closets, lavatory basins, bathtub/shower, kitchen sink;

- heating facilities, gas appliances, electrical equipment/circuits;

- hot and cold running water;

- adequate hall or stairway lighting;

- foundation, exterior walls, roof, chimney;

- floors, interior walls, ceilings;

- windows, exterior doors, basement hatchways, locks, peep holes;

- screens;

- stairways and porches;

- basement or cellar; and,

- facilities for refuse disposal.

TENANT REMEDIES

ILLINOIS   While some states have very specific rights and remedies for tenants with maintenance problems in their units, Illinois does not have such laws. Therefore, unless a local ordinance is being violated, the tenant's remedy for a maintenance problem on the property may be to take the landlord to court and claim that it was a violation of the lease or of the warranty of habitability.

However, tenants are not helpless. Tenants may also attempt to withhold all or a part of the rent (which can result in eviction) or have the repairs made and then get a reimbursement from the landlord. In cases of severe habitability problems, tenants may even report the landlord to local officials for building code or health code violations. In such case a landlord may be cited, fined and required to make repairs by the court.

Landlords should be advised that even in cases where the maintenance problem complained of seem trivial, all maintenance problems should be investigated and the investigation documented. Maintenance defects can cause injuries that the landlord may be liable for in addition to the potential of a tenant who takes his/her complaint to the city or to the courts. A tenant reimbursement for emergency maintenance done, a quick response by the landlord to maintenance problems, a janitorial fix to what the tenant is complaining of, are all less expensive that a court fight or the potential of fines from the city.

CHICAGO
The Chicago ordinance 5-12-110 specifies several tenant remedies for failure of the landlord to comply with the warranty of habitability. The remedy depends on the severity and how material the noncompliance is; the time it takes for the landlord to repair the problem; and, if there is a written lease.

The most severe material noncompliance is one that makes the premises not reasonably fit or habitable. In that case, if the condition is not corrected within a specified time period after the tenant notifies the landlord, the tenant may terminate the lease, and is entitled to the return of his or her security deposit, plus interest and any prepaid rent. In addition, a tenant may also be able to bring a lawsuit for injunctive relief and damages for a material noncompliance.

The 5-12-110 ordinance also specifies tenant remedies for landlord's failure to deliver possession of the property to the tenant, for minor defects, for failure to provide essential services, and for a failure to maintain the building. *Essential services* are heat, running water, hot water, electricity, gas, and plumbing. Material noncompliance in providing essential services are those items that constitute an immediate danger to the health and safety of the tenant, or those services that are contrary to the lease. For minor defects, the statue allows the tenant to have the damage repaired (after notifying the landlord), and, up to certain limits, deduct the repair costs from the rent. For failure to maintain, if there is a material noncompliance, a tenant can actually withhold rent. It is the responsibility to the Chicago landlord to keep up with the current Chicago Landlord and Tenant Ordinance, and to comply with these laws.

Tenant remedies for lack of maintenance are not limited to those above. Courts will take into account the circumstances of each case, the local ordinances, the terms of the lease, and the actions of both the tenant and the landlord.

WARRANTY OF HABITABILITY

In general terms, the *warranty of habitability* means that when a rental unit is turned over to a tenant, the tenant is automatically given a warranty by the landlord that the premises are in safe and habitable condition, and will remain so during the term of the lease. The building should be in accordance with all local codes and that the "dwelling unit and common areas" maintained in a "fit and habitable condition."

📖 The *implied warranty of habitability* requires that a dwelling be fit for its intended use, and habitable and fit for living. This warranty also requires that, at the inception of the lease, there are no latent defects in the premises that are vital to the use of the dwelling for residential purposes, or vital to life or safety of the tenant; and that the premises remain habitable throughout the term of the lease. (*Vanlandingham v. Ivanow*, 615 N.E.2d 1361 (Ill. App. 4 Dist. 1993).)

📖 To constitute a breach of the *warranty of habitability*, a defect must be one of a substantial nature, so as to render the premises unsafe or unsanitary, and thus unfit for occupancy. The condition complained of must truly render the premises uninhabitable in the eyes of a reasonable person. The tenant must give the landlord notice of the alleged defect, and the landlord must be given reasonable time to repair the defect. (*Fitzpatrick v. ACF Properties Group, Inc.*, 595 N.E.2d 1327 (Ill.App. 2 Dist 1992).)

📖 There is an implied warranty of habitability in all leases, and this applies even if there are no building code violations. That warranty requires that the dwelling be fit for residential use and that the premises remain habitable throughout the term of the lease. (*Glasoe v. Trinkle*, 479 N.E.2d 915 (Ill. 1985).)

COMMON AREAS

The *common areas* of a rental building are those places that are accessible to everyone. This includes interior areas (stairs, hallways, elevators, lobby, etc.); and exterior areas (walkways, walls, window frames, eaves, fence, garage, lawn, etc). Most courts have held that a landlord has a common law duty to maintain these areas in a reasonable and safe fashion. Some municipalities have enacted their own laws that specify how these common area must be cared for by the landlord or owner. Evanston has a Structures Code that regulates 212 points of a building. The first thirty-eight points are items dealing with the exterior common areas. Within the last five years, many municipalities have enacted laws that require owners of buildings to remove exterior graffiti within a short time period. Chicago has a very strict ordinance that requires owners to remove the graffiti, and also a department within the city, "Graffiti Busters," that will assist the owners if needed.

CODE VIOLATIONS

Landlords should be aware that, even for minor violations, governmental bodies can levy fines of hundreds of dollars per day. Ignoring notices of violation can be expensive.

Read governmental notices very carefully and follow any instructions in the letter. One landlord who sold his property and thought the problem was solved was fined $11,000 ($500 a day for the last twenty-two days he owned the property) for a violation. After correcting a violation, be sure that the governmental body that sent the notice gives a written confirmation.

Landlord's Liability for Utility Payments

Illinois' *Rental Property Utility Service Act* (765 ILCS 735) and the *Tenant Utility Payment Disclosure Act* (765 ILCS 740) cover the payment of utilities (water, gas, electricity) for rental property. These laws prohibit the landlord from terminating utility service to the tenants, by either not paying bills that the landlord has assumed responsibility for agreement or implication (such as having a master meter), or by tampering with the equipment or lines.

In addition, these laws allow tenants to pay for utility service, that the landlord is in default on, if the landlord's nonpayment will cause the utility to be shut off. The utility company must post notices of the service termination, and notify all tenants in buildings where there are three or more residential apartments. If the tenants do pay for the utility, the tenants are entitled to full reimbursement from the landlord. If the landlord's default is deliberate, done with reckless indifference, bad faith, or wilful disregard for the rights of the tenants—the court may award the tenants damages, costs, and attorneys' fees.

Upon receiving a notice of utility termination, either the tenants or the utility company may petition the court for appointment of a receiver. That receiver will collect rents and remit a portion to the utility company, according to a plan devised by the court. The court can also award damages, court costs, expenses, and attorney's fees.

These laws also allow the landlord and tenant to enter into an agreement where the tenant directly pays the utility bills for the entire rental property. Before entering into such an agreement, the landlord must provide to the tenant:

- written statements listing what areas of the building are served by this utility meter to be put in the tenant's name;

- history and details of the utility use in this area, including any that have not been reflected in past utility billings;

- copies of the utility bills for the previous twelve months;

- statement that the landlord neither suggests or requires that the tenant collect money from other tenants for this utility charge; and,

- a written statement of the amount of proposed rent reduction, if any, that is offered to the tenant to compensate for the payment of the utility bills.

For rental agreements where tenants must pay a proportionate amount of utility payments, these laws require a disclosure from the landlord to the tenant. This disclosure must be in writing, and can be either part of the lease or a separate document. It must provide the formula used by the landlord for allocating the utility payments among the tenants. The formula should include all areas that use the utility and reflect the variations by apartment size or usage. The formula must not allocate an amount greater than the monthly utility billing. In this case, if the tenant requests, the landlord must provide the utility bills for any billing period for which payment is demanded.

LIABILITY FOR REMOVING SNOW

For years, owners of property and landlords have been reluctant to shovel their sidewalks for fear of lawsuits. This reluctance comes from liability case law, which says things that "naturally accumulate," such as snow, ice, and flood waters, are all "acts of God." As long as these acts of God are not disturbed by humans, there is no liability to the humans.

The Illinois Snow and Ice Removal Act (745 ILCS 45) says that people who attempt to remove snow or ice from the public sidewalk that touches their property, "shall not be liable for any personal injuries allegedly caused by the snowy or icy condition" unless there was "willful or wanton" misconduct. Landlords or their employees may clear the sidewalk around their buildings without undue risk of liability. Be sure that the clearing of snow or ice does not leave the sidewalk in a dangerous condition.

The following cases illustrate how the courts impose liability under the law.

📖 By contracting with a company to remove snow, and by shoveling snow and spreading salt on hazardous areas, the landlord voluntarily undertook the task of removing snow from the parking lot, and was under a duty to perform that task with reasonable care. (*Ordman v. Dacon Management Corp.*, 633 N.E.2d 1307 (Ill.App. 3 Dist. 1994).)

📖 The landlord has no duty to remove snow and ice that have accumulated from natural causes, however, a landlord may be liable if he or she undertakes to remove ice and snow and acts negligently in doing so. This negligence would include shoveling, plowing, or moving the snow in any manner that would cause an unnatural or man-made accumulation on the walkway, making the walkway dangerous. (*Cronkhite v. Feeley*, 623 N.E.2d 748 (Ill.App. 3 Dist. 1993).)

📖 A landlord has no legal duty to remove snow and ice from areas used jointly with his tenants, when the snow and ice accumulate from natural causes. In order for a landlord to be liable for failure to remove snow and ice, it must be shown that he has in some way caused an unnatural accumulation of ice and snow; or that he aggravated a natural condition; or he undertakes to remove snow and ice from his property and does so negligently. Liability may arise where the landlord has assumed the duty to remove ice and snow by a contract with the tenants. However, even where there is such a contract, duty cannot be imposed where the precipitation is recent or continuous. (*Williams v. Lincoln Towers Associates*, 566 N.E.2d 501 (Ill.App.2 Dist. 1991).)

While the above is a state law, some municipalities require that property owners clear the public walks around their building, and the walkway that postal employees or delivery people use for access to the building. The U.S. Post Office can suspend delivery of mail if the snow or ice prevents the postal employee from gaining access to a building's mail boxes, or if the walkway is left in a dangerous condition from the snow or ice.

Some municipalities have time limits for when snow must be removed from public walks. Evanston gives owners twenty-four hours after a snowfall of four or more inches. Chicago allows owners three hours after it stops snowing, or until 10:00 A.M. the next day. Depending on the conditions and the local laws, salt, chemical melt, or sand may also be required.

Evanston used to require landlords to shovel the private walks and steps, but when the owners complained, the law was amended to read that walkways, stairs, and driveways "shall be kept from hazardous conditions." Still, in Evanston, by official reports, when a tenant complains, the owner is given a warning to clear off the snow or ice. Municipal authorities say that they enforce these laws through issuing tickets, usually after investigating a citizen's complaint.

The opinion of many who are in the business of insuring rental property is that landlords or owners should do a very good job to clear away the snow and ice, be cautious, be very thorough, and apply salt or chemical if it is needed or required by your local laws.

TENANT'S RESPONSIBILITIES

There is no state law that lists tenant's responsibilities regarding maintenance. These responsibilities would be whatever the lease requires, general duties under the common law, requirements of municipal ordinances, and any statutes that apply to specific acts on the premises.

Almost all leases contain specific tenant's duties and spell out what the landlord's remedies if the tenant fails to perform his or her duties. The more detailed a lease can be about the tenant's duties, the easier it is for the landlord in cases where the tenant must be evicted. Another important clause included in leases is one that requires the tenant to comply with local or municipal ordinances. Even if the lease is very detailed as to the tenant's duties, imposing compliance with local laws gives the landlord an additional tool to deal with unruly tenants.

The majority of Illinois municipalities that have their own landlord/tenant laws include detailed ordinances that list tenant's responsibilities. For example, under the Chicago Residential Landlord and Tenant Ordinance 5-12-040 (which applies to all rentals except when the landlord lives in a building of six or less units), tenant are required to:

- comply with obligations imposed by the municipal code;

- keep the rental unit that the tenant occupies safe;

- dispose of ashes, rubbish, garbage, and other waste in a clean and safe manner;

- keep all plumbing fixtures in the unit clean;

- use in a reasonable manner electrical, plumbing, sanitary, heating, ventilating, air conditioning, and other facilities and appliances, including elevators;

- not deliberately or negligently destroy, deface, damage, impair, or remove any part of the premises or knowingly permit or consent for another to do so; and,

- conduct himself or herself, and require guests to conduct themselves, in a manner that will not disturb any neighbors' peaceful enjoyment of the premises.

LANDLORD'S LIABILITIES 7

The law relating to a landlord's responsibility for injuries and crime on rental property has changed considerably over the last couple of decades. The law for centuries was that landlords were not liable. Now, landlords are often held liable, even for conditions that are not their fault. This change was made by judges who felt that tenants needed protection and landlords should give it to them.

INJURIES ON THE PREMISES

AREAS UNDER
LANDLORD'S
CONTROL

The parts of the rental property that are considered under the landlord's control are the *common areas*. These are the stairways, hallways, lobby, passageways, laundry room, and any other area that is for the common use of several tenants. Common areas are not usually involved in the rental of single-family homes, but can be if the landlord reserves an area that both the landlord and tenant regularly use. Whether such a common area exists in a particular situation would be a question answered by the courts. In a duplex or three-flat, the landlord may state in the lease that the tenants assume the duty to take care of the common areas. For other rentals, especially multi-unit apartment buildings, the landlord has a duty to maintain the common areas.

📖 Where only a portion of premises is rented and the landlord retains control of other parts for common use of tenants, the landlord has a duty to exercise reasonable care to keep common areas in a reasonably safe condition and is liable for foreseeable injury from the failure to perform such duty. (*St. Phillips v. O'Donnell*, 484 N.E.2d 1209 (Ill.App. 2 Dist. 1985).)

📖 If a portion of the premises is rented and the landlord retains control of other parts of the premises (such as stairways, passageways, or cellarways); or where the landlord rents the premises to several tenants, retaining control over the part of the premises for the common use of those several tenants—the landlord has a duty of exercising reasonable care to keep those common areas of the premises in a reasonably safe condition and is liable for any injury from a failure to perform such duty. (*Williams v. Alfred N. Koplin & Co.*, 448 N.E.2d 1042 (Ill.App. 2 Dist. 1983).)

📖 The landlord has a duty to exercise reasonable care to keep common areas in a reasonably safe condition and is liable for injuries to persons lawfully on those premises due to a failure to perform this duty. (*Hiller v. Harsh*, 426 N.E.2d 960 (Ill.App. 1 Dist. 1981).)

📖 If only one apartment is accessible for a particular stairway, and that stairway is used solely by the tenants of that one apartment, the stairway is not part of the common areas for which the landlord has a duty. (*Savka v. Smith*, 373 N.E.2d 1051 (Ill.App. 3 Dist. 1978).)

📖 The general duty imposed on a landlord is to use ordinary care to keep a portion of the premises that are reserved for the common use and under the landlord's control, in a reasonably safe condition. (*Finesilver v. Caporusso*, 274 N.E.2d 905 (Ill.App. 1 Dist. 1971).)

AREAS NOT UNDER THE LANDLORD'S CONTROL

The landlord is not liable for injuries on parts of the premises that are not under his or her control except in the following circumstances:

- where there is a danger known to the landlord;

- where there is a violation of law in the condition of the premises;

- where there is a pre-existing defect in construction;

- where the landlord undertakes to repair the premises or is required by the lease to do the repairs; and,

- where the landlord committed a negligent act.

CASES HOLDING A LANDLORD NOT LIABLE

The following are cases that held a landlord would not be liable for injuries. It must be kept in mind that the rulings in some of the earlier cases may have been modified by the rulings in later cases.

- The property owner/landlord of an apartment building let the building sit vacant and in a complete state of disrepair. A homeless person, who was a trespasser on the property, was beaten to death in the vacant building. The non-resident owner/landlord was sued alleging negligence which caused the death. The court found that the owner/landlord was not liable. (*Salazar v. Crown Enterprise, Inc., GLS, et. all* (WL 389862, Ill. App. 1 Dist. 2002).)

- A tenant was attacked and injured when entering the common area of the apartment complex where the tenant lived. The tenant sued the landlord stating that the landlord has a duty to protect tenants from third party criminal activity in common areas of the building. The tenant alleged that the attacker gained entrance through a security door which was broken for one month. Court found that although the landlord has such a duty to protect tenants, in this case there was no evidence that the security door had been broken for one month. Additionally there was no evidence that the attacker had gained entry through the broken door. (*Drouzas v. Drouzas* (No. 1-00-0726, Ill. App. 1 Dist. 2001).)

- Landlords are generally not liable for injuries occurring on premises leased to a tenant and under the tenant's control. (*Betts v. Crawshow*, 618 N.E.2d 1262 (Ill.App. 5 Dist. 1993).)

- An apartment complex management company was held not to owe a duty to a tenant to protect the tenant's child from falling through a screened window. This was true even though the management company knew that at least three children had recently fallen through windows in the same building. (*Best v. Services for Cooperative & Condominium Communities*, 629 N.E.2d 123 (Ill.App. 1 Dist. 1993).)

In another case, the court followed the same decision. This court added that the landlord did not agree to provide the apartment with childproof screens or sufficient safeguards to protect a child from falling from a window by merely stating they would provide "suitable aluminum screens," despite the fact that the screens had been installed improperly. (*Henstein v. Buschbach*, 618 N.E.2d 1042 (Ill.App. 1 Dist. 1993).)

    📖 Duty to inspect the premises and determine the safety and suitability falls on the tenant. (*A.O. Smith Corp. v. Kaufman Grain Co.*, 596 N.E.2d 1156 (Ill. App. 3 Dist. 1992).)

    📖 The tenant's roommate tripped over an unattached antenna wire near the second-floor deck of a leased house and fell from the deck. The court found that the tenant had known of the wire and that it could be blown onto the deck; and decided that the wire was not a "latent defect;" therefore, the landlord was not liable for the injuries. (*Housh v. Swanson*, 561 N.E.2d 321 (Ill.App. 2 Dist. 1990).)

    📖 The presence of paint chips in the apartment, that a young child might place in his mouth, did not establish a dangerous condition making injury to a child foreseeable. Therefore, the landlord had no duty to remedy the situation, even when the child developed lead poisoning as a result of contact with the paint chips. (*Garcia v. Jiminex*, 539 N.E.2d 1356 (Ill.App. 2 Dist. 1989).) (However, under recent federal lead paint rules, a landlord might be liable.)

    📖 The landlord of a farmhouse could not be held liable for injuries to a tenant who fell when rotten wood on a stair gave way. The water leakage into the basement could be considered a defect, but it was not the *proximate cause* of the injury (it was not a sufficiently direct and connected cause for liability). (*Greenlee v. First National Bank in DeKalb*, 529 N.E.2d 723 (Ill.App 2 Dist. 1988).)

    📖 Even where the landlord retains control of part of the premises, he or she is not liable for injuries that are not reasonably foreseeable. The landlord is not the absolute insurer for all injuries occurring on the premises. (*Trotter by Trotter v. Chicago Housing Authority*, 516 N.E.2d 684, (Ill.App. 1 Dist. 1987).)

    📖 Merely because the landlord makes minor repairs or cosmetic changes to the rental property, does not make the landlord accountable to fix areas under the tenant's control, nor does it make the landlord assume the liability for injuries that occur in these areas. (*Seago v. Roy*, 424 N.E.2d 640 (Ill.App. 3 Dist. 1981).)

CASES HOLDING
A LANDLORD
LIABLE

The following cases are examples of when a landlord was held liable for injuries to a tenant or a guest.

   📖 The tenant was injured by a fall on stairs in the common area. The tenant sued the landlord for not keeping the common areas maintained. The court found that the owner/landlord is responsible for a tenant's injury due to a deteriorating and dangerous condition of the common area front steps. The court reasoned that the owner/landlord had allowed the condition to continue without repair. (*Salina v. Pacheco* (Ill. Supreme Court, No. 1-00-0791, 2002).)

   📖 The landlord is liable for injuries to the tenant resulting from defective conditions in the rental unit, where the injury results from a violation of a statute or an ordinance that prescribes a duty for protection and safety of persons or property. (*Bybee v. O'Hagen*, 612 N.E.2d 99 (Ill.App. 4 Dist. 1993).)

   📖 The landlord was found liable, even though he was not in possession or control of the rental property, when a fire in the property killed and injured several tenants because there was evidence that the landlord had violated various building ordinances and was aware he was in violation. Because of these violations and the landlord's actual knowledge of the violations, the court held that the landlord owed a duty to the tenants. (*Jones v. Polish Falcons of City of Chicago Heights*, 614 N.E.2d 397 (Ill.App. 1 Dist. 1993).)

   📖 Despite the general common law relieving landlords of liability, the landlord was liable for the child's injuries when the child fell from an apartment window. The landlord had expressly assumed a duty and had contracted with the tenant to provide restraints on the windows that would be sufficient to protect a child from falling. (*Lamkin v. Towner*, 563 N.E.2d 449 (1990).)

   📖 The general rule is that a landlord is not liable for injuries sustained by a tenant as a result of a defective condition withing the rental unit. There are five exceptions to this rule: (1) where the latent defect existed at the time of the leasing, which the landlord in the exercise of reasonable care knew or should have known about, and which could not have been discovered by a reasonable examination by the tenant; (2) where there is fraudulent concealment by the landlord of a dangerous condition; (3) where the defect is causing harm that, under Illinois law, amounts to a nuisance; (4) where the landlord makes a promise to repair the condition at the time of leasing; and, (5) where the landlord violates a requirement of a law in which the tenant is in a class designed to be protected and the resulting harm is reasonably foreseeable. (*Moreno v. Balmoral Racing Club, Inc.*, 577 N.E.2d 179 (Ill. App. 3 Dist. 1991).)

📖 In Illinois, as a general rule, landlords are not liable for injuries on premises leased to and under the control of a tenant. This rule is subject to several exceptions, one of which states that the violation of a statute or ordinance that prescribes a duty for the protection and safety of persons or property may constitute negligence and be the basis of a lawsuit from those injured. (*Enis v. Ba-Call Building Corp.*, 639 F.2d 359 (C.A.7 Ill. 1980).)

These are not all the cases regarding landlord liability, but only a small sample of the cases on this topic. If all the cases were listed, it would take this entire book. Also, there are new cases happening every day, and some of the cases that are listed here may be appealed and overturned. Even if a case is not overturned, if you present it in court to support your position, that case may be rebutted by other cases that have a different outcome; or the judge may decide to disregard the case because it is not pertinent or is not from the local jurisdiction.

PROTECTION FROM LIABILITY FOR INJURIES

As is clear from these cases, the most common way for a landlord to be liable is if there are serious defects on the property, or if the landlord specifically agrees to make some sort of repair and fails to do so, or fails to do so properly. In addition, some municipalities are putting new - responsibilities on landlords.

To reduce the level of liability from injuries landlords should:

- detail responsibilities for repairs and maintenance in every lease;

- encourage tenants to report maintenance problems;

- set up a written log for each tenant complaint or request for maintenance;

- inspect these complaints and maintenance requests promptly;

- document the inspection, and every repair made;

- use a written checklist to inspect the entire building on a scheduled basis; and,

- use a written checklist to inspect a rental unit when a it becomes vacant.

Landlords should be sure that they have adequate insurance for any foreseeable liability. With jury awards going into the millions, a couple hundred thousand dollars in coverage is not enough. Some insurance companies offer "umbrella policies" that cover landlords for a million dollars or more at reasonable rates.. This type of insurance is a necessity for landlords who do not want to lose everything they own to an injured tenant, and many are raising rents to cover the cost.

Landlords should make sure the insurance coverage protects the value of the property. As property values increase, so should the amount of insurance coverage. Purchase a policy which includes coverage for physical injuries, libel, slander, discrimination, wrongful evictions, and invasion of privacy suffered by tenants and guests. Encourage your tenants to carry renter's insurance. The renter's policy should cover not only the tenant's property but damage/injuries caused by the tenant to other tenants, guests, and other rental units.

EXCULPATORY CLAUSES

An *exculpatory clause* in a lease exempts the landlord from all liability from damages or injuries on the rental property, even those injuries where (according to state law, local ordinances, or previous court cases) the landlord is legally liable.

NOTE: *Under Illinois state law, a lease provision that exonerates the landlord from liability for injuries to persons or property as a result of the negligent acts or omissions by the landlord (or the landlord's agents, servants, employees) is not enforceable.*

This law was enacted in 1971, ending years of common law which allowed landlords to avoid any liability by just inserting this type of clause in a lease.

📖 The lease in one case contained a clause that provided the tenant would "indemnify, hold harmless and defend" the landlord against all "claims and damages for all injuries or deaths" arising from the tenant's use and occupancy of the rental property. The "indemnify" portion of this clause was also supported by another lease provision that required the tenant to obtain a liability endorsement on the tenant's liability insurance policy that would indemnify the landlord. Even though the court acknowledged that there was a difference between an indemnity clause and a exculpatory clause, the court determined that Illinois State law forbids both of these types of clauses. (*McMinn v. Cavanaugh*, 532 N.E.2d 343 (Ill.App. 1 Dist. 1988).)

LIABILITY FOR CRIMES ON THE PREMISES

CRIMES AGAINST TENANTS

The liability of landlords has been greatly expanded into the area of crimes against tenants. The former theory of law was that a person cannot be held liable for deliberate acts of third parties. This has been the theory for hundreds of years, but in some parts of the country has recently been abandoned in favor of a landlord taking extra measures to protect his tenants from crimes.

If a landlord can foresee the possibility of criminal attack, the landlord must take precautions to prevent it. Some have argued that this means any time an attack is possible the landlord must protect the tenant, in nearly every tenancy. New Jersey has gone so far as to hold landlords strictly liable for every crime committed on their property, whether they knew there was a risk or took any precautions. This liability for crime, unlike the warranty of habitability, applies to both residential and commercial tenancies, but it has not yet been extended to single-family homes.

Illinois follows the former theory of law that does not hold the landlord liable from deliberate acts of third parties against tenants. Many local ordinances now require certain levels of security, that if not followed would make the landlord liable for these deliberate acts.

It should be noted that suits brought against landlords by tenants injured by third party criminal acts are on the increase. Legal duties requiring the landlord to protect tenants from criminal activity and to protect the neighborhood from the criminal tenants are starting to show up in local ordinances and codes.

It is no longer sufficient for a landlord to rely on past legal theories to protect them from the responsibilities for crimes committed on the rental property. Landlords must follow preventative measures to deter crimes. The landlord's insurance provider, local police, and private security professions can assist a landlord in setting up a workable security plan.

Other measures that may help limit a landlord's responsible for crimes committed on his or her property:

- providing all tenants with education on how to stop crimes and information on crime issues in the neighborhood;

- maintaining the rental property;

- conducting regular inspections on critical items such as security door and other means of access to the building; and,

- encouraging tenants to report dangerous situations and suspicious activity in and around the building, thus making the tenants a free security force for the landlord.

Here are some cases on this topic:

📖 Under Illinois law, the apartment building owners (and the building developer, manager, and their employees) were not negligent in providing security to a tenant who was attacked by a maintenance employee, even though the owner (manager) knew or should have known that the tenant's apartment was not secure from this employee. (*Ernst v. Parkshore Club Apartments Ltd. Partnership*, 863 F.Supp. 651 (N.D.Ill. 1994).)

📖 A landlord does not owe tenants a high degree of care to protect them from assaults by third persons. The landlord may be liable to a tenant for assaults by third persons, if the injury was due to a criminal act that occurred because of the condition of the premises (such as inadequate locks); or if the landlord attempts to safeguard the premises but does so negligently; or if the landlord, by his or her own acts, creates a hazard which did not previously exist. (*Rowe v. State Bank of Lombard*, 505 N.E.2d 1380 (Ill.App. 2 Dist. 1987).)

📖 While there is no duty upon the landlord to protect his or her tenants from harm caused by intentional or criminal act of third parties, the landlord may voluntarily assume certain duties by contracting with another party to provide protection such as security services. (*Rabel v. Illinois Wesleyan University*, 514 N.E.2d 552 (Ill.App. 4 Dist. 1987).)

📖 The general rule is that a landlord does not owe a tenant a duty to protect him or her from criminal acts. (*Carrigan v. New World Enterprises, Ltd.*, 446 N.E.2d 265 (Ill.App. 3 Dist. 1983).)

📖 Landlords do not have a legal duty to protect their tenants from the possibility of criminal action by any unidentified outsiders. (*Kosin v. Shero*, 360 N.E.2d 572 (Ill.App. 1 Dist. 1977).)

📖 The landlord/tenant relationship does not create a duty of the landlord to protect the tenants against criminal attacks of third persons. However, the landlord has a duty to correct or alleviate any dangerous condition. (*Cross v. Chicago Housing Authority*, 393 N.E.2d 580 (Ill.App. 1 Dist. 1979).)

📖 The landlord did not have a duty of care to prevent a tenant from being injured by an intruder who entered the tenant's apartment and shot the tenant in the course of a robbery and an attempted rape. (*Martin v. Usher*, 371 N.E.2d 69 (Ill.App. 1 Dist. 1977).)

📖 The landlord did not have a duty to protect tenant, who was struck and killed by a television that was thrown over a railing from above, even though the potential risk of injury from an item being thrown over the railing was known to the landlord. The intentional and criminal act of battery was that of another tenant. (*Trice v. Chicago Housing Authority*, 302 N.E.2d 207 (Ill.App. 1 Dist. 1973).)

PROTECTION
FROM LIABILITY
FOR CRIMES

The law is not clear in Illinois as to just how far courts will go in holding landlords liable for crimes against tenants. A clause in a lease that makes a tenant responsible for locks and security, may provide some protection to landlords in some situations, especially in single-family homes and duplexes.

In some inner-city apartment complexes where crime is common, landlords may be required to provide additional security or face liability. Again, insurance is a must and this cost can be covered by rent increases.

CRIMES BY
TENANTS AGAINST
NON-TENANTS

📖 In one case where a commercial tenant was selling counterfeit goods with such trademarks as Rolex and Polo, a United States District Court held that the landlords could be liable if they knew of the activities of the tenants and did nothing to stop them. (*Polo Ralph Lauren Corp. v. Chinatown Gift Shop*, 93 CIV 6783 TPG (United States District Court for the Southern District of New York, June 21, 1994).)

DRUG DEALING BY TENANTS

Landlords must be vigilant in stopping tenants who deal drugs from the rental unit. Local, state and federal drug laws penalize those who knowingly allow drug sales on their property. This can potentially include landlords and property owners. Besides the potential criminal penalties, this type of activity will drive away good tenants and drop the value of the entire rental property.

Prevention of drug dealing by tenants begins when the landlord interviews the prospective tenant. Carefully screening potential tenants is a must. Leasing and rental agreements should include a clause that prohibits drug dealing and other criminal acts, and makes violating the clause grounds for immediate eviction. This prohibition should also be part of the rules of the rental property and should be promptly enforced.

LIABILITY FOR LEAD PAINT POISONING

Rental property that was build prior to 1978 is subject to the Residential Lead-Based Paint Hazard Act—Title X in the Environmental Protection Agency regulations (40 CFR 745). This regulation requires a landlord in a property that qualifies under this act to give every tenant the EPA pamphlet "Protect Your Family From Lead In Your Home" or a state approved local version of this pamphlet. Tenants are also required to sign an EPA disclosure form stating that they were informed about lead paint dangers.

For EPA disclosure forms, pamphlets, and information on lead paint liability contact:

EPA at www.epa.gov for your local EPA office

EPA in Chicago 312-886-3000

National Lead Information Center (NLIC)
801 Roeder Road, Suite 600
Silver Spring, MD 20910
800-424-LEAD (5323)
www.epa.gov/lead/nlic.htm

There are many rental properties that are not covered by this rule. The following are not covered:

- housing which began construction after 1-1-78;

- housing that has been certified as lead free;

- lofts, efficiencies, and studio apartments;

- vacation rentals of 100 days or less;

- a single room rented in a residential home; and,

- housing designed for those with disabilities or seniors, unless children under 6 years old are expected to live in the unit.

If you have any questions as to whether your property is covered, contact the EPA or NLIC.

    📖 In 1998 the EPA brought a complaint regarding eleven housing units at Kingsville Naval Air Station. These units were built prior to 1978, housed enlisted personnel and their families. The tenants were not given the EPA pamphlet or information on lead paint dangers. The complaint was filed against several people involved in the rental including the landlord.

    📖 Tenant brought suit against the landlord due to injuries suffered by their child due to lead paint exposure. The landlord attempted to get his insurance carrier to cover legal costs and the settlement made with the tenant. The insurance company claimed that there was a lead-paint exclusion clause in the insurance contract. The court found in favor of the landlord for reimbursement of legal fees, because the landlord was not notified of the exclusion of lead paint coverage. The case is still in the court system to determine if the financial settlement was reasonable. (751 N.E. 2d 104 (May 24, 2001).)

Landlords may also be liable for lead-paint exposure when rental property is renovated, especially when other tenants continue to reside in attached units during the renovations. Again, the landlord needs to check with the NLIC and EPA prior to starting any renovations on buildings that were built before 1978. EPA requires that sixty days prior to renovations, current tenants be given information regarding lead paint dangers. This can usually be handled with a notice regarding the renovations location and date, plus the above mentioned EPA pamphlet.

Lead paint is not the only danger in renovations. Property owners may be liable for problems caused by exposure to other dangerous substances, especially during a renovation. One such substance is asbestos. Regulations issued by the Occupational Safety and Health Administration (OSHA) set very strict standards for testing, maintenance and disclosure of asbestos in buildings constructed prior to 1981. Many local communities have added regulations on asbestos through their building code ordinances. For information contact your local OSHA office or on the Internet at **www.osha.gov**.

CHANGING THE TERMS OF THE TENANCY 8

Sometimes, no matter how carefully a landlord writes a lease/rental agreement, things will come up where the landlord or the tenant needs to change the terms of the agreement. Many times the change is unavoidable; a tenant is transferred to another city, the property owner sells the building, etc. There are also some tenants who for no real reason want out of a rental lease. The landlord must then walk a narrow line between enforcing a lease against a tenant who may become a real problem, and losing rental money.

ASSIGNMENT OR SUBLEASE BY TENANT

Unless it is prohibited in a lease, a landlord cannot stop a tenant from assigning his or her lease to someone else, or from subletting all or a portion of the premises. The majority of standard lease forms in Illinois have some restrictions on a tenant's assignment or *sublease*. These restrictions are usually items such as:

- the landlord must consent to the prospective new tenant;

- the landlord can reject the prospective new tenant without cause;

- the prospective new tenant must pass the same screening process as all other prospective tenants;

- the tenant may be required to pay a fee, expenses, or an aggregate rent for the reletting;

- the new tenant must sign a lease with the landlord that is for the usual length of time for that property rental;

- the new tenant must pay rent directly to the landlord, not the former tenant; or,

- the tenant cannot sublet only a portion of the rental unit to another.

Outright denial of any assignment or sublease by the tenant is valid under Illinois state law, but is not favored by many courts. A few courts have viewed this prohibition as not absolute because of the unequal bargaining power between the landlord and the tenant. Some municipal ordinances specifically allow assignments or subleases with certain restrictions.

ASSIGNMENT   An *assignment* is where a tenant assigns all of his or her interest in a lease to another party who takes over the tenant's position.

SUBLEASE   A *sublease* is where the tenant enters into a new agreement with a third party who deals solely with the tenant. The original tenant is then the *sublessor* and the new tenant is the *sublessee*.

APPROVAL   Clauses that restrict assignment or sublease by requiring the approval of the new tenant by the landlord are very common. This approval is based upon the landlord not unreasonably withholding consent.

  Even if there is no provision in the lease that prohibits the landlord from unreasonably withholding his or her consent, "it is well established in Illinois that where a lease forbids any sublease or assignment without the consent of the landlord, the landlord cannot unreasonably withhold his/her consent." The law forbids a landlord from withholding consent if the tenant tenders a suitable subtenant or assignee. (*Jack Frost Sales, Inc. v. Harris Trust & Savings Bank*, 433 N.E.2d 941 (Ill.App. 1 Dist. 1982).)

Courts are divided as to what *unreasonable* specifically means. Generally, courts have allowed landlords to refuse consent for a prospective tenant when that tenant does not pass the objective screening process that all tenants must pass. (See Chapter 3, pages 27–30 for the screening process information.)

NOTE: *The screening must be objective and the same for every potential tenant, so that there is no violation of the Human Rights Act.*

WAIVER

If a lease contains a prohibition against subleasing or assignment, but the landlord fails to object to the sublease or assignment, that failure may constitute a waiver of the prohibition. Courts have found a waiver in instances where the landlord gave verbal approval even though the lease stated that there must be "written permission." Leases were also waived by the courts where the landlord assisted the former tenant in obtaining a subtenant by providing "For Rent" signs for the tenant's windows and posting the sublease information on the premises; and when the landlord continued to collect rent directly from the new tenant.

OBLIGATIONS

Without specific provisions in a lease or local laws, a tenant cannot discharge his or her rent obligation through a sublease or an assignment. The former tenant can be held secondarily liable if the subtenant or assignee defaults on the rent. However, it may be difficult to hold the original tenant legally liable if the landlord has approved the new tenant by an objective screening process. Also, former tenants can not always be found. Many landlords now require that the new tenant, in either a sublease or assignment, sign an agreement with the landlord in order to legally hold that new tenant responsible for the rent without the involvement of the former tenant.

SALE OF PROPERTY BY LANDLORD

A landlord has the right to sell property covered by a lease, but the new owner takes the property subject to the terms of the existing leases. The new owner cannot cancel the old leases or raise the rent while the leases are still in effect (unless the leases have provisions allowing the landlord to do so).

Most Illinois courts consider the assignment of the leases by the landlord to the new owner as part of the sale of rental property. Illinois case law has held that the new landlord will owe the tenants all of the duties that are required of a landlord under state law, local ordinance, and the terms of the lease. This also means that the new landlord is liable for a tenant's rent overpayments to the former landlord, lease obligations to the tenants that the former landlord ignored, etc.

When selling property, a landlord must specify in the sales contract that the sale is subject to existing leases. Otherwise, the buyer may sue for failure to deliver the premises free and clear of other claims. At closing, the leases should be assigned to the buyer.

As described in Chapter 5, the seller of rental property must transfer any security deposits and intent to the buyer. The seller remains liable for the deposit, and he or she should get an indemnity agreement from the buyer.

Raising the Rent

If a tenancy is for a set term (such as a one year lease) at a specified rent, then the landlord cannot raise the rent until the term ends (unless such a right is spelled out in the lease). If the tenancy is month-to-month, the landlord would be able to raise the rent if he gives notice at least thirty days prior to the end of the month. It is common law that the landlord can cancel the tenancy by giving thirty days notice, and this rule can also apply to rent increases.

If rent is raised, the tenant would not have to give thirty days notice if he or she decided not to stay at the end of the month. By raising the rent, the landlord would terminate the previous tenancy and be making the tenant an offer to enter into a new tenancy at a different rental rate.

Modifying the Lease

If you and a tenant agree to modify the terms of your lease, you should put it in an AMENDMENT TO LEASE/RENTAL AGREEMENT. (see form 19, p.260.) If you do not, and you allow a tenant to do things forbidden in the lease, you may be found to have waived your rights.

Problems During the Tenancy 9

Many problems can happen during the term of a rental agreement. The landlord may need to get into the rental unit, and the tenant believes that entry is a violation of his or her privacy. The landlord or the tenant may actually violate the terms of the lease. The tenant may violate rules of the rental community. Or, at the worst, the rental property is destroyed. This chapter reviews many of the more serious problems that landlords can encounter.

Landlord's Access to the Premises

Under Illinois common law, the landlord does not have the right to enter a rental unit during the term of the tenancy. Every lease must include a clause that reserves the right for the landlord to enter the rental premises under various circumstances. This clause will list the reasons that a landlord may enter, such as to make repairs, to inspect the premises, to show prospective tenants or buyers, and in an emergency.

The majority of the municipalities that have landlord/tenant ordinances include an ordinance that allows the landlord to enter the rental premises for certain reasons with a specified notice. Chicago requires the landlord to notify the tenant "two days" prior to the landlord entering the rental unit, and Evanston requires notice "forty-eight hours" prior entry; unless there is an emergency, in which case advance notice is not required.

In Chicago, entry must be between 8:00 A.M. and 8:00 P.M., or at any other time expressly requested or allowed by the tenant is presumed to be reasonable. Additionally, the Chicago ordinance specifies that the notice of entry be provided by mail, in person, or over the phone. For entry in cases of emergency or when repairs or maintenance elsewhere in the building unexpectedly require entry, the Chicago landlord must provide the tenant with notice that the entry has taken place within two days after the entry. Chicago's landlord/tenant ordinance allows the landlord entry:

- to make necessary or agreed upon repairs, decorations, alterations, or improvements;

- to provide necessary or agreed upon services;

- to exhibit the rental unit to prospective or actual purchasers, mortgagees, workmen, or contractors;

- as a practical necessity where repairs or maintenance elsewhere in the building unexpectedly require such access; and,

- in case of emergency.

VIOLATIONS BY THE TENANT

In a landlord/tenant relationship, serious violations of the lease by the tenant are usually considered in terms of default and remedies of the landlord. Specific actions that will be considered as violations resulting in default of the tenant, must be detailed in the lease signed by the tenant.

Most standard residential lease forms contain specific directions to the tenant about:

- paying rent;

- not abandoning the rental unit;

- upkeep or maintenance; and,

- the landlord's remedies if these directions are not followed.

It is important that the form lease used not only detail these specific requirements, but also require that the tenant comply with the local municipal ordinances.

In the Chicago Residential Landlord and Tenant Ordinance, the tenant's additional obligations are to maintain smoke detector batteries in the rental unit, keep the unit safe and clean, use provided equipment and facilities in a reasonable manner, prevent damage to the rental property, and avoid disturbing other residents. These obligations not only bind the Chicago tenant, but also bind the tenant's family and guests. However, this does not apply to tenants in buildings of six units or less in which the landlord resides.

FAILURE TO PAY RENT

Illinois state law provides that a landlord may begin taking legal action for a tenant's failure to pay rent any time after rent is due. The first step is for the landlord to give the tenant a *demand for rent*, which is a written notice stating that the overdue rent must be paid within five days or the landlord will consider the lease ended and take further steps to reclaim the premises. (See 735 ILCS 5/9-209.) If the tenant does not pay within the five days, the landlord may sue for possession under the statute on "Forcible Entry and Detainer," or maintain an *ejectment* action, without any further notice or demand. These types of legal proceedings are discussed in Chapter 12, on page 146.

If the landlord accepts the rental amount within this five day period, the landlord cannot terminate the rental agreement. The written demand for rent notice should demand the total amount of rent that is past due. However, the landlord may agree in writing to continue the lease in exchange for receiving only partial payments. The specific procedures for forcible entry and detainer and ejectment depend on the civil procedure rules in your county.

According to 735 ILCS 5/9-209, the demand for rent notice must *prominently* state:

> "Only FULL PAYMENT of the rent demanded in this notice will waive the landlord's right to terminate the lease under this notice, unless the landlord agrees in writing to continue the lease in exchange for receiving partial payment."

In addition to the above paragraph, the notice must also contain:

- the date of notice;

- the date when rent must be paid;

- the name of the tenant;

- a description of rental premises;

- the name of the landlord;

- the specific dollar amount of rent that is demanded; and,

- must be signed by the landlord or the landlord's agent.

📖 A tenant cannot be held in default in payment of rent unless there has been a legal demand for a certain dollar amount. (*Weinberg v. Warren*, 92 N.E.2d 217, (Ill.App. 1950).)

📖 The tenant's payment, without the written consent of the landlord, of an amount that was less than the total rent amount due was legally insufficient. The tenant's receipt of a five-day notice and his failure to comply with this notice for rent payment, entitled the landlord to terminate the lease. (*Elizondo v. Medina*, 427 N.E.2d 381 (Ill.App. 3 Dist. 1981).)

📖 The fact that a Chapter 13 (bankruptcy) debtor was still in possession of a rental apartment at the time she filed for bankruptcy did not change the fact that the lease was terminated due to her failure to pay rent prior to the bankruptcy filing. It was the failure to pay rent before the bankruptcy was effected, not the bankruptcy filing itself, that caused the lease termination. The tenant had received a proper fourteen-day notice of rent payment default in accordance with rule of the Chicago Housing Authority. (*In re Robinson*, 169 B.R. 171 (N.D. Ill. 1994).)

Under the Chicago Residential Landlord and Tenant Ordinance, if the entire rent or any portion of the rent is not paid on the date it is due, and the tenant fails to pay the rent or the portion within the five days after the notice, the landlord can either terminate the rental agreement or sue for rent or damages without terminating the agreement.

BAD CHECKS AND LATE CHECKS

A landlord can provide for a penalty if a tenant pays rent with a check that is returned for insufficient funds (bounced) or for rent payments that are given to the landlord after the due date. Any charge of a fee or penalty, whether for a bad check, a late payment, or for other reasons, should be included as a provision within the lease agreement. Landlords should check with the local ordinances before including a penalty or fee for bad checks or for late payments. For example, in Chicago the landlord/tenant ordinance (5-12-140 h) limit the amount of penalty by dollar amount and by percentage.

The landlord may also consider a bad check or a late payment for rent as a failure to pay rent. This requires giving the appropriate legal notice and giving the tenant five days to cure the default. As with every step prior to starting legal action against a tenant, the landlord *must* follow the applicable local law to the letter. See Chapter 10 for more details.

ABANDONMENT

A tenant is considered to have abandoned a rental unit when:

- the tenant notifies the landlord that the tenant will not return to the rental unit, or

- the tenant has been absent from the rental unit for a particular period of time, has removed his or her personal property from the rental unit, and the rent is unpaid for that period of time.

A general abandonment is one where rent is unpaid. If the landlord wants to terminate the tenancy, he or she should follow the directions under the section regarding "Failure to Pay Rent," on pages 116–117.

Some municipalities have ordinances that provide additional detail to what qualifies as an abandonment. In the Chicago ordinance [5-12-130(e)], the period of time a tenant must be absent from the rental unit (with non-payment of rent and removal of personal property) is the greater of twenty-one days or one rental period. Also under the Chicago ordinance, if a tenant is absent from the rental unit for thirty-two days and does not pay rent for that period of time, the tenant is considered to have abandoned the rental unit even if the tenant's personal property remains in the unit.

The abandonment rule rests on a non-payment of rent and an absent tenant. Landlord may wish to include a provision in the lease for those tenants who may be away from their rental property for long periods of time. This type of provision typically requires notice to the landlord and rent prepayment. As with every issue in the landlord/tenant - relationship, the landlord must check with the municipalities where the rental property is located for that municipality's ordinances.

CLASS X FELONY

The *Illinois Landlord and Tenant Act* (705 ILCS 5) can be used if the lease contains a provision requiring drug-free housing, similar to the one used in the U.S. Department of Housing and Urban Development. This law states that if a tenant or occupant is charged with having committed an offense constituting a *Class X felony* on the rental property, and there is either a judicial finding of probable cause at a preliminary hearing or an indictment by a grand jury, the lease can become void. An *occupant* is someone of any age who is living in the rental unit, but who has not signed the lease. This includes children, step-children, friends, and relatives. This law allows the landlord or building owner the choice of whether to continue to honor the lease.

If the landlord decides to terminate the lease, he or she must notify the tenant or occupant, using official forms available from the circuit court clerk of the county where the property is located. This written notice must state the basis for the lease termination. This notice is given to the tenant or occupant in person, by mail, or by posting the notice at the premises. It requires that the tenant or occupant vacate the rental unit on or before five days after the date of the notice.

GENERAL VIOLATIONS OF LEASE TERMS

Violations of provisions of a lease are viewed as either material or non-material noncompliance. *Material noncompliance* are those violations that would constitute a breach of the lease and cause the lease to terminate if the noncompliance is not remedied. In all cases, there is a required notice to the tenant, and period of time to remedy the violation, before the landlord can take further action.

A *non-material noncompliance* with the lease is a minor violation that, while not serious enough to evict, can be used by the landlord to determine if that tenant will asked to renew the lease for another term. As with material noncompliance, this is an act of not following the terms of the lease.

ORDINANCE
VIOLATIONS

In Chicago, tenants must follow the terms of the lease; plus Ordinance 5-12-040, "Tenant Responsibilities." Chicago leases usually include the terms of this particular law. In addition, Chicago landlords are required to provide the tenant with the entire Chicago Residential Landlord and Tenant Ordinance.

If a Chicago tenant does not comply with any part of Ordinance 15-12-040, or any part of the lease, it must first be determined if the non-compliance is material or nonmaterial. Material items are those listed as material in the ordinance or lease, or those actions which have severe impact. For material noncompliance, the landlord delivers a notice to the tenant. This notice specifies the acts or omissions which constitute the breach and informs the tenant that the rental agreement will terminate upon a date not less than ten days after receipt of the notice, *unless* the breach is remedied by the tenant. If the tenant does not remedy the breach within the ten day period, the lease is terminated.

The landlord can then recover damages and obtain injunctive relief for any material noncompliance. If the tenant's material noncompliance is wilful, the landlord may also recover reasonable attorney's fees for the legal work necessary in terminating the lease or obtaining injunctions.

DAMAGE TO THE
PREMISES

Tenant damage to the premises is most likely a violation of the lease. In Chicago it is also a noncompliance with the ordinance on tenant responsibilities. If the damage is what would be considered material noncompliance, the landlord may decide to repair the damage, bill the tenant for the repairs, and keep the lease in force. Another option, if the damage is not serious enough to render the place uninhabitable or will just be repeated after a repair, would be for the landlord to wait until the term of the tenancy is over, then make the repairs using the tenant's security deposit.

Under Chicago Ordinance 5-12-040, the tenant is required to maintain the rental unit. If the tenant fails to do so, the landlord must give the tenant a fourteen-day notice, telling the tenant of the problem that must be fixed and that the repair must be made withing the fourteen-day time period. If the tenant does not fix the problem within this time period, the landlord may enter the unit and have the necessary work done, following the applicable law on entering rental units. For those maintenance problems that cause an emergency in the building or affect other rental units, the landlord can enter the rental unit immediately without notice. In both cases, the landlord is entitled to a reimbursement from the tenant for the cost of repairs. However, the landlord must be able to prove that the problem was caused by the tenant's failure to maintain the rental unit as described in the lease or in the ordinance.

IGNORING TENANT VIOLATIONS

If a landlord does not take action against a tenant who violates the lease or the local ordinance, some courts have found that the landlord forfeits the ability to take action in the future. In the following cases, the landlord was proven to actually know the violation had taken place, but did nothing, not even send a notice of a violation to the tenant.

📖 Where a landlord's conduct has led the tenant to believe that the landlord will not insist on strict compliance with the terms of the lease, the court would not permit a termination of the lease because of the tenant's failure to comply strictly with the lease's terms, unless the landlord notified the tenant in writing that he intended to hold the tenant strictly to the lease's provisions in the future. (*McGill v. Wire Sales Co.*, 529 N.E.2d 682 (Ill.App. 1Dist. 1988).)

📖 Any act of the landlord that would affirm the existence of a lease with a particular tenant, after the landlord has knowledge of the tenant's breach of the lease, will result in the landlord waiving his rights to terminate the lease. (*Midland Management Co. v. Helgason*, 630 N.E.2d 836 (Ill. 1994).)

VIOLATIONS BY THE LANDLORD

The landlord has certain duties, both under the lease and in accordance with local and state law. The landlord usually is charged with the duty to maintain the common areas of the building. (See Chapter 6 for a discussion of this issue.)

DELIVERY OF
POSSESSION

Example: In a lease, the landlord implies that the tenant will have the right to possession of the rental property at the beginning of the term. However, technically there is no implied covenant that puts the new tenant in possession against a party that is wrongfully in possession, such as a hold-over tenant. Courts have found that in this case, the new tenant may have a right to damages from either the landlord or the hold-over tenant, depending upon the details of the case. However, the only damages covered are those that occurred because of the delay in moving into the rental property.

This type of incident can happen when the former tenant is unable to move out on the day specified for legitimate reasons, or when a former tenant refuses to vacate the premises. A detailed provision in the lease can explain what is considered *holding over*. The provision may also contain a clause that makes a hold-over tenancy considered a month-to-month tenancy at double the current rate, or may have a cost per day for a tenancy at sufferance. These amounts should compensate the landlord if he or she must pay the expenses of a future tenant whose moving in has been delayed. Remember to check with your local ordinances for rules on charging penalties and fees.

If the former tenant remains in possession with the knowledge and permission of the landlord, the landlord is considered to wrongfully withhold possession from the new tenant. To avoid some liability for damages of failure to deliver possession, landlords may consider additional lease provisions that limit the landlord's liability for failure to give possession, that specify that the tenant's sole remedy is the postponement of rent until the exact date of possession, or that limit the tenant's recovery to the return of prepaid rent and security deposit.

If the rental property is under construction, the landlord must be careful in setting a promised date of possession. Some leases will exempt the landlord from any liability if the construction is not finished through no fault of the landlord, while other leases will allow the tenant to decide if they wish to terminate the lease with all money returned or get a certain extension on their lease without a raise in rent. New construction, rehabbing, or extensive remodeling can cause many unforeseen delays in the availability of a building or unit. Landlords and building owners should have some plan to limit their liability for construction delays. This may be as simple as making a written agreement with each future tenant that allows for delays. Again, consult your local ordinances for requirements.

The Chicago landlord/tenant ordinance allows the tenant to:

- terminate the rental agreement by a written notice to the landlord, and receive all prepaid rent and security deposits, or

- demand performance of the lease by the landlord and maintain a court action for possession against the landlord or any person wrongfully in possession of the rental property.

The tenant may also recover any damages sustained. If the failure to deliver possession is willful, the future tenant may recover an amount equal to the greater of two months rent or twice the actual damages from the person withholding possession.

Most residential leases spell out the duties of both the landlord and the tenant. These duties and rights must be written in a non-ambiguous way, so that they are understood by both parties. Duties and rights should be detailed and use the common meaning of words. Both parties must follow these duties or they are in violation of the lease provisions. Some municipal ordinances specify what a tenant's remedies are in the instance when the landlord violates the lease.

CONSTRUCTIVE
EVICTION

A *constructive eviction* is something of a serious and substantial character, done by the landlord with the intention of depriving the tenant of the beneficial enjoyment of the premises. (*Dell'Armi Builders, Inc. v. Johnston*, 526 N.E.2d 409 (1 Dist. 1988).)

Upon a landlord's constructive eviction, the tenant is no longer liable for paying rent, and the tenant can abandon the premises without legal consequences. Constructive eviction is determined by the facts of the particular situation, including the terms of the lease and the conduct of the landlord and tenant. In court, the issue of constructive eviction has been difficult to prove.

 📖 The tenant could terminate a lease because the lease violated the Chicago Residential Landlord Tenant Ordinance as it did not provide the tenant with the same sixty-day right to termination clause as was given to the landlord. The landlord failed to deliver to the tenant a new lease that did not contain this improper provision within fifteen days of the tenant's demand. Additionally, the landlord failed to disclose, also upon the tenant's demand, that the rental property had been cited for two building code violations that had not been fixed. Even though these violations were for minor damage, it was the landlord's failure to disclose this when asked by the tenant that allowed the tenant to terminate the lease. (*Plambeck v. Greystone Management & Columbia National Trust Co.*, 666 N.E. 2d 670 (Ill.App. 1 Dist. 1996).)

 📖 Finding roaches which resisted extermination efforts in all parts of the leased premises, in addition to other serious instances of disrepair, amounted to constructive eviction. (*Applegate v. Inland R.E. Corp.*, 441 N.E. 2d 379 (Ill.App. 2 Dist. 1982).)

 📖 Following constructive eviction, the tenant is not required to vacate the premises immediately. The tenant is entitled to a reasonable time to vacate. However, even if the tenant has sufficient grounds to claim constructive eviction, the tenant waives this claim when the tenant fails to abandon the premises within a reasonable time after the untenantable condition occurs. (*JMB Properties Urban Co. V. Paolucci*, 604 N.E.2d 967 (Ill.App. 3 Dist. 1992).)

QUIET ENJOYMENT   The long standing *covenant of quiet enjoyment* requires that the landlord protect the tenant's quiet enjoinment and peaceable possession of the property during the term of the lease. (*Blue Cross Association v. 666 North Lake Shore Drive Associates*, 427 N.E.2d 270 (1st Dist. 1981).)

This means that the landlord cannot substantially interfere with the tenant's use and enjoyment of the rental property. The covenant is the consideration for the rent paid by the tenant and is implied in all leases. However, it does not protect the tenant from interference by strangers, from those with a right to title, or from interference by other tenants.

 ⌂ The covenant of quiet enjoyment is breached when the landlord substantially interferes with a tenant's use and enjoyment of the premises. In this case, building a sixty-four story office building next to the building where the tenant rented, and blocking the tenant's radio frequencies, did not breach the covenant of quiet enjoyment. There is no real or implied easement of air and light in the lease. (*Infinity Broadcasting Corp. Of Illinois v. Prudential Insurance Co. Of America*, 869 F.2d 1073 (C.A.7 Ill. 1989).)

 ⌂ A tenant's allegation that the landlord violated duties under a month-to-month tenancy, by prohibiting the tenant from subletting a portion of her rental unit, was not an intentional interference with the right to quiet enjoyment. The tenant did not have sublet rights under the original lease or under the subsequent oral month-to-month tenancy. (*Bismarck Hotel Co. v. Sutherland*, 529 N.E.2d 1092 (Ill.App. 1 Dist. 1988).)

If it is proven that the landlord has breached this implied covenant, the tenant has the right to seek damages, but must continue to pay rent for the term of the lease.

 ⌂ Damages for a breach of quiet enjoyment are the difference between the rental value of the property after the alleged incident and the amount of rent that the tenant agreed to pay under the lease. Damages may also include expenses incurred as a direct result of the landlord's breach. (*Madison Associates v. Bass*, 511 N.E.2d 690 (Ill.App. 1 Dist. 1987).)

RETALIATORY CONDUCT

The state of Illinois has a law that seeks to protect tenants from eviction, or a landlord's refusal to renew a lease, because the tenant has complained to any governmental authority about a violation of a building code, health ordinance, or any other ordinance. This law is called the *Retaliatory Eviction Act* (765 ILCS 720). The tenant must be able to prove that the landlord's actions were retaliatory, and refute any evidence of other legitimate reasons for the landlord's actions. Additionally, this law provides that any provision in a lease or rental agreement that allows the landlord to terminate a lease due to the tenant making such a complaint, is void.

  📖 The tenant could not prove in court that his lease was terminated solely because of complaints to the Department of Housing and Urban Development. There was no evidence that an inspection of the complex confirmed the existence of alleged problems. The tenant failed to specify a building code, health ordinance, or similar regulation that was applicable to alleged problem. Also, the tenant made no attempt to pay rent due. (*Shelby County Housing Authority v. Thornell*, 493 N.E.2d 1109 (Ill.App. 5 Dist. 1986).)

  📖 The tenant requested inspection by the city, violations were found by city inspectors, and the landlord was notified of the violations. Soon after, the landlord terminated the tenant's lease solely because of the tenant's complaints to the city. If the tenant can prove in court that this is the reason that the lease was terminated, the tenant can recover damages due to the retaliatory eviction. (*Morford v. Lensey Corp.*, 442 N.E. 2d 933 (Ill.App. 3 Dist. 1982).)

  📖 A landlord cannot terminate a lease, or refuse to renew the lease, because a tenant complained to a government authority about a violation in the Peoria Housing Code. The landlord is barred from terminating the lease and evicting the tenant. (*Clore v. Fredman*, 319 N.E.2d 18 (Ill. 1974).)

  📖 The Illinois Retaliatory Eviction Act only applies to residential leases. (*General Parking Corp. v. Kimmel*, 398 N.E.2d 1104 (Ill.App. 3 Dist. 1979).)

Many municipal ordinances add to the Retaliatory Eviction Act. Under the Chicago landlord/tenant ordinance, a tenant is additionally protected from retaliatory eviction for:

  ● complaining of a code violation or illegal landlord practice, or seeking assistance from a community organization or the news media;

- requesting that the landlord make repairs as required by a building code, health ordinance, other regulation, or the lease agreement;

- becoming a member of a tenant's union or similar organization;

- testifying in any court or administrative proceeding concerning the condition of the rental premises; and,

- exercising any right or remedy provided by law.

DESTRUCTION OF THE PREMISES

Municipal ordinances, or provisions in the lease itself, often provide for at least a reduction in rent if the buildings or part of the property is destroyed. A case can be made for termination of a lease when the property is destroyed, even if that is not spelled out in the lease or law, as the covenant of habitability is implied in every residential lease. If the rental property fails to meet the standards imposed by this covenant, which are usually standards based on local health and safety ordinances, or if the landlord fails to meet his obligation to maintain the building, the tenant may have the right to go into court and terminate the lease. The specifics would be listed in the municipal ordinances.

Most standard lease forms contain a provision regarding the destruction of the premises. If the landlord writes his or her own lease that includes such a provision, it must comply with the local law. In addition, some leases require that the tenant carry insurance for premise destruction. This is especially true when an entire building is being rented, or in the case of a nonresidential lease.

Under the Chicago Residential Landlord/Tenant Order, if there is a fire or casualty damage to the building or rental unit, the tenant has three options:

1. The tenant may move out immediately, and notify the landlord in writing within fourteen days of the tenant's intention to terminate the lease. In this case, the lease terminates on the date of the fire or casualty.

2. If the tenant can lawfully occupy the premises, the tenant may vacate any part of the rental unit that was rendered unusable by the fire or casualty. In this case, the tenant's liability for rent would be reduced in proportion to the area of the property that is unusable. This calculation would use the fair rental value of the property.

3. If the tenant wants to continue the tenancy, and if the landlord has promised to repair the damage but fails to make the repairs within a reasonable time, the tenant can send a written notification to the landlord within fourteen days of the tenant becoming aware that repairs are not being made. This notice informs the landlord of the tenant's intention to terminate the lease, and the termination date becomes the date of the fire or casualty.

In the case where the tenant has chosen one of the above three options, the landlord must return all security deposits, interest, and prepaid rent. This only applies if the tenant, or the tenant's family members or guests, are not responsible for the damage.

YIELD-UP CLAUSE

Many nonresidential leases and residential leases contain what are commonly called *yield-up* clauses, which direct the tenant to return the rental property at the termination of the lease in the same condition of repair as of the date the lease was begun. If this clause excludes from the yield-up condition loss by fire, casualty, and wear and tear, it may mean that the landlord will assume the risk of loss in case of fire or casualty. In this case, the landlord may wish to include a provision in the lease that holds the tenants liable for their own negligence and willful conduct in a loss by fire or other casualty.

PROBLEMS AT THE END OF THE TENANCY 10

The problems a landlord has with a tenant may not end just because the rental term has expired. Landlords need to be prepared for lingering problems from tenants who refuse to leave, tenants who damage the rental unit, and property that tenants leave behind.

TENANT HOLDING OVER

A tenant is considered to be *holding over* when the tenant does not vacate the rental property after the lease is terminated either by expiration or by termination of the lease. Two Illinois state laws cover this situation: 735 ILCS 5/9-202, titled "Wilfully Holding Over;" and 735 ILCS 5/9-203, titled "Holding Over After Notice." These laws define holding over as "a tenant not delivering up possession of the rental premises when the landlord has given the tenant notice to quit the premises or when the tenant has the right to quit as per the lease term." These laws also provide that the landlord can require a holdover tenant to pay double the rent amount required by the prior lease.

The majority of standard lease forms contain a provision on holding over, that specify what the landlord's rights are when a tenant does not leave after the lease has terminated. The most common provisions require that a landlord notify the tenant, within thirty days from the date of the hold over, what the landlord has chosen as a remedy for the hold over. Some common remedies are:

- renewal of lease for one year at double the rent;

- creation of a tenancy at sufferance with a daily rental rate;

- creation of a month-to-month tenancy at double the rent; or,

- a legal action for eviction.

📖 It is an option of the landlord whether a tenant at sufferance is evicted as a trespasser or treated as a holdover tenant. If the landlord decides to treat the tenant as a holdover, the holdover tenancy is governed by the terms of the original lease. (*Meyer v. Cohen*, 632 N.E.2d 22 (Ill.App. 1 Dist. 1993).)

📖 Double rent cannot be recovered under holdover statutes when the landlord terminates the lease. (*Stride v. 120 West Madison Building, Corp.*, 477 N.E.2d 1318 (Ill.App. 1 Dist. 1985).)

📖 A landlord can unilaterally change the terms that bind a holdover tenant by notifying the tenant before the holdover term begins. (*Brach v. Amoco Oil Co.*, 570 F.Supp. 1437 (N.D. Ill. 1983).)

📖 Failure to vacate the rental premises, without the permission of the landlord, following expiration of the lease creates a tenancy at sufferance. A tenant at sufferance presumptively creates a holdover tenancy, which the landlord can terminate at anytime. (*In re Generes*, 69 F.3d 821 (N.D. Ill. 1994); also *Bransky v. Schmidt Motor Sales, Inc.*, 584 N.E. 2d 892 (Ill.App. 2 Dist. 1991).)

DAMAGE TO THE PREMISES

If the landlord finds damage to the property at the end of a *tenancy*, the landlord may deduct the cost of repairs from the tenant's security deposit. To make such a deduction from the security deposit, the landlord must adhere to the local law which requires notice to the tenant, inclusion of the bills from the repair, and that this be done within a specific time period. See Chapter 5 on "Security Deposits" for details.

PERSONAL PROPERTY ABANDONED BY TENANT

When a tenant abandons the rental property or exits at the specified end of the lease, and leaves personal property behind, the landlord may be able to seize that personal property to offset any rent due. What may be seized and the procedures that need to be followed to perform the seizure are covered by state law and municipal ordinances.

The applicable state law is Chapter 735 ILCS 5/9, Part 3, "Distress for Rent." In this law, the word *distress* refers to the common law right of a landlord to seize a tenant's goods to satisfy an arrears of rent. Throughout the series of laws in Part 3, the word *distraint* is also used, which refers to the act of seizing this property. The theory is that the landlord is holding the tenant's personal property until the tenant pays the rent that is past due.

These state laws date back to the late 1800s and early 1900s, and may not be applicable because of municipal ordinances. Also, most standard lease forms address the holding of personal property when there is an abandonment of the rental unit. In the past, some landlords have used this law to lock the tenant out of his or her apartment because of back rent. The majority of local ordinances, such as the one in Chicago, do not allow that tactic to be used anymore. This area of law is very unstable, and a landlord would be wise to check with a local attorney before taking this type of action.

📖 "Distress for rent" denotes the landlord's right to seize a tenant's property in lieu of unpaid rent. (*In re Marriage of Logston*, 469 N.E.2d 167 (1984).)

Within the *Distress for Rent Act* there are procedures that must be followed. The landlord must file a *distress warrant* combined with a written inventory of the property to be seized. The warrant is filed with the county clerk's office. The clerk then issues a summons against the party against whom the distress warrant has been issued (the tenant). If the tenant cannot be found, there still must be a legal notice given, and this is usually done by publication. The procedures in this act are very specific and complex. This act also includes rules for the taking of crops off abandoned farm land, liens upon crops not yet mature, and seizure of products or labor in a nonresidential rental.

📖 If a landlord does not comply with the procedures for commencing a distress for rent action, he is not entitled to distress for rent against the property of the tenant. (*Schiller Park Compressed Steel Corp. v. Boerema*, 359 N.E.2d 852 (Ill.App. 1 Dist. 1977).)

In most instances, the personal property left when a tenant abandons the rental unit is probably not worth as much as the rent due. In addition, there are other legal remedies available to the landlord, that will be discussed in the following chapters.

A landlord's municipal ordinance may also provide for the acquisition of a tenant's personal property after that tenant has abandoned the rental property. For example, in Chicago's landlord/tenant ordinance, the first step is to determine if the tenant has abandoned the rental unit as defined under the law.

If the tenant has truly abandoned the rental property and has failed to remove personal property from the premises, or has left the personal property after a termination of the lease, the landlord can leave the property in the rental unit or store it. After seven days, the landlord can dispose of the property by any method. If the landlord reasonably believes that the abandoned property is valueless; or of such little value that, if sold, the amount recovered would not exceed the cost of storage, the landlord can immediately dispose of the property. The landlord can also immediately dispose of property that is perishable. (Chicago Ordinance 5-12-130 (f).)

NOTE: *The above procedure is not to be used while the tenant still occupies the property—even if rent is seriously in arrears.*

Chicago Ordinance 5-12-160 prohibits the landlord from interrupting the tenant's occupancy "by plugging, changing, adding or removing any lock or latching device." This ordinance also lists several other actions that the landlord is prohibited from doing in order to keep the tenant out of the property without going through the proper eviction procedure of forcible entry and detainer (see Chapter 12 on "Evicting a Tenant").

If the landlord violates this law, he or she can be liable for a fine of between $200 to $500 for each day the violation takes place. Plus, the tenant may be able to receive the greater of an amount equal to two months rent or double the amount of damages, in addition to being able to recover possession of the rental property.

TERMINATING A TENANCY 11

A tenancy may be terminated in several ways, but unless the tenancy is terminated properly, the tenant may not be evicted. Whether the lease is oral or written, Illinois law is very strict about how the tenancy may be terminated. Any variation from the required procedures can seriously delay an eviction, and cause a court battle that may go on for months or even years. An eviction without proper termination of the tenancy, will allow that the tenant may win the case. A landlord may then be ordered to pay damages to the tenant as well as the tenant's attorney fees—and the tenant will remain in the property.

TENANCIES WITH NO SPECIFIC TERM

In this section we will discuss terminating a tenancy when the rental agreement, either oral or written, does not specify when the tenancy will end. This typically occurs when the lease is open-ended from the beginning, or when the original lease term ends and the parties verbally agree to continue the lease indefinitely. Terminating such a tenancy is primarily a matter of giving the tenant the correct amount of notice.

To determine the amount of notice required, you will need to consider the following factors:

- terms of the written lease (if there was one) regarding renewals, extensions, otherwise continuing the tenancy beyond the expiration date;

- timing of rent payments under the lease.

    Example: If rent is paid weekly, it will be considered a week-to-week tenancy. If rent is paid monthly, it will be considered a month-to-month tenancy; and,

- reason for the termination.

    Example: If your agreement with the tenant is for rent to be paid monthly, you have a month-to-month lease that generally requires a thirty-day notice to terminate. However, if you are terminating because the tenant failed to pay the rent, another law comes into play and only a five-day notice is required.

The following cases help illustrate these factors.

📖 A month-to-month tenancy will abide by the terms of an original lease, if there was one. Otherwise, the tenancy will last indefinitely. To terminate a month-to-month tenancy, the landlord is required to give the tenant a thirty day notice. (*A.O. Smith Corp. v. Kaufman Grain Co.*, 596 N.E. 2d 1156 (Ill.App. 3 Dist. 1992).)

📖 The tenant remained in possession after the lease had expired. The landlord sent the tenant monthly bills, in increasing amounts, and the tenant paid the bills. The court found that the conduct of the two parties established a month-to-month tenancy. (*Bismark Hotel Co. v. Sutherland*, 415 N.E.2d 517 (Ill.App. 1 Dist. 1980).)

The following is a list of the number of days notice required to terminate a particular tenancy, and the state law that supports this:

- Week-to-week lease—seven day notice is required (735 ILCS 5/9-207);

- Month-to-month lease—thirty day notice is required (735 ILCS 5/9-207);

- Year-to year-lease—sixty day notice is required, and may be given at anytime within the four months before the last sixty days of the year (735 ILCS 5/9-205); and,

- Year-to-year tenancy of farm land, occupied on a crop share, live-stock share, cash rent, or other rental basis—written notice must be given not less than four months before the term end of the lease—even if the lease for farm land is an oral lease, the notice must be written.(735 ILCS 5/9-206).

The above time periods are those listed in the Illinois state law. Municipal ordinances may differ. Landlords must consult the municipal laws governing the location of the rental property.

EXPIRATION OF RENTAL TERM

When the term of a tenancy expires according to the lease, the tenant is required to surrender possession and neither the tenant nor the landlord need a notice (735 ILCS 5/9-213).

Some leases have an *automatic renewal provision*. This provides that the lease is renewed at the same rental rate for the same length of time, unless either the landlord or the tenant gives the other a notice of intent not to renew. Even without an automatic renewal provision, most tenants assume that they will have the option to renew their lease at the end of the rental term. Many municipal ordinances address this assumption of renewal by requiring landlords to notify the tenant if the landlord will not renew the lease.

Under the City of Evanston ordinance (5-3-8-3), landlords are required to give a tenant a thirty-day written notice if the landlord will not renew the lease. In this ordinance, the landlord is not required to give a reason for a refusal to renew.

For those in Chicago who are under the Chicago Residential Landlord and Tenant Ordinance must follow strict requirements to end a lease even when the written term is over. Landlords must provide a written NOTICE OF NON-RENEWAL before the last month of the lease. (see form 18, p.259.) Tenants who do not receive this thirty-day notice can extend their lease for up to sixty days past the termination date at the old rent rate if they notify the landlord in writing. So it is in the landlord's best interest to promptly notify any tenant who's lease is not being renewed. A thirty-day notice not to renew the lease is also required state wide for those who are in a month-to-month rental agreement.

EARLY TERMINATION BY TENANT

Generally, a tenant who vacates the property before the end of the lease term is liable for damages to the landlord. However, a tenant may legally terminate a residential lease early because of:

- a provision in the lease that allows this option;

- the complete destruction of the premises;

- the noncompliance of the landlord to the terms of the lease; or,

- provisions in state laws or municipal ordinances.

A provision in a lease that allows either the landlord or tenant to terminate a lease early, is usually called an *option*, which is discussed later in this chapter. Destruction of premises and the rights of the tenant is addressed in Chapter 18. For the duties of the landlord, see Chapters 6 through 7. Also, many municipal ordinances spell out the precise duties of the landlord and what remedies the tenant has if the landlord does not comply. (For Chicago, see Residential Landlords and Tenants 5-12-110.) Depending on the municipal ordinance, not every noncompliance of a landlord will result in allowing a tenant to terminate his or her lease early.

EARLY TERMINATION BY LANDLORD

STRICT
REQUIREMENTS

Much of this chapter addresses how a landlord can terminate a lease early, but there are some things that should be repeated because of their importance. Illinois law demands strict compliance with the procedural requirements for terminating a tenancy. The courts require that the termination notice be given a certain number of days in advance, as listed in the state laws. If the landlord attempts to shorten this number of days, he or she may not be able to complete the eviction and can be liable to the tenant for damages.

NOTICE

Before a residential lease can be terminated, the landlord must satisfy certain legal requirements. The primary requirement, and the one that causes the most problems, is "the landlord must serve the tenant with the proper notice" within the appropriate number of days. For the number of days required for a notice to be effective, reference the list on this page or review the state law indicated there. If the landlord does not comply with the exact number of days required, the landlord may be barred from completing the eviction process and may be sued by the tenant.

The notice *must be in writing.* This is true even if the tenancy was based on an oral agreement. Illinois state law does not require any exact wording or the use of a particular form.

TIME ALLOWED

The amount of time the tenant must be given in the notice depends upon the reason for termination:

- if the tenant has failed to pay rent—five day notice is required (735 ILCS 5/9-209), or

- if the tenant violates the terms of the lease—ten day notice is required (735 ILCS 5/9-210).

WORDING

The wording of the termination notice is also important. The state statutory rules are contained in Chapter 735, Act 5 under Forcible Entry and Detainer. Some municipalities also have requirements so be sure to check these before posting your notice. One thing that is often required is a date. If the date is missing the court may find that it is not effective. Also, lack of a signature can void the notice. Termination notices are included in Appendix D of this book, but be sure to check if your municipality has any local requirements before using them.(See forms 20-23, pages 261–264.)

the landlord's legal guide in illinois

DELIVERY Correct delivery of the notice is just as important as the notice itself. An easy mistake to make with delivery of the notice is neglecting to fill out the AFFIDAVIT OF SERVICE portion of the form and have it notarized. A landlord who is laying the foundation of an eviction must be able to prove that the notice was served upon the tenant. A court looks to the AFFIDAVIT OF SERVICE as the proof of proper service. If the AFFIDAVIT OF SERVICE has not been filled out properly or not notarized, a court may find that there has been no legal service made.

NOTE: *The wording and delivery rules may seem insignificant, but not complying with these items can cost the landlord in time, court fees, and possibly damages.*

LOCAL LAWS Along with complying to Illinois state laws for notice, delivery, and eviction, the landlord must be familiar with the laws of the municipality where the rental property is located. Some of these municipalities are very involved in the eviction process and can add more requirements for the landlord.

The City of Chicago has given landlords additional support for dealing with problem tenants. The Chicago Municipal Code ordinances 8-4 and 13-4, are being used to force landlords to begin eviction proceedings to remove those tenants that are involved in illegal activity (drug use, drug dealing, prostitution, solicitation for prostitution, or gang activities). This applies even if the illegal activity is done outside the area of the rental property. If a tenant is arrested twice for this type of behavior, the City of Chicago can force an eviction. If the landlord refuses to act, he or she may be subject to a fine of up to $500 or six months in jail.

NONPAYMENT OF RENT When the tenant has failed to pay rent, Illinois Statutes (735 ILCS 5/9-209) gives some direction as to the required content of the notice. The notice must contain:

- the names of the tenants;
- the amount of rent that is due;
- the location of the rental premises;
- a demand for payment of the rent due;
- the date of the notice; and,
- the signature of the landlord or the landlord's agent.

116

Wording. Within this type of notice the "demand for the rent due" may be worded something like:

> "You are notified that payment of the amount due is now demanded of you and that unless this entire payment is made on or before the expiration of five days after service of this notice, your lease of the above rental premises will be terminated immediately."

This is merely a suggestion of language to use in the notice. The only legal requirement is that the notice include a "demand" for rent and a statement of consequences that will result if the rent due is not paid before the end of the five-day notice period.

State law does requires the following clause to appear on a notice for back rent. According to the law, this is the exact language that must be used. The law states: "To prevent invalidation, the notice must prominently state:

> "Only FULL PAYMENT of the rent demanded in this notice will waive the landlord's right to terminate the lease under this notice, unless the landlord agrees in writing to continue the lease in exchange for receiving partial payment."

Amount. If the termination notice is due to nonpayment of rent, the landlord must double-check that the amount due is correct. A review of the lease terms is a must. Indicating the wrong amount of rent due is the most common mistake made. Depending upon the municipal ordinance, the amount due may be restricted to only rent, with other charges being listed in the suit for damages.

According to state law, if the tenant pays the amount past due within the time limit of the five-day notice, the landlord cannot proceed with the eviction. In some cases, even after the five-day notice, if the landlord accepts rent due, then the eviction cannot proceed.

> 📖 Once a landlord has given notice due to nonpayment of rent, the landlord can "waive his right of forfeiture" (not be able to proceed with the eviction) by accepting any rent, including partial payments, from the tenant. (*Robinson v. Chicago Housing Authority*, 54 F.3d 316 (7th Cir. 1995).)

VIOLATION
OF LEASE

Illinois Statutes (735 ILCS 5/9-210), says that a notice to a tenant in default "may be substantially in the following form:

> "To *(tenant/s)*: You are hereby notified that in consequence of your default in *(insert the nature of the default)* of the premises now occupied by you, being, etc., *(insert a description of the premises)*. I have elected to terminate your lease, and you are hereby notified to quit and deliver up possession of the same to be within 10 days of this date *(insert date)*."

TERMINATING
TENANCY OF
FARM LAND

This notice must be signed by the landlord or the landlord's agent. The description of the premises can be as simple as a street address that includes the rental unit number (such as "100 Oak Lane, Building 3, Apartment 3b"). Besides the signatures of the landlord or agents, the notice should also include the typed or printed name of the person who signs the document, and his or her address.

   📖 A letter sent by the landlord to the tenant adequately provided the tenant with a notice of the termination. The letter stated how the tenant had allegedly violated the lease, that the tenant could cure the default by taking certain actions within a specified period of time, and that the tenant would be able to present a defense should there be a hearing. (*Cunningham v. Lifelink Corp.*, 159 B.R. 230 (N.D. Ill. 1992).)

The Illinois Statutes (735 ILCS 5/9-206) state that the notice to terminate tenancy of farm land "may be substantially in the following form:

> "To ____: You are hereby notified that I have elected to terminate your lease of the farm premises now occupied by you, being *(describe the premises)*, and you are hereby further notified to quit and deliver up possession of the same to me at the end of the lease year, the last day of such year being *(insert the last day of the lease year)*."

In looking at other notices, the termination of farm land should be dated, signed by the owner or landlord, and be signed by the owner, landlord, or agent. This statute only applies to farm land tenancies.

LONG TERM
DEFAULT

There are occasions when the landlord must terminate a lease in a different manner. The provisions of 735 ILCS 5/9-204 allow the landlord to re-enter a rental property and begin an action for the tenant's ejectment if the tenant is six months behind in paying rent. In this case, the landlord does not have to give the tenant any formal demand to enter the rental property. The landlord must file an *ejectment action* in the county were the property is located, and follow that county's rules for commencing this type of action. If the court allows the ejectment order, the lease is terminated. However, before there is a judgment in the court case, a tenant may pay the amount of rent in arrears plus the cost of bringing the case, and the ejectment action will be dismissed. Ejectments will be discussed in Chapter 12.

SERVICE OF NOTICE

Besides following the required time limits for notice, the notice must be *served on* (delivered to) the tenant in the proper manner to be valid. Not only is there the physical service of the notice document, but the person who delivered the document must swear that the service was done and have that statement notarized in order for the service to be valid. The state law that covers the service of the notice is 735 ILCS 5/9-211 and 5/9-212.

Proper service of the notice can be done in one of several ways:

- by personally delivering the written notice to the tenant;

- by leaving the written notice with a person thirteen years old or older, who is living in or in possession of the rental property;

- by sending the written notice to the tenant by certified or registered mail, with a returned receipt from the addressee; or,

- if no one is residing in or in actual possession of the rental property, by posting the written notice on the rental property.

Along with the proper method of service, the server must swear as to how the service was made and have that sworn statement notarized. On notice forms, a portion of the notice is titled AFFIDAVIT OF SERVICE. The AFFIDAVIT OF SERVICE section must be fill out by the person doing the serving. It lists the date that the service was made, who made the service, and how the service was made. The person who makes the service must have this statement notarized.

A landlord can arrange for a deputy sheriff to serve the notice to the tenant. You need to contact the sheriff's office in the county where the rental property is located. The sheriff's office is usually closely associated with (often in the same building as) the office of the clerk of the court for the county because the sheriff serves legal documents. Using a sheriff to serve any legal papers does cost a certain fee. However, it may be worth it if you do not live close to the rental property, or if you want to avoid any potential confrontation with the tenant. If you wish to use a sheriff for this, contact the sheriff's office to check fees and any other requirements (such as the number of copies of the document they require).

MITIGATION OF DAMAGES

Whenever a lease is terminated, the landlord must take steps to preserve his or her right to sue for unpaid rent or damages to the premises. The primary step and a requirement according to Illinois law (735 ILCS 5/9-213.1) is for the landlord to try to reduce his or her economic loss (e.g., by making efforts to rent the premises to a new tenant or to prevent further damage to the premises). Such effort to reduce the economic loss is referred to as the landlord's duty to *mitigate damages*.

📕 The landlord has the burden to prove that he has acted in a way to mitigate the damages when the tenant defaults. Before a landlord can get a court to award damages because of the tenant's default, the mitigation must be proved. (*Snyder v. Ambrose*, 639 N.E.2d 639 (Ill.App. 2 Dist. 1994).)

This statute requires that the landlord take "reasonable measures to mitigate the damages," but does not define what would constitute "reasonable measures." As a result, Illinois courts have held that the lease between the landlord and tenant can define what acts the landlord must do in order to mitigate damages, as long as those acts are reasonable.

 📖 A court found that a landlord properly mitigated damages caused by the tenant's default when it re-let the abandoned unit for half the amount of rent paid by the defaulting tenant. The tenant had abandoned the rental property with two years left on the lease. After it sat vacant for seven months, the landlord re-let the property to the first available tenant after the tenant left and before the landlord rented out other available property. The court found that this was reasonable mitigation of damages and the landlord could sue the tenant for damages, including the other half of the amount of rent. (*JMB Properties Urban Co. v. Paolucci*, 604 N.E.2d 967 (3d Dist. 1992).)

 📖 The court found that the landlord had made a reasonable effort to mitigate damages after the tenant's default. The landlord's records showed that the landlord had sought and obtained some short-term rentals. The landlord's expert witness said that the rental price and the marketing strategy was reasonable for this type of property in this area. The landlord had put up a sign about an available rental unit, and the landlord had placed calls to brokers and developers about renting the property. (*MXL Industries, Inc. v. Mulder*, 623 N.E.2d 369 (Ill.App. 2 Dist. 1993).)

Some of the confusion in interpreting this law comes when the lease provision differs from the actual law. The lease may provide the rate at which the property may be re-let. Several courts have found that the landlord acted reasonably, even if the landlord's act caused a delay in renting the unit, when he re-let the rental property at the rate listed in the lease, and did not use the current market value rate. In addition, courts have found that a landlord acted reasonably when the new tenant was required to fill out the same application and pass the same security checks as all other tenants, even though the damages would have been less if the landlord had accepted the first tenant willing to re-let the rental property. The bottom line is that the landlord must do something to reduce the total amount of damages.

 📖 The statute on mitigation of damages means that the landlord cannot just sit and do nothing, while the total amount of damages continues to increase against the tenant who is in default. (*Stein v. Spainhour*, 521 N.E.2d 641 (Ill. App. 4 Dist. 1988).)

DEATH OF A TENANT

The majority of Illinois standard lease forms contain a clause that states that all parties to the lease agree to the terms and "…all the covenants and agreements herein contained shall be binding upon, and inure to, their respective successors, heirs, executors, administrators, and assigns…" For the landlord, this means that even if the tenant dies, the lease is still enforceable against the estate of the tenant. A lease with this provision becomes a debt of the deceased and should be paid from the estate, provided the estate has enough money to cover the rent due. This provision also binds the landlord to handle the matter of the security deposit and security deposit interest with the executor of the tenant's estate, in the same way as if the tenant was still alive.

OPTIONS TO CANCEL

A lease can require certain notices or other actions, as long as the lease conforms to both state and local laws. Some leases provide for an option to terminate prior to the expiration date. This option will have both penalties and requirements on the party exercising the option. This type of option may be applicable to rental properties that are in high demand, or to tenants who are unsure of the time they will remain in the area.

 📖 A lease can provide for termination before the expiration date, at the option of the landlord or tenant. There must be an option provision in the lease, and the terms of the provision must be followed. (*Cox v. Grant*, 373 N.E.2d 820 (Ill.App. 5 Dist. 1978).)

EVICTING A TENANT 12

Eviction is the dirty word that both landlords and tenants alike dread. For the landlord it means more work, following court rules that don't seem to make sense, and having to spend yet more money on a "lousy" tenant that the landlord doesn't want on the premises. For the tenant it is the loss of a home, the result of a failed financial venture, and a blot on the tenant's credit history for years to come.

SELF-HELP BY LANDLORD

Illinois law has long recognized that a landlord cannot evict a tenant by means of *self-help*. A landlord taking action to shut off electricity, discontinue heating the rental unit, change locks, or other things meant to prevent the tenant from using the property or annoy the tenant into leaving on his or her own are forms of self-help. That type of action is against many laws and may result in the landlord paying fines and not being able to proceed with a normal eviction. It may also result in the tenant being able to sue the landlord for damages, court costs, and attorney's fees, or, in the worst case—bring a discrimination suit. For a proper legal eviction, the landlord must go through the process as required under law.

📖 In a case for the court of appeals of Wisconsin, the landlord attempted to use self-help in evicting a tenant by shutting off both heat and electricity to the rental unit. The tenant sued. The court awarded the tenant recover of security deposits, two rent abatement awards due to code violations (which were doubled), the tenant's costs for an alternate residence, and the tenant's attorney's fees. (Peterson v. Tucker (no. 01-1738, 2002 EL 43614, (March 21, 2002).)

📖 In a Missouri case a landlord took the refrigerator, washing machine, and stove because the tenant failed to pay rent. The tenant was awarded $10,000 in damages. (*Smiley v. Cardin*, 655 S.W.2d 114 (Mo.Ct.App. 1983).)

📖 In a District of Columbia case, where purchasers of a tax deed to property kept changing the locks on the property, nailing the door shut, and nailing "for sale" signs on the property when the occupant was away, a jury awarded the occupant $250,000 in punitive damages. The purchasers had used those tactics to try to force the occupant to sue them, so that the government would have to defend their tax deed. The appeals court upheld the verdict. (*Robinson v. Sarisky*, 535 A.2d 901 (D.C.App. 1988).)

📖 In a Florida case, a landlord posted a three-day notice; but when the tenant was absent from the premises, the landlord entered and removed the tenant's possessions. In a lawsuit the tenant testified that her possessions were all heirlooms and antiques, and since the landlord had disposed of them he could not prove otherwise. The tenant was awarded $31,000 in damages. (*Reynolds v. Towne Mgt. of Fla., Inc.*, 426 So.2d 1011 (Fla. 2 DCA 1983).)

SURRENDER OR ABANDONMENT

In most standard lease forms, the word *surrender* is associated with the tenant returning the keys for the property to the landlord at the end of the rental term. There are instances when a tenant may surrender the property other than at the end of the lease, such as when a lease provisions requires surrender, in case of a court ordered surrender, when the tenant exercises a legal option to surrender, or when the landlord and tenant agree to end the lease.

The difference between surrender and *abandonment* is that, in most cases, the landlord must assume that the tenant has abandoned the rental property; and in a surrender the landlord knows that the tenant has left the property because the landlord has agreed to let the tenant out of the lease early. By the landlord agreeing to a surrender, the lease is terminated, as is the tenant's obligation under the lease to pay rent. In some cases, it may be in the landlord's best interest to agree to a surrender just to be rid of the tenant, rather than spend the time and money to take the tenant to court. Abandonment is discussed in more detail in Chapter 10.

📖 An agreement between the landlord and tenant to end a lease can be oral or written. (*Inland Real Estate Corp. v. Slymon*, 371 N.E.2d 1187 (1st Dist. 1977).)

SETTLING WITH THE TENANT

Although in more than half of all Illinois evictions the tenants do not answer the complaint and the landlord wins quickly, some tenants can create nightmares for landlords. Clever tenants and lawyers can delay the case for months, and vindictive tenants can destroy the property with little worry of ever paying for damages. Therefore, in some cases, lawyers advise their clients to offer the tenant a cash settlement to leave.

Example: A tenant may be offered $200 to be out of the premises and leave it clean within a week.

GROUNDS FOR EVICTION

A tenant can be evicted for violating one of the terms of the lease, the Illinois state or local landlord/tenant law, or failing to leave at the end of the lease. The most common violation of a lease is the tenant failing to pay the rent, but a tenant can also be evicted for violating other terms of the rental agreement.

The five requirements for evicting a tenant for nonpayment of rent in Illinois are:

1. the tenant must be delinquent in his or her rent;

2. the landlord must notify the tenant in writing that the rent must be paid within no less than five days;

3. the specified time period mentioned in the notice must pass without the tenant tendering the payment;

4 the landlord must sue for possession or ejectment and obtain a judgment for possession; and,

5. the writ of possession must be issued pursuant to the judgment for possession. (*Robinson v. Chicago Housing Authority*, 54 F.3d 316 (C.A.7 Ill. 1995).)

TERMINATING THE TENANCY

It is an old rule of law that an eviction suit cannot be filed until the tenancy is legally terminated. There are cases from the 1500s that dismiss evictions because the landlord failed to properly terminate the tenancy. A judge will not overlook this mistake. What the judges often do is order the landlord to pay the tenant's attorney fees. There are two ways to terminate a lease:

TERMINATION FOR CAUSE
A tenancy may be terminated, by action of the landlord, for some breach of the lease terms by the tenant. If you need to evict a tenant whose tenancy has not expired, you should carefully read Chapter 11, page 114–119 and follow the procedures to properly terminate the tenancy.

TERMINATION BY EXPIRATION
If parties to a rental agreement do not agree to renew or extend the agreement, it automatically ends at its expiration date. (This does not occur when there is a lease provision that the lease is automatically renewed unless notice is given that it is not being renewed.)

USING AN ATTORNEY

Many municipal landlord/tenant ordinances, as well as many leases, provide that the loser in a landlord/tenant case can be charged with the winner's attorney fees. It is important to do an eviction carefully because of these ordinances or leases. In some cases, the tenant may just be waiting for the eviction notice before leaving the premises, and in such a case the landlord may regain the premises no matter what kind of papers he files. In other cases, tenants with no money and no defenses have attained free lawyers who find technical defects in the case. This can cause a delay in the eviction and cause the landlord to be ordered to pay the tenant's attorney fees. A simple error in a landlord's court papers can cost him or her the case.

A landlord facing an eviction should consider the costs and benefits of using an attorney compared to doing it without an attorney. One possibility is to file the case without an attorney and hope the tenant moves out. If the tenant stays and fights, the landlord can hire an attorney to finish the case. Some landlords who prefer to do their evictions themselves, start by paying a lawyer for a half-hour or hour of time to review the facts of the case and point out any problems.

Whenever a tenant has an attorney, the landlord should also have one. It is, of course, important to find an attorney who both knows landlord/tenant law and charges reasonable fees. There are many subtleties of the law that can be missed by someone without experience. Some attorneys who specialize in landlord/tenant work charge very modest fees to file the case. Others charge an hourly rate that can quickly add up to thousands of dollars. Check with other landlords or a local apartment association for names of good attorneys, or try calling the manager of a local apartment complex.

WHO CAN SUE

An owner can represent himself or herself in court, and does not necessarily need an attorney. No one can represent another person in a court case except an attorney who is licensed to practice in that state. It is a criminal offense for a non-lawyer to represent another party in court. In cases where an agent of the landlord signed the lease in their own name, that agent may be considered a party to the contract and therefore would go into court with the owner.

Example: Rental property owner John Doe has a secretary named Mary Smith. John Doe authorizes Mary Smith to sign certain contracts as his agent. Mary must sign "Mary Smith as agent for John Doe." If she merely signs a contract with her own name and no indication that she is John Doe's agent, Mary Smith will be considered as a party to any court procedure regarding that contract.

COURT PROCEDURES

Illinois evictions are governed by the Illinois Forcible Entry and Detainer Act (735 ILCS 5/9-101). The Act must be strictly complied with in order to ensure a successful and legal eviction. The goal of an eviction is to obtain an ORDER FOR POSSESSION from the court, which grants the landlord the right to take possession of the rental property, and may also include a judgment for the rent due. (see form 35, p.277.)

NOTE: *In many cases where the landlord is attempting to evict a family with small children, especially winter evictions of a low-income family, the judge may grant a Stay of Enforcement of the Order for Possession. This stay delays the actual eviction for a period of time in the hope that the family will be able to find another place to live instead of being thrown out on the street. Once the stay expires, a landlord may then direct the sheriff's department of forcibly remove the tenant from the rental property.*

FORMS   It can be difficult to determine what forms to use in any court case because of home rule and the autonomy of the circuit courts that handle each county. As stated in earlier chapters, most stationery and office supply stores sell the everyday forms needed by landlords, such as various types of leases, applications for a lease, even five-day and ten-day notices. These forms do not always adhere to the requirements of the state law and the municipal ordinance where the rental property is located, so you should check local requirements before using them.

When the landlord decides to take court action against the tenant, he or she has to use forms that conform to the rules of the circuit court in the county where the landlord is filing suit. Usually this is the county where the rental property is located. The courts that handle that county's cases are familiar with the intricacies of the applicable municipal ordinances.

A particular form may look different in each of the twenty-one circuit courts throughout Illinois. Some of the possible differences between forms of different circuits are:

- the heading of the top of each form that says either:

    "IN THE CIRCUIT COURT OF THE _____
    JUDICIAL CIRCUIT"

    or

    "IN THE CIRCUIT COURT OF _____
    COUNTY, ILLINOIS"

- form number;

- name of the Clerk of the Court;

- circuit division name, if the circuit is broken into various divisions

Occasionally, forms will have varyng titles in different circuits, or even have the same title but a different use. In the circuit court of Cook County there are individualized forms for just about every type of legal action that anyone may ever file; while other circuits use a few generic form types that the person who files the action must be able to fill in correctly.

The landlord who is planning to go into court should go to the Office of the Clerk of Circuit Court where the suit will be filed. (See Appendix A for the circuit court in your county.) That office should be able to provide you with the appropriate forms, however, the clerks will not be allowed to assist you with filling out the forms. Unfortunately, this part of any court action is the most confusing. The local circuit court rules may be of some help, as are the Illinois Statutes that have been cited in Appendix B.

While you are at the clerk's office, ask to see one or more court files for an eviction case, especially those where an attorney represented the landlord. When looking through such files notice the necessary forms and how they are filled out. It would also be beneficial to sit in on an eviction trial. The clerk should know when eviction hearings will be held in the circuit court. By sitting in on a few hearings, it will become apparent what to expect, what types of issues arise, and how the judge deals with this type of case.

In Appendix D there are basic court forms. These forms are included to give an idea of what certain forms look like, and to use as a starting point if the court does not provide forms. Make changes to the forms in this book to comply with local law.

COURT
DIVISIONS

In circuit court, the case is filed in a particular division, if that particular county has circuit court divisions; or just with the clerk of the circuit court if there are no such divisions. In circuit courts in heavily populated counties, judges who are in one division do not hear cases that belong to another division. Cook County Circuit Court has the following divisions: Chancery, Law, Probate, County, Criminal, Juvenile, Child Protection, Child Support, and Domestic Relations. This is in addition to the Municipal Departments that are divided into six Districts.

The type of case determines in which division to file. For property in the City of Chicago, a case for eviction or property damage would be heard in the First Municipal District—Civil Division. (The Second through Sixth Districts are located in Cook County suburbs). The First

Municipal District—Civil Division is responsible for handling civil cases and where the defendant or the occurrence are within the Chicago city limits. Other circuits are not as complex. Check with your local circuit court clerk if you need more information.

A *forcible entry and detainer action* is the remedy for obtaining possession of premises by a person who is entitled to possession. Usually, a forcible entry and detainer action is filed by a landlord who wants to recover possession of property from a tenant who has not paid the rent. This action can be brought for only possession, or for rent and possession. If the complaint seeks both rent and possession, it is called a *joint action*.

COMPLAINT

This suit is started by writing and then filing a COMPLAINT against the tenant in the county court where the rental property is located. (see forms 26–29, pages 267–271.) The COMPLAINT should have:

- the name of the landlord;

- the names of all the tenants or people living in the rental property

  NOTE: *All adults residing in the rental property must be named on the COMPLAINT—those not listed may be allowed to remain;*

- the statement that the plaintiff (landlord) is suing the defendant (tenant) for possession, or,

- for possession and rent or damages.

Other information in the COMPLAINT is the legal or street address of the rental property, if the lease was oral or written, the total amount of rent due, the dates that the tenant failed to pay, and the date the notice was given. The landlord should also attach a copy of the lease and a copy of the notice. The landlord's name, address, and telephone number should appear at the bottom of the COMPLAINT.

FILING

The COMPLAINT form, an Appearance form (in some courts), and a SUMMONS (form 31, p.273) are all filed with the court of the county where the rental property is located. These forms are filed by taking the appropriate number of copies to the office of the Clerk of the Circuit

Court. The usual rule of thumb on the number of copies to make is: one for the court, one for each person listed as defendant (each adult tenant), and at least one for yourself; however, some counties may require additional copies. One of the clerks then reviews the forms, and assignees a case number and a court date. In order to file these forms, the landlord must pay a filing fee.

After the filing fee is paid, the clerk stamps each copy with a date/time stamp. This date/time stamp is proof that the COMPLAINT has been filed with the court. The court date, or *return date*, is set by the court. In Cook County, the return date for forcible entry and detainer actions is from fourteen to forty-two days after the complaint is filed. The time in other counties will vary.

THE SUMMONS AND SERVICE OF PROCESS

A SUMMONS lists defendant information such as the defendant's name, address, and the location where the defendant is to be served.

NOTE: *The actual form used for a* SUMMONS *and the number of copies required varies by county.*

The SUMMONS, along with the COMPLAINT, are the documents that are served upon the tenant. After the COMPLAINT is filed with the clerk of the court, a copy of the COMPLAINT that has been stamped by the clerk, and the SUMMONS are taken to the sheriff's office to arrange for service.

The sheriff will serve these legal papers on the tenant, record the date and time of service on a copy of the SUMMONS, and return that copy to the clerk of the court to be filed with the other documents of the case. The sheriff will charge a fee for service; the fee will vary by county and the distance the sheriff travels to serve the documents.

Prior to the court date, the sheriff must find the tenants and serve the legal papers on them. If the sheriff cannot serve the summons in time, the court date must be delayed until there is proper service. The case cannot proceed to trial until the tenant has been served with these papers. Sometimes a tenant who knows that there is going to be an eviction action, will be absent when the sheriff shows up to serve him or her with the eviction papers. If the landlord continues to have problems with service on the tenant, the landlord may decide to hire a specially licensed process server. The special process servers usually cost more, but they have a high degree of success in finding and serving people who attempt to hide.

Once the tenant is served, he or she can file an answer and contest the case, which will require a trial. The tenant may request a jury trial, meaning even more delay. In the City of Chicago, statistics show that the majority of tenants who have been served with a COMPLAINT do not contest the case, but just move out of the rental unit.

HEARINGS AND ORDERS FOR POSSESSION

The hearing will be held in the circuit court on the date listed in the SUMMONS, or on an alternative court date if the tenant could not be served in time. If the tenant does not appear in court or provide an answer, and all documentation and notices have been prepared and presented in accordance with the law, the case is considered *uncontested*. Most judges will usually enter an *ex parte* judgment (the term *ex parte* means that a court is taking action for one party without the other party).

If the landlord presents proof that he or she complied with the lease and statutes as to giving the tenant a notice (this is the five or ten day notice form), the court may enter an ORDER OF POSSESSION that will become effective in one to four weeks. Depending on the court and whether the landlord properly requested damages, the judge may also enter a "default judgment" for the amount claimed as damages or rent due.

Once the ORDER FOR POSSESSION becomes effective, the sheriff's office or the Police Department of the municipality in which the property is located can forcibly remove the tenant. This process can also take a few weeks. The entire eviction process may take a long as four months to complete, and that is without the tenant contesting the eviction.

If the tenant files an ANSWER and plans to contest the case, the tenant or the tenant's attorney will appear at the hearing. At that point, depending on the court calendar, the judge will either set a trial date or try the case immediately. The length of time from the hearing to the actual trial date will depend upon the number of cases pending in the circuit. Courts are aware that eviction suits need to be processed quickly, and most circuits try to speed these types of cases along, while allowing both sides ample time to prepare their case.

Depending on the rules of the court, along with the trial date, the judge may order a status date or a pretrial conference date. A *status date* is usually at a pre-determined number of days after a case is filed. The number of days depends on the case, the county, and the judge's calendar. At a status date, both sides meet with the judge to inform the judge of the progress being made in the case.

A *pretrial conference* is also a meeting between the parties and the judge. It can be called automatically by the court system (as with the status date), by any of the parties to the suit, or by the judge. In addition to informing the judge of the progress made in the case, a pretrial conference can be used to iron out any difficulties in complying with court rules, or to try to bring about a settlement agreement.

Each county, and sometimes each judge, has their own way of scheduling these dates. Some judges encourage pre-trial conferences in order to try to get a settlement and avoid a trial; while other judges will not use court time for settlement negotiations. To add to the confusion, these two terms (*status date* and *pre-trial conference date*) are sometimes used to mean the same thing, depending upon the county.

MANDATORY ARBITRATION

Mandatory arbitration is used in Illinois to reduce the number of cases that are waiting for trial. Only certain types of cases are required to participate in mandatory arbitration. Currently, only civil cases with a claim not exceeding $50,000 are required to go through arbitration. The type of case and the dollar amount are subject to change by state law, and can vary by county (735 ILCS 5/2-101).

In an arbitration hearing, both sides are given a short period of time (two to four hours) to present their case. After presentation, an arbitration panel (usually made up of three experienced attorneys) evaluates the case and prepares a decision that is filed with the court. If a case goes to mandatory arbitration, the decision of the arbitration panel will be imposed on the parties. However, either side can reject the decision of the arbitration panel and pay a fee to the court (currently $200) for the rejection. The case will then proceed to trial.

If the landlord fails to appear on the trial date, but the tenant appears, the case may be dismissed. Then, if there is a good reason for failing to appear, the landlord would have thirty days to file a motion asking the court to vacate the dismissal (735 ILCS 5/2-1301).

If the landlord wins, the judge will enter an Order for Possession and may enter a Final Judgment for damages (depending on the case). The Order for Possession is handled as described above, with the assistance of the local sheriff's office or police department.

TENANT'S ATTORNEY

If the answer of the tenant is filed by an attorney, that tenant has hired an attorney to represent him or her in the court case. In that case, the landlord should also get an attorney. Only a small percentage of eviction cases are contested. However, if the landlord makes a mistake in one of those cases, the landlord may be liable for fines and the fees of the tenant's attorney, which can be very costly. If the tenant appears at the hearing with an attorney, the landlord should ask the judge for a *continuance* so that he or she can get an attorney.

The courts generally do not give any special consideration to a person who has neglected to obtain his or her own attorney. Judges expect that those who represent themselves have done some homework on how the process is handled. Although a landlord may want to avoid attorney costs, occasionally the landlord will need legal representation. The way to avoid needing to hire an attorney is to implement plans that try to eliminate, not litigate, the problems, such as:

- have a tough, thorough, organized, and documented screening procedure before a person is accepted as a tenant;

- have procedures for handling tenant problems before those problems get to the eviction stage;

- use lease provisions that allow the landlord the most flexibility;

- have and enforce rules for the rental property;

- know and follow the municipal ordinances and the state law for your rental property; or,

- determine a plan for handling potential evictions before the tenants make the errors.

> **Example:** Decide whether you will ever accept a surrender, and at what point. Decide if you should try meeting with a tenant face to face prior to starting an eviction.

MEDIATION

In some areas, *mediation* services are recommended or required before trial. At a mediation, the parties are encouraged to resolve their differences. This may mean establishing a planned date of departure for the tenant, or perhaps allowing the tenant to stay in the premises with a timetable for paying the back rent. In some cases, damage to the premises or animosity between the parties may make it impossible to continue the tenancy.

STIPULATION

If a settlement is reached, it should be in the form of a *stipulation*, which is a document that is filed with the court as described below. If you merely dismiss your case as part of the settlement, you will have to start all over from scratch if the tenant again defaults.

SETTLING WITH THE TENANT

The parties may be able to resolve the matter without going through a hearing, either on their own, through their attorneys, or through mediation. This will allow the landlord to recover some back rent and avoid the hassle of cleaning and re-renting the unit. If you wish to settle with the tenant and come to an agreement where the rent will be paid over time, you can enter into a stipulation to delay the case. You should never accept any rent from the tenant once the case is filed, without signing a stipulation. Some counties may have their own stipulation forms, but one is included in Appendix D in case your county does not provide one. (see form 25, p.266.) The *stipulation* is an agreement that the tenant will pay the back rent in installments and keep current in the rent, and that the landlord will not proceed in the case. If the tenant fails to pay as agreed, the landlord can go to the judge, without a hearing, and get a Order for Possession upon presentation of a sworn, notarized statement that the tenant has defaulted on the stipulation.

TENANT'S POSSIBLE DEFENSES

A tenant who is behind in rent usually has one objective—to stay in the property rent-free as long as possible. Tenants and lawyers sometimes come up with a variety of creative defenses. The following are some of the defenses, both fanciful and appropriate, that a tenant may attempt to use in an eviction trial. Many of the legitimate defenses can also be used as a basis for a suit against the landlord for damages, or as a countersuit in the eviction case.

SECURITY DEPOSIT

A tenant says that he is not in default because the landlord has his security deposit that covers the default. The tenant may attempt to show that the landlord did not comply with the state laws or the municipal ordinances on security deposits or security deposit interest. Assuming the landlord did not violate any security deposit law, the defense should not work because the security deposit is meant to be held until the end of the lease. Depending upon the municipal ordinances, the terms of the lease, and other details of the case, a court may find that this is not a proper defense. If the court does determine that this is a proper defense, then, as the state law currently stands, the penalty to the landlord would be an amount equal to twice the amount of the security deposit, plus court costs and the tenant's attorney's fees.

INCORRECT AMOUNT

Disputing the amount of rent due is not a defense because if any rent is due, the landlord is entitled to eviction. However, if the amount stated in the five-day notice is wrong, the case may be dismissed.

TITLE

A tenant claims that the landlord has not proved that he or she has good title to the property. This is not a valid defense because a tenant who has entered into a rental agreement with a landlord is prohibited from denying that the landlord has good title.

WAIVER OF
RENT

A tenant may argue that the landlord created a waiver because the landlord refused to accept rent *after* the five-day notice expired. As stated in Chapter 11 on "Terminating Tenancy," the landlord is not required to accept rent after the five-day notice period. The landlord's refusal to accept rent due after this time does not effect the eviction action.

However, if the landlord refused to accept the rent amount listed as due on the notice *before* the five-day notice expired, the landlord waives the right to evict the tenant for this particular incident of not paying the rent. The landlord must wait until the tenant is in arrears on the rent again to evict because of nonpayment of rent.

RENT PAID

The tenant may attempt to prove to the court that the rent has been paid. Tenants can come up with different theories regarding what constitutes rent being paid. For example, the tenant may be deducting the cost of repairs to the rental property from the rent due. This may be an accurate defense, if the municipal ordinance allows these costs to be deducted. However the tenant would have to comply with the rest of such an ordinance that usually limits the amount deducted and restricts the repairs for that a tenant can legally pay.

📖 Amounts paid for scavenger service for commercial property was not considered "additional rent." (*La Salle National Bank v. Khan*, 547 N.E.2d 472 (Ill.App. 3d 1989).)

REG. Z

A tenant says that the landlord has not complied with "Reg. Z" of the Code of Federal Regulations. This federal regulation is a truth-in-lending requirement that does not apply to the rental of property (12 CFR 226.1(c)(1).)

BREACH OF
LEASE

If the landlord has failed to follow a certain provision in the lease, the tenant may raise this breach in an eviction action. In some municipal ordinances, there are rules as to what the tenant must do, such as send a written notice to the landlord, to get the landlord to comply with the entire lease. If the tenant did not follow those local rules, the court may not allow this defense to be used.

CONSTRUCTIVE EVICTION

Constructive eviction occurs when the landlord has made the premises so untenantable, such as depriving the tenant of essential services, that the tenant is unable to reside in the property. The landlord's interference must be substantial and a result of matters that are under the landlord's control. Constructive eviction does not require that the landlord intentionally did these acts to get the tenant to leave. All that is required is that the landlord do something, or neglect to do something, that makes the rental property useless to the tenant, either in whole or in part.

Constructive eviction is the result of a landlord denying the tenant the quiet enjoyment of the premises. Past cases have required that a tenant move out in order to be able to raise this issue, however, the current view is that the tenant need not abandon the premises to be able to use this as a defense against eviction.

📖 To prove constructive eviction, the tenant must show that the landlord failed to keep the premises in a tenantable condition. *Untenantability* is when the rental property cannot be used for the purposes for which it was rented, and cannot be restored to a fit condition without making extensive repairs that would interrupt the use of the property. (*RNR Realty, Inc. v. Burlington Coat Factory Warehouse of Cicero, Inc.*, 522 N.E.2d 679 (1st Dist. 1988).)

BREACH OF IMPLIED WARRANTY OF HABITABILITY

The modern trend in landlord/tenant law is that a residential tenant should be able to expect that the rental property is of adequate quality for its purpose. This imposes an obligation on the landlord to keep the rented premises *habitable* throughout the terms of the lease. Courts have found that, at a minimum, the landlord must keep the rental property free from substantial building code violations. Some courts go beyond this and require that the rental property be kept safe, sanitary, and fit to occupy.

Some municipal ordinances do allow the tenant to make a reduction in rent in proportion to the loss of habitability. It is then possible that the amount of damages from this breach could equal or exceed the amount of rent due, which gives the tenant a defense against an eviction based on nonpayment of rent.

Additionally, some local ordinances allow the tenant to make rent payments into an escrow account, while the tenant sues the landlord for the breach of the implied warranty of habitability. Courts and the law-makers are becoming very pro-tenant on this issue. As evidence of that, since 1979, any clause in a lease by which the tenant waives the implied warranty of habitability is deemed void and against public policy.

FAILURE TO
REPAIR

When the landlord has failed to make agreed-on repairs, and the tenant makes the repairs, the tenant may deduct the cost from the rent—to the extent that it is allowed by the lease and by any municipal ordinances. Typically, the tenant is required to give the landlord adequate, timely, and written notice about the need to repair, before the tenant assumes the repairs himself. The deduction allowed usually does not exceed one month's rent.

PUBLIC AID
DEDUCTION

The tenant has a defense to an eviction when the tenant is a public aid recipient and the rent is withheld by the Illinois Department of Public Aid. By law, the Illinois Department of Public Aid is authorized to with-hold all rent on the behalf of a public aid tenant, when the tenant is living in rental property that is in violation of the building code or similar regulations. The public aid office sends notices of this action to the landlord, so this should not be a surprise defense in an eviction case.

FAILURE OF THE
LEASE
CONTRACT

Like all contracts, if it can be proven that the landlord induced the tenant to sign the lease by fraud or duress, the lease may be considered void. The court would look at the details of the terms and conditions in the contract, and the actions of the landlord in getting the tenant to sign the lease. The court would also look at the actions of both landlord and tenant after the lease was signed—did the tenant act as if he or she were following the contract? If the court ultimately found that the tenant was forced to sign the lease by fraud or duress, the landlord could be liable for hefty fines, a return of the rent paid by the tenant (perhaps double that amount), court costs, and the tenant's attorney's fees.

RETALIATORY
CONDUCT

A tenant may claim the eviction is in retaliation for some lawful action, and that this is illegal under 765 ILCS 720/1. This defense does not apply if the landlord is evicting the tenant for good cause, such as non-payment of rent, violation of the lease or reasonable rules, or violation of the landlord/tenant law. (see Chapter 8.)

DISCOVERY

A tenant may want more time in order to take *discovery*. This means asking questions of the landlord and any witnesses under oath before a court reporter.

ATTORNEY BUSY
OR UNPREPARED

The tenant's attorney may say that he or she just got on the case and needs time to prepare or has a busy schedule and is not available for trial for a month or so. If the attorney appears at the hearing and makes this argument to the judge, you might suggest to the judge that, if the tenant's attorney is so busy, he should not have taken the case. Also, if the tenant has a lawyer; you should have one too.

GRIEVANCE
PROCEDURE

In federally subsidized housing, the regulations require that tenants be given a grievance procedure in some evictions. However, where the tenant is a threat to the health and safety of other tenants or employees, Title 24 CFR 966.51(a) states such hearing is not required.

PROCEDURAL
DEFENSES

There is an entire category of defenses that may be raised by the tenant in an eviction action that goes after the procedure, or format, used to bring about the eviction. Some of these defenses, if true, will result in the eviction case being dismissed. Others can be cured by action on the part of the landlord.

Wrong jurisdiction or venue. This is a claim that the complaint was not filed in the county and district where the rental property is located. The landlord may be able to solve this by just filing a MOTION FOR CHANGE OF VENUE to move the complaint to the proper venue.

Legal capacity. This is a claim that the person who filed the complaint does not have the required legal relationship with the property to entitle him or her to file a complaint. Generally, the person who files the complaint must be the property owner or the owner's agent. In a sublease, the sublessor or the sublessor's agent may file the complaint. If the property is held in a land trust, only the trustee, not the beneficiary, can file the complaint.

Notice was not proper. If the AFFIDAVIT OF SERVICE on the notice form was not filled out or not notarized, the tenant may have a good defense. Depending upon other conditions, this may cause the case to be dismissed. Illinois state law requires certain information to be included on the notices, and that the notice contain an AFFIDAVIT OF SERVICE that is to be signed and sworn to by the person who delivers the notice. Also, if the landlord filed the eviction suit before the number of days listed on the notice had passed, then the court will dismiss the case for having been filed prematurely.

Summons or complaint was not served properly. In this case, check with the sheriff's office where the service was arranged. Some courts have allowed the case to be delayed in order to obtain proper service, others have found that proper service was made even if there were irregularities, and still others have dismissed the case. This depends on the individual case, whether certain actions were done, the local ordinances, and the court itself.

Improper joinder of defendant. This is a claim that one of the people listed on the complaint is not in possession of the rental property. This may be because of a sublet or assignment. If this defense is true, most courts will allow a motion to substitute the proper defendant, again depending upon the circumstances of the individual case.

ABANDONMENT AFTER DISMISSAL

In some cases, the tenant will fight the eviction, have it dismissed on a technicality, and then move out. In such a situation, if you are given the right to refile and you wish to continue pursuing the tenant for monetary damages, correct the error and refile.

TENANT'S BANKRUPTCY

If a tenant files for bankruptcy, the bankruptcy laws require that all legal actions against the tenant must stop immediately. This provision is automatic from the moment the bankruptcy petition is filed (11 USC 362) and called an *automatic stay*. If you take any action in court, seize the tenant's property, try to impose a landlord's lien, use the security deposit for unpaid rent, or take any other action against the tenant, you can be held in contempt of federal court. It is not necessary that you receive formal notice of the bankruptcy—verbal notice is sufficient. If you do not believe the tenant, you should call the bankruptcy court to confirm the filing. The automatic stay lasts until the debtor is discharged or the bankruptcy case is dismissed, until the property is abandoned or voluntarily surrendered, or until the bankruptcy court lifts the stay.

RELIEF FROM AUTOMATIC STAY

The landlord may ask for the right to continue with the eviction by filing a **MOTION FOR RELIEF FROM STAY** and paying the filing fee (this is done in the bankruptcy court). Within thirty days a hearing is held, which may be held by telephone. The motion is governed by Bankruptcy Rule 9014, and the requirements of how the tenant must be served are contained in Rule 7004. However, for such a hearing the services of an attorney are usually necessary.

POST-FILING RENT

The bankruptcy stay only applies to amounts owed to the landlord at the time of filing the bankruptcy. Therefore, the landlord can still sue the tenant for eviction and rent owed for any time period *after* the filing of the bankruptcy petition, unless the bankruptcy trustee assumes the lease. The landlord can proceed during the bankruptcy without asking for relief from the automatic stay under three conditions (*In re Knight*, 8 B.R. 925 (D.C. Md. 1981).):

- the landlord sues only for rent due *after* the filing;

- the trustee has rejected the lease (If the trustee does not accept the lease within sixty days of the Order for Relief, then 11 USC 365(d)(1) provides that it is deemed rejected.); and,

- the landlord sues under the terms of the lease and may not treat the trustee's rejection as a breach.

In Chapter 13 (reorganization bankruptcy), the landlord should be paid the rent as it comes due.

FILING AFTER JUDGMENT

If the tenant filed bankruptcy after a judgment of eviction has been entered, there should be no problem lifting the automatic stay since the tenant has no interest in the property.

If the tenant files bankruptcy and you decide it is worth hiring a lawyer, you should locate an attorney who is experienced in bankruptcy work. Prior to the meeting with the attorney you should gather as much information as possible (type of bankruptcy filed, assets, liabilities, case number, etc.).

APPEALS

The process of filing an appeal is covered in Illinois Supreme Court Rules 301 through 375. The first step is filing a NOTICE OF APPEAL. That NOTICE OF APPEAL must be filed within thirty days of the entry of the final judgment or appealable order. If the NOTICE OF APPEAL is not filed within that time, a party can petition the court for an additional thirty days *if* there are facts showing a "reasonable" excuse for not filing on time. It is up to the court to determine what is "reasonable."

GROUNDS FOR APPEAL

Our legal system allows one chance to bring a case to court. If you did not prepare for your trial, or thought you would not need a witness, and you lost; you do not have the right to try again. However, you may be able to have your case reviewed in certain limited circumstances, such as if the judge made a mistake in interpreting the law that applies to your case, that is grounds for reversal. Also, if new evidence is discovered after the trial that could not have been discovered before the trial, a new trial might be granted.

REHEARING

There are certain other grounds for rehearing by the judge who heard your original case, such as misconduct of an attorney or errors during the trial.

NOTICE OF
APPEAL

According to the Supreme Court Rule 303(b) the title of the NOTICE OF APPEAL must include:

- At the top of the notice, the statement:

  APPEAL TO THE _____COURT

- Below the court's name is the name of the trial court.

  For example, in Cook County this entire statement would be:

  APPEAL TO THE ILLINOIS APPELLATE COURT, FIRST DISTRICT FROM THE CIRCUIT COURT OF COOK COUNTY

- The case title appears next (This includes the parties names as "Plaintiff-Appellant" and "Defendant-Appellee.")

- The trial court case number is put on the right-hand side, across from the names of the parties

- After all of the above, center the words: "NOTICE OF APPEAL"

- Within the body of the NOTICE OF APPEAL there must be the order, decision, judgment, or decree (or the part of these) being appealed.

- The date of the appealed order, a brief description of the order, and the relief requested must be in the body of the NOTICE OF APPEAL.

- The NOTICE OF APPEAL must also be signed.

APPELLATE
PROCEDURE

There are many detailed procedural steps that must be taken in order to proceed in an appellate case. Appellate work is considered a complex area of law, and a person who wishes to appeal a judgment may wish to consider turning things over to an attorney who regularly practices in the appellate courts.

SATISFACTION OF JUDGMENT

Once a judgment is entered in a lawsuit, if the tenant pays the amount due, a document called a SATISFACTION OF JUDGMENT may need to be filed with the court. (see form 37, p.279.) This would be true if the tenant's payment came after a court case where the landlord won, or if the payment came after a settlement agreement between the parties which was incorporated in a judgment. The tenant would want this filed to clear his or her monetary obligations that show up on credit reports. The landlord may need to file this because of a requirement in a settlement agreement. In addition, if the Clerk of the Court is involved in collecting payment, a SATISFACTION OF JUDGMENT may be required before the funds are released to the landlord.

EJECTMENT

A suit on *ejectment* is different from a suit for forcible entry and detainer. In forcible entry and detainer, the only question is: who has the right of possession? Since it is easy to prove that an owner or landlord has that right and because the forcible entry and detainer law has been modified for ease of use, it is the law of choice. An ejectment case includes two questions of law. The first question is 'who has the right of possession?' exactly as in a suit for forcible entry and detainer. The second question is concerned with people other than the landlord and tenant, and their rights to the property. These other people include those who have a mortgage on the building, the heirs of the building owner, the heirs of the tenant, someone who has illegally taken possession of the building/rental unit, and anyone who is attempting to assert ownership. Ejectment suits are complicated and should probably be left to those attorneys who regularly work in this type of law.

Money Damages and Back Rent 13

Trying to collect a judgment against a former tenant is usually not worth the time and expense. Most landlords are just glad to regain possession of the property. Tenants who do not pay rent usually do not own property that can be seized, and it is very difficult to garnish wages in Illinois. Occasionally former tenants come into money, and some landlords have been surprised many years later when called by a former tenant wanting to pay off their judgment. Therefore, it is usually worthwhile to put a claim for back rent into an eviction complaint.

Making a Claim

Making a claim for damages and back rent is easy in Illinois when suing under the forcible entry and detainer laws. Using the forcible entry and detainer forms supplied by the clerk of the court is the best way for a landlord to get possession of the rental property and a judgment for the monetary amount. These forms (see Appendix D) contain places for the landlord to enter the dollar amounts for both damages and back rent.

At a trial, the landlord will have to prove the dollar amounts. For the rent due, the proof will typically consist of the lease between the landlord and tenant, and the landlord's records of rent received. For the damages claim, a landlord might bring photographs of the damages, estimates for repair, bills for repairs, or any other evidence that would tend to prove that the damages existed, caused by the tenant, and cost a certain amount to repair.

A claim for attorney's fees, cost of eviction, court costs, and/or late charges will usually NOT be allowed by the court UNLESS there is a provision in the rental agreement/lease which states that such fees are collectible if the landlord evicts the tenant.

AMOUNT

The local rules of the circuit court determine the maximum amount that can be claimed in a particular lawsuit within that court. If the dollar amount that the landlord wishes to sue for is above what a particular court will allow, the suit may have to be filed in a different division, split into two or more separate suits, or limited by that amount—it depends on the court rules. In Cook County, eviction cases are heard in a court that allows civil cases.

Municipal landlord and tenant ordinances may allow the landlord to sue for interest, double rent, future rent, and court fees. These local rules may also restrict what is allowed as reimbursable damages. Landlords cannot include "normal wear and tear" in the damages amount.

DEFENSES

Since the forcible entry and detainer complaint puts damages, back rent, and possession in the same suit, the defenses used would be those discussed in Chapter 12, pages 137–142. Against damage claims, the tenant may attempt to prove that he or she did not damage the property or that the repair did not cost as much as the landlord claims. The tenant may also try to rely on local ordinances that sometimes limit the amounts for which tenants are liable. Landlords must be familiar with local ordinances regarding damages. Landlords should also keep good records in order to prove back rent. In addition, the landlord may be required to prove the dollar amount required to repair the damages.

ENFORCING A JUDGMENT

In a forcible entry and detainer action, the ORDER FOR POSSESSION may be the easiest to enforce. (see form 35, p.277.) The portion of a judgment that relates to back rent and damages will probably be tough, if not totally impossible, to enforce. Once the court has made a judgment for a monetary amount, it is up to the landlord or owner to make sure that this is enforced. This may mean additional court time, such as actions for wage garnishment and attachments. That part of the law is called *collections*. Consult a book on collections law if serious about pursuing such a claim.

There are many ways that a person can avoid paying a judgment. Some leave the state, change their name, or just become scarce. Once the landlord has the court judgment for damages or back rent, it may be worth turning that judgment over to a law firm or collection agency experienced in pursuing debtors. Finding the debtor will cost the landlord a percentage of the judgment amount, but it may be worth it, especially if the judgment is for a large amount.

Judgments need to be renewed with the court every seven years. Renewing a judgment is done by submitting documents to the court by way of a motion to the court that the judgment is still outstanding. Check with your clerk of the circuit court for specialized forms and procedures.

REPLEVIN

In a nonresidential tenancy there is a procedure called *replevin*, by which the property of the tenant may be sold to pay the rent owed to the landlord. The sale must be advertised and the landlord has the right to bid for the tenant's property.

NOTE: *A replevin action is complicated and should be handled by an attorney.*

SELF-SERVICE STORAGE SPACE 14

ILLINOIS LAW

The Self-Service Storage Facility Act (770 ILCS 95) covers any real property designed and used for the purpose of renting or leasing as individual storage space to occupants who will have access to the space. These facilities may also be covered under municipal ordinances, but they are not considered a "warehouse" for purposes of the Uniform Commercial Code. The Self-Service Storage Facility Act does not apply if the owner of a storage facility issues warehouse receipts, bills of lading, or other documents of title for the person's property.

LEASES

Usually, like other rentals, the individual storage space is covered by a lease or rental agreement. This rental agreement can be written or oral, although a written agreement is better because it eliminates confusion about the terms of the rental and is easier to enforce in court. Like other leases, one for a storage should establish the terms, conditions, rules, and any other provisions about the use of this facility.

LIENS

The owner of the self-service storage facility has an immediate lien on the personal property as it is brought into the storage facility. This lien is superior to any other lien or security interest, except those that have been perfected by filing the proper legal documents prior to the property being stored. The lien can be enforced for the payment of rent, labor, or other charges of the storage facility as listed in the rental agreement. The enforcement of the lien begins with a notice to the tenant.

First, a notice must be sent by registered mail to the last-known address of the tenant, and posted in a conspicuous place at the facility. The notice must include:

- an itemized statement of the owner's claim, showing the sum due at the time of the notice, and the date when the sum became due;

- the same description, or a reasonably similar description, of the personal property as provided in the rental agreement;

- a demand for payment within a specified time, not less than fourteen days after delivery of the notice;

- a conspicuous statement that, unless the claim is paid within the time stated in the notice, the personal property will be advertised for sale or other disposition, and will be sold or otherwise disposed of at a specified time and place; and,

- the name, street address, and telephone number of the owner whom the tenant may contact to respond to the notice.

After the fourteen days have passed, an advertisement for the sale or other disposition (which could mean to throw away) must be published once a week for two consecutive weeks in a newspaper of general circulation in the area. The property of several tenants may be listed in one ad if one sale will be held. The ad must include:

- a brief and general description of what is believed to constitute the personal property contained in the storage unit;

- the address of the self-service storage facility and the name of the tenant; and,

- the time, place, and manner of the sale or other disposition (the sale or other disposition may take place not sooner than fifteen days after the first publication).

The final disposition must conform to the terms in the ad, and must be in a "commercially reasonable manner," which means the property may be sold in one lot, or as individual items if that is more reasonable, and the owner may buy at the sale.

Any time before the sale the tenant may redeem the property by paying the money due plus the expenses in preparing for the sale.

The rights of purchasers at the sale, and rights of the landlord to the proceeds, are complicated by the laws of lien priority. For larger, expensive items of personal property, such as vehicles and machinery, a search for liens should be made through the Department of Motor Vehicles, the County Recorder's office, or the Secretary of State UCC division. Prior liens of this type would remain on the property.

In most cases, the property is inexpensive personal items that would not have liens against them, and no future claims can be expected.

If there are excess funds after the sale, a notice must be sent to the tenant's last known address (even if the last notice came back unclaimed) and to any known lienholders. Either the tenant or a secured lienholder may claim the excess proceeds from the landlord within two years of the sale. If they are not claimed within this time the landlord may keep them.

MOBILE HOME PARKS 15

The state of Illinois has an extensive mobile home rental law, the *Mobile Home Landlord and Tenant Rights Act* (765 ILCS 745). The state laws that cover non-mobile home rentals are lacking in detail, and fail to cover so many important aspects of the landlord/tenant relationship that the majority of municipalities have been forced to enact ordinances under the home rule theory just to protect their residents. On the other hand, the state law covering mobile home rental is extremely detailed and leaves very little for the municipalities to regulate. Municipal ordinances are usually limited to building code restrictions or an outright ban on mobile home parks. As with all landlord/tenant issues, the landlord should check with the municipalities where the rental is located.

QUALIFICATIONS

The Mobile Home Landlord and Tenant Rights Act covers both *park owners* and *tenants*. The term *park owner* means

- the actual property owner whose name appears on the deed for the mobile home park, or

- a person or legal entity (corporation, association, company, etc.) authorized by the owner to exercise "any aspect of management," including those people who merely receive the rent. (765 ILCS 745/3.)

The Mobile Home Landlord and Tenant Rights Act does not apply to mobile home parks or park land that is operated by the state or the federal government, or to trailer parks that are run for use by recreational campers or travel trailers. Mobile home parks must be completely within the state of Illinois, and contain five or more mobile homes to come under this Act.

If a mobile home park qualifies under this Act, the mobile homes offered for rental and the lot that the home sits upon must conform to the sanitation, housing, and other ordinances of the state, county, and municipality where the mobile home park is located.

MOBILE HOME LEASES

Mobile home leases must fully comply with the Mobile Home Landlord and Tenant Rights Act. Any provision of the mobile home lease that does not comply with this Act becomes void. In that case, the remaining provisions of the lease would still be in effect, and only the conflicting provisions would be considered invalid.

The landlord or park owner must provide a potential tenant with a copy of the lease prior to that tenant agreeing to rent a mobile home. Unless the parties agree to a different time period, all mobile home leases are for a term of twelve months or more.

UNSIGNED LEASES

A tenant will be deemed to have accepted a written lease offered by the landlord where the tenant fails to sign the lease, does not provide the landlord or owner with a written rejection of the lease, and continues to live in the mobile home and pay rent.

LEASE PROHIBITIONS

A lease between a mobile home park landlord or owner and a tenant cannot contain a provision:

- charging the tenant a penalty fee for late payment without giving the tenant a minimum of five days from the date the rent is due to pay the rent;

- charging a security deposit greater that one month's rent;

- allowing the owner or landlord to charge additional fees which are not fully specified in the lease;

- allowing the owner or landlord to transfer or move the mobile home to a different lot during the term of the lease; or,

LEASE
PROVISIONS

- requiring the tenant to purchase a mobile home from the park owner.

A lease between a mobile home park owner and a tenant must contain the following items which bind the owner during the term of the lease. The owner must:

- specifically identify that lot area for which the tenant is responsible;

- keep all exterior mobile home park property areas that do not belong to a tenant free from weeds and plant growth that are generally noxious or detrimental to the health of the tenants;

- maintain all electrical, plumbing, gas, or other utilities that are provided by the owner;

- provide that emergency repairs to utilities must be made within a reasonable period of time;

- maintain all subsurface water and sewage lines and connections in good working order;

- respect the privacy of the tenants;
  - if only the lot is rented, agree not to enter the mobile home without permission of the mobile home owner;
  - if the mobile home is the property of the owner, enter only after notice to the tenants; or,

- park owners or their representative may enter without notice only in the case of emergencies;

  📖 Provisions that authorize owners or landlords to enter the mobile home to make certain repairs, do not impose a duty on the owners to make all repairs. (*Hurt v. Pershing Mobile Home Sales, Inc.*, 404 N.E.2d 842 (Ill.App. 4 Dist. 1980).)

- maintain all roads within the park in good condition;

- include in the lease a detailed statement listing specifically which services and facilities are provided by the owner for the tenant;

- provide the full names and addresses of all individuals who hold all or part of the title to the mobile home park;

- provide the name and address of the owners' designated agent, if there is one; and,

- provide a custodian's office and furnish each tenant with the name, address, and telephone number of the custodian and the designated office.

Additionally, a mobile home lease must contain:

- terms for payment of the rent (including ground, lot rent, and unit rent), and

- charges for services, specifically itemized.

REQUIRED LEASE NOTICE

Illinois requires that the following notice be printed verbatim in a "clear and conspicuous manner" in each lease or rental agreement for a mobile home or lot:

> ## "IMPORTANT NOTICE REQUIRED BY LAW:
>
> The rules set forth below govern the terms of your lease of occupancy arrangement with this mobile home park. The law requires all of these rules and regulations to be fair and reasonable, and if not, such rules and regulations cannot be enforced against you.
>
> You may continue to reside in the park as long as you pay your rent and abide by the rules and regulations of the park. You may only be evicted form non-payment of rent, violation of laws, or for violation of the rules and regulations of the park and the terms of the lease.
>
> If this park requires you to deal exclusively with a certain fuel dealer or other merchant for goods or services in connection with the use or occupancy of your mobile home or on your mobile home lot, the price you pay for such goods or services must not be more than the prevailing price in the locality for similar goods and services.
>
> You may not be evicted for reporting any violations of law or health and building codes to boards of health, building commissioners, the department of the Attorney General or any other appropriate government agency."

RENEWAL OF LEASE

Mobile home leases are required to "contain an option which automatically renews the lease." (765 ILCS 745/8.) In order for the tenant to prevent the lease from being automatically renewed, the tenant must notify the landlord or owner thirty days prior to the expiration of the lease that he or she does not want to renew. In order for the landlord or owner to prevent the lease from being automatically renewed, he or she must notify the tenant in writing thirty days prior to the expiration of the lease that the lease will not be renewed and specify the reasons why it is not being renewed. Valid reasons for the landlord or owner to not renew a lease are:

- violations of park rules, health, and safety codes;

- irregular or non-payment of rent; or,

- the owner has decided to cease operation of all, or part of, the mobile home park.

Tenants are entitled to at least twelve months notice if the mobile home park is ceasing operation. Tenants are entitled to the balance of their of existing leases when there are more than twelve months remaining on the lease. Tenants with less than twelve months remaining on their lease are entitled to a written month-to-month rental so that they may also receive a full twelve months notice.

📖 There was not a month-to-month lease when the tenant began paying the monthly rate without protest or reservation. The annual lease was automatically renewed with a valid rent increase. (*Fyke v. Melton*, 664 N.E.2d 1070 (Ill.App. 4 Dist. 1996).)

📖 Park owners must show cause and provide reasons for nonrenewal of a lot lease. This protects the tenants from arbitrary termination of their tenancy. In this case the mobile home park owner had not met his burden of showing a reason for nonrenewal. The reasons provided to the tenant in the nonrenewal notice, were continual violation of two park rules. In court, there was no evidence presented regarding violation of the one rule; and for the other rule, the tenant presented evidence that contradicted what the owner considered to be a violation. (*Beeding v. Miller*, 520 N.E.2d 1058 (Ill.App. 2 Dist. 1988).)

When a lease comes up for renewal, the rent or any service charges may increase. A notification of such an increase must be in writing and delivered to the tenant sixty days prior to the expiration of the lease.

📖 Under Illinois law, a letter that included a notice of an increase in rent (which was not provided for in the original lease), and the operator's willingness to enter into a new lease at the increased rental, was an offer to enter into a new lease. (*Aydt v. DeAnza Santa Cruz Mobile Estates*, 763 F.Supp. 970 (N.D. Ill. 1991).)

DEPARTMENT OF PUBLIC HEALTH PAMPHLET

State law provides that a pamphlet produced by the Department of Public Health on the topic of "Tenant's and Park Owner's Rights and Obligations" be given to each new tenant at or before the time they are offered a written lease. Current tenants should also get these pamphlets by hand distribution or mailing. If the owner did not provide these pamphlets to tenants, the lease would still be considered enforceable.

SECURITY DEPOSITS

Upon termination of the lease, the security deposit must be returned to the tenant—minus any rent due and the cost of repairing actual damages to the premises.

If there are damages to the premises, the park owner must provide the tenant with an itemized list of damages, and the estimated cost for the repair of each item. This notice is to be furnished to the tenant within fifteen days after termination or expiration of the lease. If the tenant fails to object to the itemized list within fifteen days, the tenant is considered in agreement to the amount of damages that are on the list. If the owner does not provide the tenant with an itemized list of damages and repair costs within the fifteen-day time limit, that will be considered as an agreement that there were no damages and the entire security deposit will be due immediately to the tenant. If a tenant fails to furnish the park owner with a forwarding address for this correspondence, the park owner is excused from furnishing the itemized list of damages and repair costs.

If a mobile home park contains twenty-five or more mobile homes, the owner must pay interest on security deposits held for more than six months. The rate of interest is "equal to the interest paid by the largest commercial bank, as measured by total assets, having its main banking premises in this State on minimum deposit passbook savings accounts as of December 31 of the preceding year." During the term of the lease, if any portion of the security deposit is used to compensate the owner for nonpayment of rent or to make a good faith reimbursement for damages, then the calculation will reflect the lowering of the principal.

At the end of each twelve month period, the owner must pay the interest to the tenant. This can be paid in cash, or applied to rent due if the owner and tenant so agree. A park owner who fails or refuses to pay the security deposit interest can be forced by a court to pay the tenant the entire amount of the security deposit, court costs, and attorney fees.

TENANT'S DUTIES

State law requires that the tenant agree to:

- keep the mobile home interior, if rented, or the mobile home lot, if rented, in a clean and sanitary condition—free of garbage and rubbish;

- refrain from storing any inoperable motor vehicles;

- wash all vehicles only in areas designated for such by the park management;

- refrain from performing major motor vehicle repairs at any time;

- refrain from storage of any icebox, stove, building material, furniture, or similar items on the exterior premises;

- keep all interior mobile home supplied basic facilities; including plumbing fixtures, cooking and refrigeration equipment, and electrical fixtures in a clean and sanitary condition; and be responsible for the exercise of reasonable care in the proper use and operation of these items;

- not deliberately or negligently destroy, deface, damage, impair, or remove any part of the premises, or knowingly allow any other person to do so;

- conduct himself, and require other persons that the tenant invites to conduct themselves, in a manner that will not affect or disturb the neighbors' peaceful enjoyment of their premises;

- abide by all rules and regulations concerning the use, occupation, and maintenance of the premises; and,

- abide by any clearly stated, reasonable rules for guest parking.

Rules

Rules of a mobile home park are enforceable against a tenant only if:

- a written copy of all rules was delivered by the owner to the tenant prior to the tenant signing a lease;

- the rules apply to tenants in a fair manner;

- the purpose of the rules is to promote convenience, safety, and welfare of the tenants; preserve park property from damage; or fairly distribute park services and facilities to the tenants;

- the rules are reasonably related to the purpose for which adopted;

- the rules are written sufficiently explicit in prohibition, direction, or limitation of a tenant's conduct in order to fairly inform the tenant of what must be done or not done in order to comply; and,

- the rules are not for the purpose of evading a legal obligation of the park owner.

Rules and regulations adopted within a term of a lease are enforceable against a tenant only if the tenant is given a thirty day notice of the adoption of the rule or regulation, and the rule or regulation is not in violation of the terms and conditions of the lease.

MASTER ANTENNA TELEVISION SERVICES

A park owner cannot require that a tenant remove a conventional, outdoor television antenna unless the owner makes master antenna television services available at no additional charge to the tenant. Owners cannot require that a tenant subscribe to and pay for master antenna television services.

OTHER RESTRICTIONS ON MOBILE HOME PARK OWNERS

Various other laws in the state's Mobile Home Landlord and Tenant Rights Act affect the actions of the park owners. Park owners cannot:

- prohibit tenant meetings, as long as these meeting are held at reasonable hours and when facilities are available;

- require that a tenant purchase fuel oil or bottled gas from a particular dealer or distributor—this does not apply to the owner who provides a centralized distribution system for fuel oil or bottled gas, providing that the tenants are not charged more that a reasonable retail price;

- restrict a tenant in the choice of a seller of furnishings, accessories, goods, or service, unless the restriction is necessary to protect health or safety of the residents (owners can restrict the access of the park by service vehicles if they are in such number and frequency as to create a danger for pedestrian traffic in the park);

- require or accept a payment or gift from anyone who wishes to obtain an advantage in the rental of a mobile home or a mobile home site. (An example of this situation would be a waiting list for the rental or a particular mobile home or site. Anyone acting

LANDLORD'S FIVE-DAY NOTICE

STATE OF ILLINOIS   )
)   SS.

COUNTY OF _____)

To: _____

_____

YOU ARE HEREBY NOTIFIED that there is now due the undersigned Landlord the sum of $_____, being rent for the premises situated in the City of _____, and County of _____, Illinois _____, and described as follows:

The property at _____,
Unit Number _____, together with all buildings, sheds, closets, out-buildings, garages, and other structures used in connection with said premises.

YOU ARE NOTIFIED that payment of the amount due is now **DEMANDED** of you, and that unless the entire payment is made on or before the expiration of five days after the service of this notice, your lease of the above rental premises will be terminated immediately.

ONLY FULL PAYMENT of the rent demanded in this notice will waive the Landlord's right to terminate the lease under this notice, unless the Landlord agrees in writing to continue the lease in exchange for receiving partial payment.

Dated this _____ day of _____, _____.

_____
LANDLORD

AFFIDAVIT OF SERVICE

I, _____, being duly sworn on oath, deposes and says that on the _____ day of _____, _____, I served the foregoing notice on the tenant(s) named herein:

   __1. By delivering a copy hereof to the Tenant _____.
   __2. By delivering a copy hereof to _____, a person
         above the age of 13 years, residing or in charge of the described premises.
   __3. By sending a copy hereof to said Tenant by certified/registered mail, with a request for return
         receipt from the addressee.
   __4. By posting a copy hereof on the main door of the described premises, because no one was in
         actual possession of the premises.

Signed:_____

Subscribed and sworn to before me
this _____ day of _____, _____.

_____
Notary Public

LANDLORD'S TEN-DAY NOTICE

STATE OF ILLINOIS   )
)   SS.

COUNTY OF   )

To: _____

_____

_____

YOU ARE HEREBY NOTIFIED that you are not complying with your lease in that
_____
_____
_____.

Demand is hereby made that you remedy the noncompliance within ten (10) days of receipt of this notice or your lease shall be deemed terminated and you shall vacate the premises upon such termination. If this same conduct or conduct of a similar nature is repeated within twelve months, your tenancy is subject to termination without you being given an opportunity to cure the noncompliance.

Dated this _____ day of _____, _____.

_____
                             LANDLORD

AFFIDAVIT OF SERVICE

I, _____, being duly sworn on oath, deposes and says that on the
_____ day of _____, _____, I served the foregoing notice on the tenant(s) named herein:

    __ 1. By delivering a copy hereof to the Tenant _____.

    __ 2. By delivering a copy hereof to _____, a person
           above the age of 13 years, residing or in charge of the described premises.

    __ 3. By sending a copy hereof to said Tenant by certified/registered mail, with a request for return
           receipt from the addressee.

    __ 4. By posting a copy hereof on the main door of the described premises, because no one was in
           actual possession of the premises.

Signed:_____
                   Subscribed and sworn to before me
                   this _____ day of _____, _____.

                   _____
                   Notary Public

as the owner's agent would also be bound by this law. If a court finds that a person made such a payment to an owner in order to gain an advantage, the owner may be liable for twice the payment amount plus the cost of taking legal action.]; or,

- in any way restrict, limit, obstruct, interfere with, or prohibit the owners of mobile homes from selling the mobile home. (In the case of a mobile home sale, the park owner cannot require a fee or commission on the sale price, nor require that the new owner of the mobile home remove it from the park unless there is significant deterioration and substantial disrepair.)

TENANT'S REMEDIES

During the first thirty days of a lease, if the park owner fails to substantially conform to the provisions of the lease or fails to comply with any applicable code, statue, or ordinance; the tenant may terminate the lease with a written notice, and vacate the mobile home. After the first thirty days of the lease, the tenant can terminate the lease only if the tenant remained in possession in reliance on the owner's written promise to correct all or part of the compliance with the lease, code, statute, or ordinance.

If a condition deprives the tenant of substantial benefit and enjoyment of the property, and the owner fails to remedy that condition within thirty days of receiving a written notice of the condition, the tenant may terminate the lease and vacate the unit. A written notice is not required if the condition makes the mobile home uninhabitable, or if it poses an imminent threat to the health, welfare, and safety of any occupant. If these conditions are caused by the willful or negligent acts or omissions of the owner, then the tenant may be able to recover any damages, including a reasonable expenditure to obtain adequate housing while the mobile home is uninhabitable.

PARK OWNER'S REMEDIES

If the tenant does not conform to the provisions of the lease or the rules and regulations of the mobile home park, the owner must notify the tenant in writing of the breach. This notification must specify the violation in detail, and advise the tenant that if the violation continues for more than twenty-four hours after receiving the notice, the park owner may terminate the tenant's lease.

Any time the rent is overdue, the tenant must be notified in writing that, unless the payment is made within the time specified in the notice (not less than five days from receipt of the notice), that the lease will be terminated. If the tenant remains in default for the rent payment, then the park owner may institute legal action for eviction, recovery of possession, rent due, and reimbursement of any damages.

EVICTIONS

According to Illinois law, a mobile home park owner can terminate a lease and evict a tenant for any of the following:

- nonpayment of rent;

- failure to comply with the park rules and regulations; or,

- failure to comply with local ordinances or applicable state law.

A mobile home park owner cannot terminate a lease to retaliate against a tenant who:

- makes an effort to secure or enforce any rights given to the tenant under the lease or the law;

- complains in good faith to governmental authorities about the park owner's violations of health or safety laws, regulations, codes, ordinances, or state statutes; or,

- is an organizer, member, or involved in any activities relative to a home owners association.

The Forcible Entry and Detainer Act provides that "the rental of land upon which a mobile home is placed or the rental of a mobile home and the land on which it is placed, for more than 30 days, shall be construed as a lease of real property" (735 ILCS 5/9-103). Therefore, evictions will be governed by the Forcible Entry and Detainer Act.

COMMERCIAL RENTALS 16

This book is primarily directed towards residential rentals, however many landlords are involved in both commercial and residential rental property. While this one chapter can not contain a complete summary of commercial rentals, the following should give both commercial landlords and commercial tenants an overview of the subject.

LAWS

Commercial rental property is not subject to most consumer protection laws that govern residential leases. However it is subject to the larger area of contract law, federal laws on discrimination (such as the ADA), federal & state laws for specific businesses, tax laws, and many more local ordinances that cover the operation of a business.

BEFORE YOU SIGN A COMMERCIAL LEASE

The biggest step that a business owner will take is securing a location for that business. Businesses that rely on the public as customers need to be concerned with location, neighborhood, access to parking, ability to enter and exit the parking lot, and the appearance of the business. Before you start renting space for your business you need to look at the details of the rental building, the lease, and the neighborhood.

TENANT BALANCE

If you are planing to locate your business in a building with other tenants, take the time to look at the other tenants. Problems which will effect your profits can happen due to a bad tenant mix. For example, if your business needs a level of quiet (tax preparation, accounting, real estate) being located next to a rock music store probably will cause problems for you and your customers. Likewise you may not want to locate a florist shop next to a garden center that also sells cut flowers, or a dentist office next to a machine shop. Before deciding on a particular building to locate your business in visit that building at different times. Check during rush hours to see how easy it is to enter and exit the parking lot. Check during off hours to see if there is loitering around the building. Note the type of people who are customers for the other tenants in the building.

USE EXCLUSIVES

A landlord can give a tenant what is called a *use exclusive* in a particular building occupied by other tenants. This is a clause in the lease which guarantees that other tenants will not be allowed to market certain items. This effectively prevents a tenant's competition from moving into the same building. Use exclusives are usually offered to strong tenants as an incentive to get them into a building. Any such offer must be written in the lease with details as to what activities are prohibited, what activities are allowed, and the remedies that a tenant with a use exclusive is entitled to if that is violated. This is frequently used in shopping centers in order to get a good mix of retail stores.

On the other hand a landlord may wish to only rent to tenants in a certain profession in order to provide a center for such activities to the public. An example of this is a building with several doctors, a pharmacy, and a medical lab. In such a case the use exclusive may go to the pharmacy, lab, or maybe to a doctor practicing a certain type of medicine.

Special Licenses

Commercial tenants must be aware that some business operations also require special state and/or community licenses, permits, approvals or sanctions in order to operate. One common example of this is an *occupancy permit*. An occupancy permit is issued to a business upon the passing of inspections by local agencies such as health department, building and codes, etc. Without such a permit, a business may not be allowed to open. Because most commercial tenants make their own changes to the interior of a building, a new tenant may invest a lot of money in renovations only to find out that building code violations prevent opening until the premises are brought up to code.

Another example of a special license is one to sell liquor, which is governed by federal, state, and local community laws. Illinois has very strict laws which govern all aspects of selling liquor such as: location of the business to schools, hospitals, churches, military bases; qualifications of those who will be dispensing the liquor; the type of business that can dispense liquor; the times a business can be open; and how to obtain a liquor license; among many other things. Most Illinois cities add additional laws that a business must comply with in order to sell liquor within that city.

One such law may take a new business owner who intends to sell liquor by surprise: If a location previously had a license to distribute liquor and that license was revoked, a new liquor license cannot be issued for that location for a period of time—even in the case where there is a new store tenant. In the worst case, the new tenant signs the lease and then contacts the city only to find out that he/she cannot get a liquor license at that location for many months and he/she is locked in a lease.

Commercial tenants should make sure that there is a contingency clause in the lease that covers special licenses needed. This clause should allow the tenant to get out of a lease if the special license can not be obtained within a certain period of time. At the minimum, the tenant must review the local ordinances and commercial building codes before signing the lease. Most cities will gladly assist a potential commercial tenant before the lease is signed.

THE COMMERCIAL LEASE

Commercial leases are very different from residential leases. One major difference is that there is no standard form, all commercial leases can be changed with a little effort. Large corporations and owners of large commercial buildings often speak of the 'standard lease', in reality this is the lease which they most often use. That so called 'standard lease' may not really be a standard within the commercial renting industry, and it will almost always favor the landlord. It is up to the commercial tenant to read, review and propose changes to the lease. Before signing a lease or an "intent" to sign a lease, the commercial tenant would be well served to obtain the assistance of an attorney who is familiar with this type of document. This is not to say that all commercial landlords will attempt to push an unfair lease upon the tenant. However, because commercial leases do not come under the scrutiny of laws that residential leases do, the commercial tenant must actively look out for his/her own interests.

LENGTH

The length of a lease is called its term. The term of a commercial lease is also a matter of negotiation. Nowadays, most commercial leases will include an increase (called escalations) in rent for each year the lease is in effect. This is a change from years past when the majority of commercial leases kept the same rental amount for the entire term, which made long term leases very favorable. Long term leases still may save the tenant money, if the percentage of rent increase in the lease is lower than what the property is renting for in a new lease. Short term leases can also be beneficial for a business that needs to be flexible. This is especially true for new business and for new property in an area.

Build Outs

Build outs or improvements are what is required to be done to commercial property in order to comply with the tenant's business. These build outs are things done to the property which cannot be taken by the tenant at the end of the lease. Examples would be bringing the building up to code, upgrading electricity, adding walls, etc. Traditionally all build outs are paid for by the tenant. However, this is a fertile area for the tenant to negotiate with the landlord. Besides getting the landlord to pay for some or all of the build outs, negotiations may include a longer term or lower rent depending on who pays for build outs.

In some commercial businesses, such as restaurants, build outs can come at considerable cost. Before negotiating and signing a lease the commercial tenant must get accurate estimates as to the cost of such improvements to the property. Also, as stated prior, commercial tenants may also want to involve different departments in the city in order to determine if the property needs build outs in order to comply with building codes, health regulations, and other ordinances.

Other Items

Commercial leases are flexible and should be negotiated to fit the business of the tenant. The lease should spell out in detail what is included in the rent. Is this a 'gross lease' where the rent includes building insurance, maintenance, repairs, and property tax; or a 'net lease' where the tenant will be charged separately for these items. It should also include disposition of security deposits, restrictions on subleasing, options to renew, how the lease is terminated, and how disputes are handled. If there are common areas, the lease should detail them and provide for responsibility for maintenance. The exact space being rented should be detailed in any commercial lease, this may include professional blueprints and architectural renderings. In multiple tenant office buildings, a tenant's signage should also be specified.

It is in both the landlord's and the tenant's best interest to include every detail in a commercial lease. Unlike residential leases, there are very few laws which will protect the parties of a commercial lease because it is assumed that all parties are professional business people. Commercial leases are contracts and courts will look to contract law between two business people in a commercial lease dispute. Generally, unless the commercial lease specifies otherwise, courts will assume that the tenant assumes the commercial rental space 'as is'. The landlord has no responsibility for the property being safe, up to local code, or suitable for the purpose rented.

CASES

In a lease between landlord and a commercial renter, the lease stated only that the rent be paid semi-annually. The lease originated at the beginning of July. The court stated that a reasonable person would presume that the following payments be made at the beginning of January and the beginning of July, and the landlord was correct by enforcing this time frame. (Fox v. Commercial Coin Laundry Systems; 325 Ill.App.3d 473, 757 N.E.2d 529, 258 Ill. Dec. 840 (Sept. 13, 2001)).

Landlord sued former office tenant for lost rent after the tenant vacated the offices before the end of the lease. Tenant told the court that he left because the landlord could not fix temperature and humidity variations in the offices rented. The court found in favor of the landlord citing several reasons; the tenant remained in the offices several months after he stopped paying rent, the tenant did not supply ample evidence about the problems with the temperature and humidity or any damages that resulted. (Shaker v. Medical technologies Group, Ltd., 315 Ill.App.3d 125, 733 N.E.2d 865, 248 Ill. Dec. 190, (June 30, 2000)).

    📖 Landlord sued tenant for breach of lease in that tenant, who operated a gas station, expanded the use of the property resulting in necessary EPA damage clean up. Court awarded landlord $875 in reimbursement for clean up, but refused to allow the claim for $38,000 in legal fees. The reason that the tenant was not required to reimburse the landlord for legal fees was that the lease stated that each party pays their own legal fees. (Powers v. Rockford Stop-N-Go Inc., 326 Ill.App.3d 511, 761 N.E.2d 237, 260 Ill. Dec.393 (2001)).

    📖 Tenant sued landlord to get landlord to repair damages to tenants business because the building's sump pump did not work. The court looked at the commercial lease and determined that the lease made the tenant responsible for repairs and that a commercial lease did not carry the presumption that the landlord had a duty to repair common areas as a residential lease did. (Midwest Laundry, Inc. v. Vainikos, Appellate Court First District No. 1-99-3566 (2001)).

SECTION 8 AND LOW-COST HOUSING 17

The *Housing Choice Voucher Program* is tenant-based and project-based financial assistance from the Federal Government. It is operated by Housing and Urban Development (HUD) and gets its name because the law which covers this program is at Title 24, Chapter IX, Part 982 -- Section 8. While most people know this as Section 8 Housing, it is also called The Housing Choice Voucher Program. The primary goal of this program is to provide very low-income families, the elderly, and the disabled with the ability to chose safe, decent, and affordable housing.

RESPONSIBILITIES AND OBLIGATIONS

Both the landlord and the tenant in Section 8 Housing are subject to rules and duties as specified by HUD.

LANDLORDS

Landlords and property owners who provide Section 8 rental units are subject to an additional governing body, the Housing Authority. Some cities have their own local HUD office that would be the landlord's direct contract. Housing Authority rules require that the rental facilities be maintained in a decent, safe, and sanitary condition. The unit must pass the local program's housing standards and continue to be maintained at that level. HUD will also enforce the terms and services which are listed in the lease.

In the actual renting to those with Section 8 vouchers, the landlord is under an additional obligation to avoid discriminating against tenants because of race, religion, sex, age, sexual orientation, or disability. HUD provides tenants and potential tenants several methods to file discrimination complaints including filling out a form on the Internet.

In April 2002, the Lawyers' Committee For Better Housing did a study and test of the voucher system under the Chicago Housing Authority. What they found was that landlords in the Chicago area rejected more African Americans and Latinos than Caucasians under the voucher system. Landlords have disputed this study and have pointed to a shortage in Section 8 rental units because the Housing Authority is very slow in performing the investigation necessary to register the unit as Section 8.

This points to another instance when a landlord must use the same criteria in selecting tenants. Also the majority of the above study was done via phone calls with the landlord. Landlords should make it a policy to avoid screening potential tenants over the phone and require a face to face meeting where the potential tenant can fill out an application and provide financial information.

TENANTS

Before even looking for a rental unit, the potential tenant must apply to HUD for a rent voucher. HUD will determine if the person is eligible based on several factors such as income, assets, and number of people in the family. This information is verified and the person is investigated to make sure the information is accurate. Once the potential tenant qualifies for a rental voucher, their local HUD office may be able to give them a list of housing which accepts the rental voucher or the potential tenant may be on his/her own to find a rental unit. The potential tenant then views the rental unit and goes through the same screening that the landlord does for other tenants.

HUD information for tenants consistently reminds them that a lease is a legal contract and that they must abide by the contents of the lease. Tenants must also follow local ordinances and the rules of the rental community. They must provide accurate information regarding their eligibility for the voucher at all times. Section 8 tenants must also pay the correct amount of rent at the time specified by the lease.

Under responsibilities, HUD reminds tenants that they are responsible for keeping their rental unit clean, disposing of garbage properly, complying with local health and safety codes, and reporting any building defects to the landlord.

RESEARCH

Federally assisted housing can financially benefit a landlord with loans and grants. Landlords who are interested need to contact their local Housing Authority, review their local ordinances to see if this is feasible, and review HUD information.

Most HUD information is online at **www.hud.gov.** That site is also the place for tenants to file a discrimination complaint online and locate your local HUD office.

HOUSING OTHER THAN SECTION 8

Tenants with low income may be eligible of housing other than Section 8 vouchers. Federal Assistance is also available for:

- *Public Housing.* This is low income housing that is operated by the local Housing Authority.

- *Privately Owned Subsidized Housing.* In this case the Federal Government provides a level of subsidies to the property owner. The owner then applies this money toward the rent payment of housing for specific people under different programs. There are programs for the elderly, disabled, low income families, and low income individuals. This is also operated by the local Housing Authority.

- *HUD's HOME Program.* This provides grants to state and local governments to offer low income housing.

- *Rural Housing Service.* The local Rural Development office operates this program which is funded by the Department of Agriculture. It provides financial assistance and low cost loans for those who qualify.

CASES

☷ This case was decided in Kane County. The landlord filed to evict a tenant in a federally assisted housing project after police found cannabis in the rental unit of the tenant. At the time of the police search the named tenant was upstairs and a guest was the source of the criminal activity. The appellate court found that the lease did not state that the tenant was strictly liable for criminal activity on the premises, that there was no evidence that the cannabis was the tenants' or that that tenant condoned such activity. The tenant was not evicted. (Kimball Hill Management Co. v Roper, 314 Ill.App.3d 975, 733 N.E.2d 458, 248 Ill.Dec. 11, (July 20, 2000).)

☷ This case was decided in Will County. The landlord filed to evict a tenant in a federally assisted housing tenant due to criminal activity in the rental unit. While the tenant was in the hospital, family members of the tenant committed a crime. The court held since the tenant was in the hospital at the time of the crime and had no knowledge of the crime, she had no control over the family member. The tenant was not evicted. (Housing Authority of Joliet v. Keys, 761 N.E.2d 338, Ill.App. 3 Dist., (Dec. 14, 2001).)

NOTE: *Both of these cases are outside of the reach of the Chicago ordinances. If these cases were in Chicago the result may have been different. Also the decision of these cases, especially the one in Joliet cause a lot of controversy and a move to hold the named tenant responsible for all activity no matter what the circumstances are. If you are a landlord who wants to evict a federally assisted housing tenant, you will need to have the backing of a well written lease, evidence, and you may want to obtain the assistance of an attorney who is familiar with this type of housing.*

SPECIAL RULES FOR PUBLIC HOUSING TERMINATIONS

For nonpayment of rent in a public housing unit, the a fourteen-day notice is required rather than a three-day notice; and it must be mailed or hand delivered, not posted (24 CFR 866.4(1)(2).) The notice must inform the tenant of his or her right to a grievance procedure. At least one court has held that both a fourteen-day notice and a three-day notice must be given. (*Stanton v. Housing Authority of Pittsburgh*, 469 F.Supp. 1013 (W.D.Pa. 1977).) Other courts have disagreed. (*Ferguson v. Housing Authority of Middleboro*, 499 F.Supp. 334 (E.D. Ky. 1980).)

   📖 The housing authority must prove both that the tenant did not pay the rent and that the tenant was at fault for not paying. (*Maxton Housing Authority v. McLean*, 328 S.E.2d (N.C. 1985).)

   📖 A Louisiana court held that a tenant was not at fault for not paying rent because her former husband did not pay child support. (*Housing Authority of City of New Iberia v. Austin*, 478 So.2d 1012 (La.App. 1986); writ denied, 481 So.2d 1334 (La. 1986).)

   📖 One Florida court held that posting both a fourteen-day notice and a three-day notice is too confusing. It suggested that the landlord only use a fourteen-day notice, or else deliver the three-day notice on a date so that the deadline was the same as for the fourteen-day notice. (*Broward Co. Housing Authority v. Simmons*, 4 F.L.W.Supp. 494 (Co.Ct. Broward 1996).)

For breach of the terms of the lease, other than payment of rent, a thirty-day notice must be given, except in emergencies. The thirty-day notice must inform the tenant of the reasons for termination, his or her right to reply, and his or her right to a grievance procedure [24 CFR 366(4)(1)]. If the tenant requests a grievance hearing, a second notice must be given, even if the tenant loses at the hearing. (*Ferguson v. Housing Authority of Middleboro*, 499 F.Supp. 432 (E.D. Ky. 1980).)

FEDERALLY SUBSIDIZED SECTION 236 APARTMENTS

For nonpayment of rent in federally subsidized Section 236 apartments, tenants must be given a three-day notice, and be advised that if there is a judicial proceeding they can present a valid defense, if any. Service must be by first class mail, and also hand delivered or placed under the door [24 CFR 450.4(a)].

For breach of the terms of the lease other than payment of rent, the tenant must first have been given notice that in the future such conduct would be grounds for terminating the lease. The notice of termination must state when the tenancy will be terminated, specifically why it is being terminated, and must advise the tenant of the right to present a defense in the eviction suit (24 CFR 450).

The legal provision that acceptance of rent is a waiver of past noncompliance does not apply to the subsidized portion of the rent. However, waiver will occur if legal action is not taken within forty-five days.

SECTION 8 SUBSIDIZED APARTMENTS

For Section 8 housing under 24 CFR 882.215(c)(4), the landlord must notify the housing authority in writing at the commencement of the eviction proceedings. The previous paragraph regarding acceptance of rent also applies to Section 8 housing.

EVICTIONS DUE TO ILLEGAL ACTIVITY

The eviction of a tenant living in rental property that is owned or managed by a public housing authority established under the Housing Authorities Act is covered by 735 ILCS 5/9-118. Under this law, a tenant can be evicted if there is direct evidence of:

- "trafficking in cannabis, narcotics, or controlled substances; within or upon the rental premises, or with the knowledge, consent, or in concert with a person named in the complaint", or

- "the possession, use, sale, or delivery of a firearm, (which is prohibited by state law); within or upon the rental premises, or with the knowledge, consent, or in concert with a person named in the complaint."

If there is evidence of such illegal activity, you would need to file a verified complaint demanding possession of the rental property. A *verified complaint* includes a statement made under oath that the information and allegations in the complaint are true. The complaint is then served upon the tenant at lease fourteen days before the day of a hearing.

If the tenant does not appear at the hearing, the court will enter a default judgment for eviction. If the tenant does appear at the hearing, there will be either an immediate trial, or a trial date will be set for less than seven days from the original hearing date. At trial, if there is proof of the listed violations, the court will enter a judgment for immediate possession and immediate re-entry of the rental premises.

TENANT'S RIGHTS 18

This book is aimed at landlords and property owners, their rights and responsibilities. However, a good landlord should not only be aware of his/her rights but of those that are specifically important for the tenants. This chapter reviews some of the more important issues of being a good tenant.

BEING A PROSPECTIVE TENANT

Before you start touring available rental units get the facts about the neighborhoods and about your available housing funds. Pre-shop the neighborhood, the stores, the parking, the length of commute to your job, look at the night activity. Are there gangs in the area? Will you have the peace and quiet needed to sleep?

Once you determine what neighborhood you want to live in, realistically determine what you can spend in housing. Remember your rent may not include all utilities. Telephone service is usually paid for by the tenant as is renters insurance. Be honest about this. Do not waste your time or a landlord's time by viewing rental units that are not within your budget. Above all do not sign a rental agreement for a rental unit that is over what you can pay. Tenants who have a past of evictions due to non-payment of rent may end up being rejected from renting in locations that they desire.

Tenants should inspect potential rental units carefully for working water, toilets, appliances, windows and doors. Check for damage to the unit, and if there is damage make sure it is noted in writing as part of your signed rental agreement. A tenant who accepts a rental unit that has damage may end up losing part of his/her security deposit to pay for repairs, unless the damage was noted at the time of the rental.

PETS

Tenants with pets need not abandon their pets in order to get a rental unit. There are an increasing number of landlords and property owners who are willing to rent to responsible tenants with pets. Local humane societies sometimes have listings of rental communities which allow pets. Landlords may advertise that pets are allowed. No matter how tenants with pets plan to find a place to rent, those with pets need to give themselves additional time to find accommodating landlords.

A responsible tenant with pets should provide a potential landlord with proof that the pet is well behaved and has proper medical care. Certificates of puppy training, a letter from your veterinarian stating that the animal is current on vaccinations, and a letter from a current landlord may help. Also the prospective tenant should offer to pay and additional security deposit for the pet.

Once you convince a landlord to allow your pet, get it in writing. If you are an existing tenant or a new tenant, make sure that you and the landlord sign a pet addendum to the rental agreement. The reason to do this is simple. If the rental community is considered 'no pets' but your landlord allows you to keep a pet, that personal favor may be forgotten if the landlord no longer works at that rental community.

An interesting internet site for those renting with pets:

www.rentwithpets.org

Rental Agreement

Most landlords will require that you bring in certain information before you can sign a lease. Lying about this information can cause the lease to be voided. Be honest and prompt in providing what the landlord requires.

Get everything in writing from rules, promises, to the lease. Make sure that you get a copy of everything that you sign. READ THE LEASE and THE RULES. Once you sign the lease you are responsible for everything in it just as the landlord is. Courts will not accept the excuse that you never read the lease in order to get you out of a lawsuit brought by the landlord. It is the tenant's responsibility to read and to abide by the lease and the rules of the rental agreement. As one court recently said "Tenants are bound by the lease too."

It is also important that tenants have some knowledge of local ordinances. In Chicago The Chicago Residential Landlord and Tenant Ordinance is free from the city, it is also printed in the back of this book. In order to insist on your rights as a tenant, you must know what those rights are. Besides local ordinances, there are many internet sites which can educate tenants.

Repairs

Items that need repair should always be reported to the landlord first. If a tenant has problems getting repairs, he/she should inform the landlord in writing about the problem. Landlords who are not prompt in repairs may be pushed by certified letters regarding such repairs. Also, if a tenant wants to pay for the repair him/herself, the landlord must be told in writing using a certified letter.

Problems which make the rental unit uninhabitable, should be brought to the attention of the landlord immediately. Landlords who do not respond with repairs may be liable for building code violations, fines, and suits by tenants.

TENANT'S RESPONSIBILITIES

A tenant should follow his/her duties as listed in the rental agreement and the rules provided by the landlord. Tenants who cannot follow these rules are subject to eviction. In several chapters of this book, we have covered what the law requires of a tenant: Chapter 6 on "Maintenance," Chapter 8 on "Changing the Terms of the Tenancy," Chapter 9 on "Problems During the Tenancy," and Chapter 12 on "Evictions." A tenant who repeatedly causes problems is not only subject to losing the right to rent that unit, he/she may also be liable for civil penalties.

One common mistake that tenants make is to take on a roommate without informing their landlords. Before you let another person live with you a tenant must check with their landlord. Most landlords will require that this roommate be considered a co-tenant and go through the same screening as the original tenant did. Also landlords are legally entitled to set reasonable occupancy limits and an additional roommate may violate this limit. Legally, landlords can charge an additional rent and security deposit for roommates who are considered co-tenants.

INJURIES

Landlords are usually held responsible for injuries to tenants or their visitors when it can be proven that: the landlord had control over the problem, an accident resulting in serious injury was foreseeable if the problem was not fixed, the fix would not be unreasonably expensive, the landlord failed to fix the problem and this failure caused the accident, and that the injury is real. This is a long list of things that must be proven for a court to hold the landlord responsible.

In cases where the above criteria is obviously met, the insurance provider for the landlord may be willing to settle with the injured. However the trend with insurance companies is to allow all such cases to proceed in the court system before offering to settle. Many insurance companies have their own attorneys on staff or have an agreement with law firms who are willing and able to spend years going through the court system. The era when a minor injury was met with a large settlement check is over.

Noise

One of the largest reported problems with tenants is noise. Noise from other tenants can drive the good tenants from a rental community leaving behind those who enjoy a nightly battle of the stereo speakers. In some cases the noise of neighbors may be against the law, depending on time of day and volume. If the noise is coming from a barking dog the local animal control ordinances may apply. This is yet another case where the tenant should be knowledgeable of local ordinances. Also your rental agreement and rental rules may prohibit certain levels of noise and may even list what steps tenants need to follow to file a complaint with the landlord. Your neighbors loud stereo could be a violation of the rental agreement and the landlord may be able to threaten the noisy neighbors with eviction. Most rental agreements contain a clause which gives all tenants the right to "quiet enjoyment" of the premises and requires that tenants not disturb others.

There are many solutions to the noise problems, including involving the landlord. Sometimes a quiet talk with a neighbor may resolve the problem, but face to face confrontations can also result in many other problems. Sometimes reporting a loud party or constantly barking dog to the proper authorities may result in quiet. However irresponsible neighbors may simply resort to their noisy ways once the authorities have left the area. Tenants and landlords have also resorted to professional mediation in order to curb noise from neighbors. There is not one sure way to resolve the noise problem.

Tenants who are bothered with noise may also need to look inward for a solution. There is a certain level of noise that will happen in any multi-family building. The noise of a late night flushing toilet, an early morning shower, creaking floors in older buildings, are all noises that should be expected. Also, tenants who work odd shifts and sleep during the day should not expect the other tenants to keep quiet during the daytime. Earplugs, sound machines, or other audio distractions may be of help in dealing with noisy neighbors.

DISPUTES

It is inevitable that landlords and tenants will disagree. Disagreements and disputes need to be resolved quickly and fairly for both parties. Again the best defense to disagreements with your landlord is to know what is required of both you and the landlord in the lease, the rules of the property, and the local law. Arguing with a landlord about paying for or repairing something which is listed in the lease as the tenant's responsibility is a waste of time and will probably result in hard feelings. Also a tenant who has a history of not causing trouble and being responsible has a better chance of getting what he or she wants than a tenant who has been a problem to the landlord.

Tenants who have severe problems with the landlord or property owners should first try to work out the differences without the assistance of attorneys. People are more apt to negotiate a problem without the perceived threat of litigation that an attorney brings. Tenants should document problems, keep copies of communication between the tenant and landlord and keep all communication civil. If the dispute does end up in court, a knowledgeable tenant who can prove that he/she did everything possible to resolve the problem in a business like manner will go far in impressing the court to listen to the tenant's side.

INSURANCE

For a tenant, renters insurance is a must. Many rental agreements will hold a tenant liable if they cause damage to the rental building, even if the cause was an accident. A fire caused by a forgotten pot can result in major damage and the landlord may be able to hold the tenant financially liable. Additionally a tenant's property is probably not covered by the landlord's insurance. A tenant can lose everything due to a fire, theft or natural disaster. Rental insurance is relatively low-cost and can be obtained from those who sell other types of insurance.

TENANT'S HELP

In addition to the Internet sites that have been mentioned in this book, those in federally assisted housing can find information and what to do about housing discrimination at **www.hud.gov**. There are also low cost legal clinics that can help tenants. One of Illinois' premier assistance groups is Prairie State Legal Services, Inc. Prairie State has several offices within the state, contact the closest office to you for assistance.

GLOSSARY

A

actual damages. Money awarded by the court to compensate a person for losses that are proved to the court by receipts or testimony.

affidavit. A statement of facts in writing that is made under oath. It is usually witnessed and/or signed by a notary.

agreement to lease. Legal and binding contract that the landlord and tenant enter into regarding the tenant renting a certain unit/building from the landlord in the future. This is often used in new construction to reserve a unit not yet built and in commercial leases for offices/building that will be vacant at some future date.

C

client-attorney representation agreement. Term used for the attorney/client contract.

common areas. Parts of the rental property that are considered under the control of the landlord. These areas include stairways, hallways, lobby, laundry room, and other such areas that are for the common use of all tenants.

constructive eviction. This occurs when the landlord makes the rental unit "unlivable." Things such as locking the tenant out, not providing the minimal service of habitability, etc., are actions that make the unit "unlivable."

D

decree. The final decision made by the court.

deep pockets. A legal theory used in personal injury law. Under the theory, the plaintiff sues as many people as can be connected to injury, especially those who are wealthy or have insurance providers, to get the most amount of money in a settlement.

default order or judgment. An order or judgment made on only the plaintiff's or petitioner's complaint because there was no response from the other person (defendant) within a certain time.

defendant. Person being sued.

deposition. Testimony given under oath outside a courtroom.

discovery. A court ordered period (done before the actual trial) when attorneys for both sides obtain information about the case.

docket. The calendar or schedule of cases in a particular court.

domicile. The place where a person lives and is considered as primary residence by the IRS.

E

ejectment. A type of eviction which deals not only with the tenant, but with others who may or may not have a legal right to the property.

emancipation. When a child is legally not considered a minor.

escalation. Word used in commercial leases to indication how much the rent increases from one year to the next.

estate. The interest in property or the actual property of a deceased person.

eviction. Legal process to remove tenant from rental property.

F

foreign order. Any court order that was issued by a state other than Illinois or in another country.

G

gross lease. Term used in commercial leases to indicate that the rent includes building insurance, maintenance, repairs, and property tax.

H

hearing. A proceeding which takes place in a courtroom in front of a judge.

hearsay. What someone claims he/she was told by some other person. Usually cannot be used as a statement of fact in court.

holding over. Term used for a tenant who does not vacate the rental property after the lease is terminated.

home rule. In the state of Illinois, laws have priorities. Federal laws are applied, unless there is a state law which covers the issue. Then state laws are applied, unless the local community has a law covering the issue. Home rule is when the community (city, town) has such a law.

I

in camera. Legal proceeding held in a judge's chambers with or without the participating parties. (Frequently done when children testify.)

injunction. A court order which prevents someone from doing some act.

interrogatories. Questions in writing from the other side in a case. These questions require written answers that are sworn under oath. Is used instead of a deposition or as a supplement to a deposition.

J

jurisdiction. The power of the court to rule on a legal issue.

L

landlord. Person who rents out property to tenant, can also be an owner of the property or a property management company.

lease. Legal contract between landlord and tenant to secure rental property.

litigation. Process of fighting a legal dispute in the court system.

M

majority age. A person who is of legal age; no longer a minor.

mediator. An independent, professional who attempts to resolve the differences between two parties without legal action.

mitigate damages. Whenever a lease is terminated, the landlord usually takes steps to reduce his or her economic loss.

modification. A court order that changes the terms of an existing court order.

motion. A written or oral request to the court asking the court to do something.

N

net lease. Term used in commercial leases to indicate that the rent does not include building insurance, maintenance, repairs, and property tax.

O

objection. A verbal interruption by an attorney at a trial or deposition. (This action occurs when the attorney believes that something inappropriate was said.)

option to purchase. A clause in a lease that a portion of the rent will be applied toward a down payment if the tenant decides to purchase the rental in the future. This portion can only be applied to a future down payment and is usually not refundable to the tenant if the tenant decides not to purchase the rental.

oral lease. An unsigned lease that cannot be enforced by either the landlord or tenant for more than one year.

order. A court ruling on a disputed issue.

order to show cause. A court order which requires a party to a legal action to appear in court and present evidence as to why the court should not do something.

P

party. A plaintiff or defendant (petitioner or respondent) in a legal action.

perjury. Lying under oath.

personal injury. An area of law which concentrates on resolving disputes due to an injury this is not necessarily criminal but is the result of an accident.

plaintiff. Person who files the suit against the defendant.

pleadings. This is another term for the formal written documents that are filed with the court.

pro se. Acting as your own attorney.

punitive damages. Money awarded by the court, above and beyond the compensation for money which a plaintiff or defendant has paid out. This is commonly known as "pain and suffering" damages.

R

rental agreement. Legal contract between landlord and tenant to secure rental property, same as lease.

replevin. An old term for returning property to its rightful owner. Some eviction laws still use this term, however it is most commonly referred to as eviction forcible entry and detainer.

rescission period. A period of time when a contract can be cancelled by a party without penalty. This information will be included within the actual contract.

residence. The place were a person lives, considered their home.

restraining order. Court order that restricts a person's action.

retainer. Amount of money given in advance to a law firm by a client to pay towards legal bills.

S

sanctions. Court ordered punishment.

self-help eviction. A landlord taking action to shut off electricity, discontinue heating the rental unit, or other things meant to prevent the tenant from using the property.

service of process (or service). Act of giving the other side in a lawsuit a copy of the complaint and summons.

summons. A written notification that a legal action has been filed in the court system.

T

temporary orders. Are those formal requests to the court for relief that will only last for a period of time or are for an immediate emergency situation.

tenancy. Length of time that a unit is rented.

tenant. Person who rents property.

term. Word used in commercial leases to indicate the length of time a lease is in effect.

testimony. Statements made under oath at a hearing, deposition, or trial.

transcript. A written copy of testimony given.

U

use exclusive. Phrase used in commercial leases to indicate that a select tenant will be the only one selling a certain item or the only business of a particular type in a rental property.

W

warranty of habitability. The guarantee that the rental property will be in such condition that a reasonable person could live in the property. Covers only the basic necessities such as minimal heat, electricity, water, and construction.

Appendix A
Judicial Circuit Courts

On the following pages, you will find a listing of the twenty-two circuit courts in Illinois. Twenty-one circuits are designated by a number, and one circuit (Cook County) by the name of the county. These listings give the circuit identification, the address and main telephone number of the court, and the county or counties which the circuit covers.

STATE OF ILLINOIS—JUDICIAL CIRCUIT COURTS

COURT	ADDRESS	SERVING COUNTIES OF:
Cook County Circuit	50 W. Washington St. Chicago, IL 60602 312-443-4732 www.cookcountycourt.org	Cook
First Judicial Circuit	1001 Walnut Street Murphysboro, IL 62966 618-687-7300 http://www.circuitclerk.co.jackson. il.us/index.html	Alexander, Jackson, Johnson, Massac, Pope, Pulaski, Saline, Union, Williamson
Second Judicial Circuit	Courthouse Mt. Vernon, IL 62864 618-244-8036	Crawford, Edwards, Franklin, Gallatin, Hamilton, Hardin, Jefferson, Lawrence, Wabash, Richland, Wayne, White
Third Judicial Circuit	155 N. Main St. Edwardsville, IL 62025 618-692-7040	Bond, Madison
Fourth Judicial Circuit	Montgomery County Courthouse 120 N. Main, Room 231 Hillsboro, IL 62049 217-532-9501 http://www.effingham.net/4thcircuit/	Christian, Clay, Clinton, Jasper, Effingham, Fayette, Marion, Montgomery, Shelby
Fifth Judicial Circuit	Courthouse Paris, IL 61944 217-465-1315	Clark, Coles, Cumberland, Edgar, Vermilion
Sixth Judicial Circuit	Courthouse Monticello, IL 61856 217-762-5861	Champaign, DeWitt, Douglas,Macon, Moultrie, Piatt
Seventh Judicial Circuit	Sangamon Co. Courthouse Springfield, IL 62701 217-753-6813	Greene, Jersey, Macoupin, Scott, Sangamon

COURT	ADDRESS	SERVING COUNTIES OF:
Eighth Judicial Circuit	Adams Co. Courthouse 521 Vermont Street Quincy, IL 62301 217-223-2055 http://www.co.adams.il.us/courts/	Adams, Brown, Calhoun, Cass, Mason, Menard, Pike, Schuyler
Ninth Judicial Circuit	Courthouse Macomb, IL 61455 309-837-9278	Fulton, Hancock, Henderson, Knox, McDonough, Warren
Tenth Judicial Circuit	Peoria Co. Courthouse 324 Main St., Rm 215 Peoria, IL 61602 309-672-6036	Marshall, Peoria, Putnam, Stark, Tazewell
Eleventh Judicial Circuit	McLean County Law & Justice Center 104 W. Front St. Bloomington, IL 61701 309-888-5282	Ford, Livingston, Logan, McLean, Woodford
Twelfth Judicial Circuit	Courthouse Joliet, IL 60431 815-727-8540	Will
Thirteenth Judicial Circuit	LaSalle Co. Courthouse 119 W. Madison, Rm. 204 Ottawa, IL 61350 815-434-0779 http://www.lasallecounty.com	Bureau, Grundy, LaSalle
Fourteenth Judicial Circuit	Courthouse Rock Island, IL 61201 309-786-4451	Henry, Mercer, Rock Island, Whiteside
Fifteenth Judicial Circuit	Courthouse Mt.Carroll, IL 61053 815-244-0271	Carroll, Jo Daviess, Lee, Ogle, Stephenson

COURT	ADDRESS	SERVING COUNTIES OF:
Sixteenth Judicial Circuit	Kane Co. Judicial Center 37 W 777 Route 38 St.Charles, IL 60175 630-232-3440 http://www.co.kane.il.us/judicial/ index.htm	DeKalb, Kane, Kendall
Seventeenth Judicial Circuit	Courthouse Rockford, IL 61101 815-987-2522 http://www.co.winnebago.il.us/ trialct/main.html	Boone, Winnebago
Eighteenth Judicial Circuit	505 N. County Farm Rd. Wheaton, IL 60187 630-682-7300 http://www.co.dupage.il.us/circuitcourt	DuPage
Nineteenth Judicial Circuit	Lake County Courthouse and Administration Building 18 North County Street Waukegan, IL 60085 847-360-6380 http://www.19thcircuitcourt.state.il.us/	Lake, McHenry
Twentieth Judicial Circuit	Monroe County Courthouse 100 South Main Streeet Waterloo, IL 62298 618-939-8681 http://www.htc.net/~jacobbj/mcc/ index.htm	Monroe, Perry, Randolph, St.Clair, Washington
Twenty-First Judicial Circuit	Kankakee County Circuit Court 450 East Court Street Kankakee, IL 60901 815-937-2915 fax: 815-937-3903 http://www.prairenet.org/fordiroq/ 21st/21st.htm	Iroquois, Kankakee

APPENDIX B
EVICTION FLOWCHARTS

On the next two pages are flowcharts which show each step in the eviction process. The first one is for an *eviction for nonpayment of rent*. The second one is for *evictions based on the tenant's breach of some clause of the lease* other than payment of rent, or for the tenant's violation of some aspect of the state or local laws regarding landlords and tenants.

Eviction Flowchart - Nonpayment of Rent

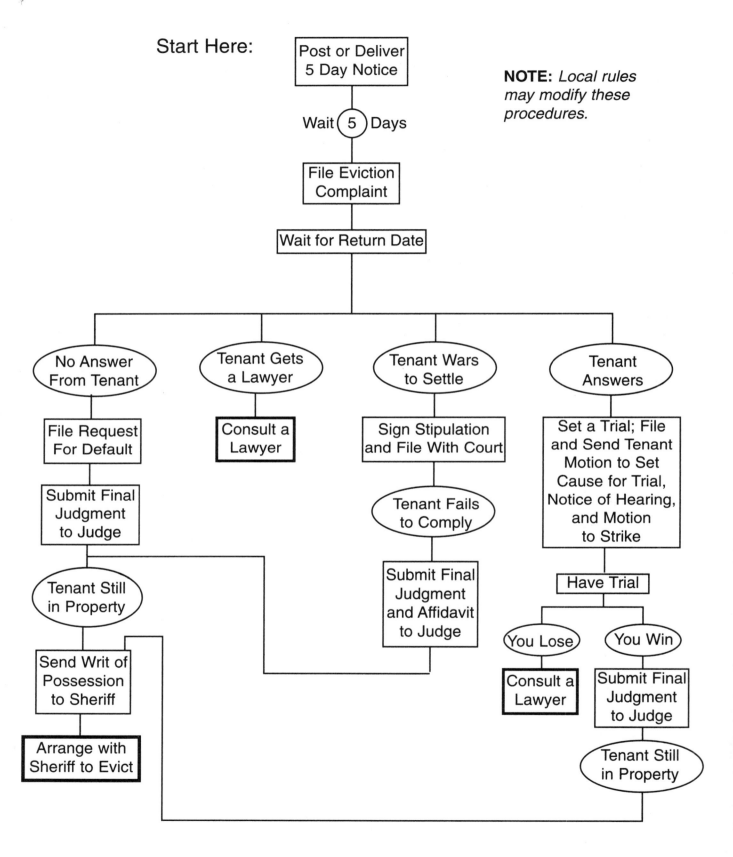

Start Here:

Post or Deliver 5 Day Notice

Wait (5) Days

File Eviction Complaint

Wait for Return Date

NOTE: *Local rules may modify these procedures.*

No Answer From Tenant

File Request For Default

Submit Final Judgment to Judge

Tenant Still in Property

Send Writ of Possession to Sheriff

Arrange with Sheriff to Evict

Tenant Gets a Lawyer

Consult a Lawyer

Tenant Wars to Settle

Sign Stipulation and File With Court

Tenant Fails to Comply

Submit Final Judgment and Affidavit to Judge

Tenant Answers

Set a Trial; File and Send Tenant Motion to Set Cause for Trial, Notice of Hearing, and Motion to Strike

Have Trial

You Lose

Consult a Lawyer

You Win

Submit Final Judgment to Judge

Tenant Still in Property

EVICTION FLOWCHART - BREACH OF LEASE

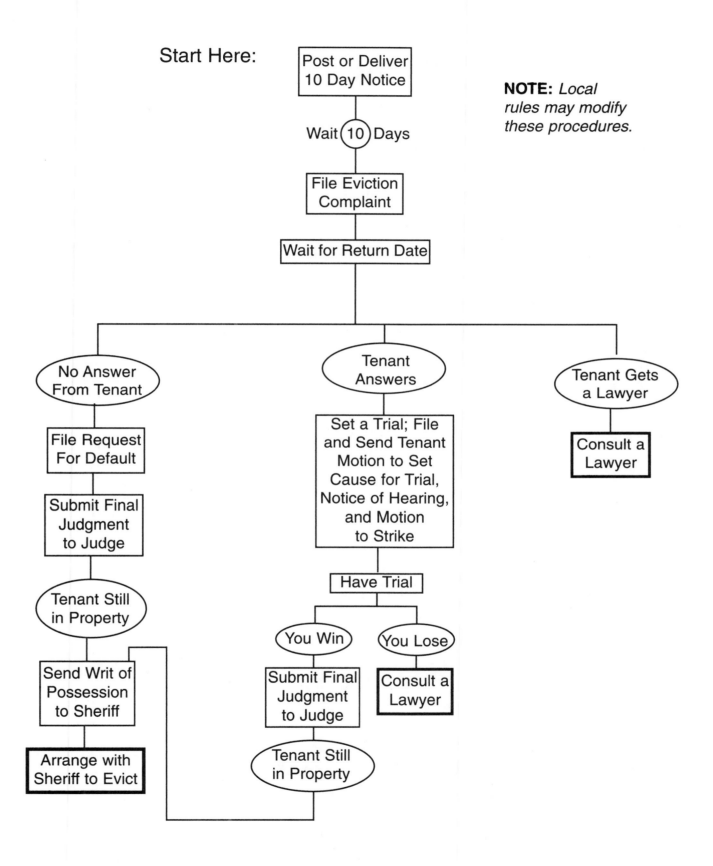

Start Here:

Post or Deliver 10 Day Notice

Wait (10) Days

NOTE: *Local rules may modify these procedures.*

File Eviction Complaint

Wait for Return Date

No Answer From Tenant

Tenant Answers

Tenant Gets a Lawyer

File Request For Default

Set a Trial; File and Send Tenant Motion to Set Cause for Trial, Notice of Hearing, and Motion to Strike

Consult a Lawyer

Submit Final Judgment to Judge

Tenant Still in Property

Have Trial

Send Writ of Possession to Sheriff

You Win

You Lose

Submit Final Judgment to Judge

Consult a Lawyer

Arrange with Sheriff to Evict

Tenant Still in Property

205

APPENDIX C
STATUTES AND ORDINANCES

This appendix contains selected portions of the following laws:

Illinois Compiled Statutes:

Chapter 735, Act 5:   Forcible Entry and Detainer Act

Snow Removal

Chapter 765, Act 705: Landlord and Tenant Act

Chapter 765, Act 710: Security Deposit Return Act

Chapter 765, Act 715: Security Deposit Interest Act

Chapter 765, Act 745: Mobile Home Landlord and Tenant Rights Act

City of Chicago Landlord and Tenant Ordinance

Keep in mind that these laws are subject to change at any time, and are also subject to the interpretation of the courts. Also, counties and municipalities may have laws that cover these same matters.

Illinois Compiled Statutes

Chapter 735

Act 5

ARTICLE IX. FORCIBLE ENTRY
AND DETAINER

PART 1. IN GENERAL

5/9-101.   Forcible entry prohibited

No person shall make an entry into lands or tenements except in cases where entry is allowed by law, and in such cases he or she shall not enter with force, but in a peaceable manner.

5/9-102.   When action may be maintained

(a) The person entitled to the possession of lands or tenements may be restored thereto under any of the following circumstances:

(1) When a forcible entry is made thereon.

(2) When a peaceable entry is made and the possession unlawfully withheld.

(3) When entry is made into vacant or unoccupied lands or tenements without right or title.

(4) When any lessee of the lands or tenements, or any person holding under such lessee, holds possession without right after the termination of the lease or tenancy by its own limitation, condition or terms, or by notice to quit or otherwise.

{other sections dealing with sales of land are omitted}

5/9-104.   Demand—Notice—Return

The demand required by Section 9-102 of this Act may be made by delivering a copy thereof to the tenant, or by leaving such a copy with some person of the age of 13 years or upwards, residing on, or being in charge of, the premises; or in case no one is in the actual possession of the premises, then by posting the same on the premises. When such demand is made by an officer authorized to serve process, his or her return is prima facie evidence of the facts therein stated, and if such demand is made by any person not an officer, the return may be sworn to by the person serving the same, and is then prima facie evidence of the facts therein stated. The demand for possess may be in the following form:
"To...

I hereby demand immediate possession of the following described premises: (describing the same.)"

The demand shall be signed by the person claiming such possession, his or her agent, or attorney.

5/9-114.   Judgment against plaintiff

If the plaintiff voluntarily dismisses the action, or fails to prove the plaintiff's right to the possession, judgment for costs shall be entered in favor of the defendant.

PART 2. RECOVERY OF RENT

5/9-201.   Recovery of rent

The owner of lands, his or her executors or administrators, may sue for and recover rent therefor, or a fair and reasonable satisfaction for the use and occupation thereof, by a civil action in any of the following instances:

1. When rent is due and in arrears on a lease for life or lives.

2. When lands are held and occupied by any person without any special agreement for rent.

3. When possession is obtained under an agreement, written or verbal, for the purchase of the premises, and before a deed is given the right to possession is terminated by forfeiture or non-compliance with the agreement, and possession is wrongfully refused or neglected to be given upon demand, made in writing, by the party entitled thereto. All payments made by the vendee, or his or her representatives or assigns, may be set off against such rent.

4. When land has been sold upon a judgment of court, when the party to such judgment or person holding under him or her, wrongfully refuses or neglects to surrender possession of the same, after demand, in writing, by the person entitled to the possession.

5. When the lands have been sold upon a mortgage or trust deed, and the mortgagor or grantor, or person holding under him or her, wrongfully refuses or neglects to surrender possession of the same, after demand, in writing, by the person entitled to the possession.

5/9-202. Wilfully holding over

If any tenant or any person who is in or comes into possession of any lands, tenements or hereditaments, by, from or under, or by collusion with the tenant, wilfully holds over any land, tenements or hereditaments, after the expiration of his or her term or terms, and after demand made in writing, for the possession thereof, by his or her landlord, or the person to whom the remainder or reversion of such lands, tenements or hereditaments belongs, the person so holding over, shall, for the time the landlord or rightful owner is so kept out of possession, pay to the person so kept out of possession, or his or her legal representatives, at the rate of double the yearly value of the lands, tenements or hereditaments so detained to be recovered by a civil action.

5/9-203. Holding over after notice

If any tenant gives notice of his or her intention to quit the premises which are held by him or her, at a time mentioned in such notice, at which time the tenant would have a right to quit by the lease, and does not accordingly deliver up possession thereof, such tenant shall pay to the landlord or lessor double the rent or sum which would otherwise be due, to be collected in the same manner as the rent otherwise due should have been collected.

5/9-204. Rent in arrears—Re-entry

In all cases between landlord and tenant, where one-half year's rent is in arrears and unpaid, and the landlord or lessor to whom such rent is due has the right by law to re-enter for non-payment thereof, such landlord or lessor may, without any formal demand or re-entry, commence an action of ejectment for the recovery of the demised premises.

In case judgment is entered in favor of the plaintiff in the action of ejectment before the rent in arrearage and costs of the action are paid, then the lease of the lands shall cease and be determined, unless the lessee shall by appeal reverse the judgment, or by petition filed within 6 months after the entry of such judgment, obtain relief from the same. However, any tenant may, at any time before final judgment on the ejectment, pay or tender to the landlord or lessor of the premises the amount of rent in arrears and costs of the action, whereupon the action of ejectment shall be dismissed.

5/9-205. Notice to terminate tenancy from year to year

Except as provided in Section 9-206 of this Act, in all cases o tenancy from year to year, 60 days' notice, in writing, shall be sufficient to terminate the tenancy at the end of the year. The notice may be given at any time within 4 months preceding the last 60 days of the year.

5/ 9-206. Notice to terminate tenancy of farm land

In order to terminate tenancies from year to year of farm lands, occupied on a crop share, livestock share, cash rent or other rental basis, the notice to quit shall be given in writing not less than 4 months prior to the end of the year of letting. Such notice may not be waived in a verbal lease. The notice to quit may be substantially in the following form:

To A.B.: You are hereby notified that I have elected to terminate your lease of the farm premises now occupied by you, being (here describe the premises) and you are hereby further notified to quit and deliver up possession of the same to me at the end of the lease year, the last day of such year being (here insert the last day of the lease year).

5/9-206.1. Life tenancy termination; farmland leases

(a) Tenancies from year to year of farmland occupied on a crop share, livestock share, cash rent, or other rental basis in which the lessor is the life tenant or the representative of the life tenant shall continue until the end of the current lease year in which the life tenant's interest terminates unless otherwise provided in writing by the lessor and the lessee.

(b) Whenever the life tenancy of the lessor terminates not more than 6 months before the end of the tenancy of the lessee but before the beginning of the next crop year, the lessee of the farmlands is entitled to reasonable costs incurred in field preparation for the next crop year, payable by the succeeding life tenant or remainderman.

As used in this Section "farmland" means any property used primarily for the growing and harvesting of crops; the feeding, breeding and management of livestock; dairying, or any other agricultural or horticultural use or combination thereof, including, but not limited to, hay, grain, fruit, truck or vegetable crops, floriculture, mushroom growing, plant or tree nurseries, orchards, forestry, sod farming and greenhouses; the keeping, raising and feeding of livestock or poultry, including poultry, swine, sheep, beef cattle, ponies or horses; dairy farming; fur farming; beekeeping; or fish or wildlife farming.

5/9-207. Notice to terminate tenancy for less than a year

In all cases of tenancy from week to week, where the tenant holds over without special agreement, the landlord may terminate the tenancy by 7 days' notice, in writing, and may maintain an action for forcible entry and detainer or ejectment.

In all cases of tenancy for any term less than one year, other than tenancy from week to week, where the tenant holds over without special agreement, the landlord may terminate the tenancy by 30 days' notice, in writing, and may maintain an action for forcible entry and detainer or ejectment.

5/9-208. Further demand

Where a tenancy is terminated by notice, under either of the 2 preceding sections, no further demand is necessary before bringing an action under the statute in relation to forcible detainer or ejectment.

5/9-209. Demand for rent — Action for possession

A landlord or his or her agent may, any time after rent is due, demand payment thereof and notify the tenant, in writing, that unless payment is made within a time mentioned in such notice, not less than 5 days after service thereof, the lease will be terminated. If the tenant does not within the time mentioned in such notice, pay the rent due, the landlord may consider the lease ended, and sue for the possession under the statute in relation to forcible entry and detainer, or maintain ejectment without further notice or demand. A claim for rent may be joined in the complaint, and a judgment obtained for the amount of rent found due, in any action or proceeding brought, in an action of forcible entry and detainer for the possession of the leased premises, under this section.

Notice made pursuant to this Section shall, as hereinafter stated, not be invalidated by payments or past due rent demanded in the notice, when the payments do not, at the end of the notice period, total the amount demanded in the notice. The landlord may, however, agree in writing to continue the lease in exchange for receiving partial payment. To prevent invalidation, the notice must prominently state:

"Only FULL PAYMENT of the rent demanded in this notice will waive the landlord's right to terminate the lease under this notice, unless the landlord agrees in writing to continue the lease in exchange for receiving partial payment."

Collection by the landlord of past rent due after the filing of a suit for possession or ejectment pursuant to failure of the tenant to pay the rent demanded in the notice shall not invalidate the suit.

5/9-210. Notice to quit

When default is made in any of the terms of a lease, it is not necessary to give more than 10 days' notice to quit, or of the termination of such tenancy, and the same may be terminated on giving such notice to quit at any time after such default in any of the terms of such lease. Such notice may be substantially in the following form;

"To A.B.: You are hereby notified that in consequence of your default in (here insert the character of the default) of the premises now occupied by you, being, etc., (here describe the premises) I have elected to terminate your lease, and you are hereby notified to quit and deliver up possession of the same to me within 10 days of this date (dated, etc.)."

The notice is to be signed by the lessor or his or her agent, and no other notice or demand of possession or termination of such tenancy is necessary.

5/9-211. Service of demand or notice

Any demand may be made or notice served by delivering written or printed, or partly written and printed, copy thereof to the tenant, or by leaving the same with some person of the age of 13 years or upwards, residing on or in possession of the premises; or by sending a copy of the notice to the tenant by certified or registered mail, with a returned receipt from the addressee; and in case no one is in the actual possession of the premises, then by posting the same on the premises.

5/ 9-212. Evidence of service

When such demand is made or notice served by an officer authorized to serve process, the officer's return is prima facie evidence of the facts therein stated, and if such demand is made or notice served by any person not an officer, the return may be sworn to by the person serving the same, and is then prima facie evidence of the facts therein stated.

5/9-213. Expiration of term

When the tenancy is for a certain period, and the term expires by the terms of the lease, the tenant is then bound to surrender possession, and no notice to quit or demand of possession is necessary.

5/9-213.1. Duty of landlord to mitigate damages

After January 1, 1984, a landlord or his or her agent shall take reasonable measures to mitigate the damages recoverable against a defaulting lessee.

5/9-214. Lease defined

The term "lease," as used in Part 2 of Article IX of this Act, includes every letting, whether by verbal or written agreement.

5/9-215. Remedies available to grantee

The grantees of any leased lands, tenements, rents or other hereditaments, or of the reversion thereof, the assignees of the lessor of any lease, and the heirs, legatees and personal representatives of the lessor, grantee or assignee, shall have the same remedies by action or otherwise, for the non-performance of any agreement in the lease, or for the recovery of any rent, or for the doing of any waste or other cause of forfeiture, as their grantor or lessor might have had if such reversion had remained in such lessor or grantor.

5/9-216. Remedies available to lessee

The lessees of any lands, their assigns or personal representatives, shall have the same remedy, by action or otherwise, against the lessor, his or her grantees, assignees or his, her or their representatives, for the breach of any agreement in such lease, as such lessee might have had against his or her immediate lessor. This section shall have no application to the covenants against incumbrances, or relating to the title or possession of the premises demised.

Sec. 9-217. Rent recoverable by representative, from subtenant

When a tenant for life demises any lands and dies on or after the day when any rent becomes due and payable, his or her executor or administrator may recover from the subtenant the whole rent due, but if such tenant for life dies, before the day when any rent is to become due, his or her executor or administrator may recover the proportion of rent which accrued before his or her death, and the remainder man shall recover for the residue.

Chapter 765

Act 705

LANDLORD AND TENANT ACT

705/1. Every covenant, agreement or understanding in or in connection with or collateral to any lease of real property, exempting the lessor from liability for damages for injuries to person or property caused by or resulting from the negligence of the lessor, his or her agents, servants or employees, in the operation or maintenance of the demised premises or the real property containing the demised premises shall be deemed to be void as against public policy and wholly unenforceable.

705/5.   Class X felony by lessee or occupant.

(a) If, after the effective date of this amendatory Act of 1995, any lessee or occupant is charged during his or her lease or contract term with having committed an offense, on the premises constituting a Class X felony under the laws of this State, upon a judicial finding of probable cause at a preliminary hearing or indictment by a grand jury, the lease or contract for letting the premises shall, at the option of the lessor or the lessor's assignee, become void, and the owner or the owner's assignee may notify the lessee or occupant by posting a written notice at the premises requiring the lessee or occupant to vacate the leased premises on or before a date 5 days after the giving of the notice. The notice shall state the basis for its issuance on forms provided by the circuit court clerk of the county in which the real property is located. The owner or owner's assignee may have the same remedy to recover possession of the premises as against a tenant holding over after the expiration of his or her term. The owner or lessor may bring a forcible entry and detainer action.

(b) A person does not forfeit his or her security deposit or any part of the security deposit due solely to an eviction under the provisions of this Section.

(c) If a lessor or the lessor's assignee voids a contract under the provisions of this Section, and a tenant or occupant has not vacated the premises within 5 days after receipt of a written notice to vacate the premises, the lessor or the lessor's assignee may seek relief under Article IX of the Code of Civil Procedure. Notwithstanding Sections 9-112, 9-113, and 9-114 of the Code of Civil Procedure, judgment for costs against the plaintiff seeking possession of the premises under this Section shall not be awarded to the defendant unless the action was brought by the plaintiff in bad faith. An action to possess premises under this Section shall not be deemed to be in bad faith if the plaintiff based his or her cause of action on information provided to him or her by a law enforcement agency or the State's Attorney.

(d) The provisions of this Section are enforceable only if the lessee or occupant and the owner or owner's assignee have executed a lease addendum for drug free housing as promulgated by the United States Department of Housing and Urban Development or a substantially similar document.

Act 710

SECURITY DEPOSIT RETURN ACT

710/1. Withholding security deposit—Statement of Damages—Liability of lessor

A lessor of residential real property, containing 5 or more units, who has received a security deposit from a lessee to secure the payment of rent or to compensate for damage to the leased property may not withhold any part of that deposit as compensation for property damage unless he has, within 30 days of the date that the lessee vacated the premises, furnished to the lessee, delivered in person or by mail directed to his last known address, an itemized statement of the damage allegedly caused to the premises and the estimated or actual cost for repairing or replacing each item on that statement, attaching the paid receipts, or copies thereof, for the repair or replacement. If the lessor utilizes his or her own labor to repair any damage caused by the lessee, the lessor may include the reasonable cost of his or her labor to repair such damage. If estimated cost is given, the lessor shall furnish the lessee with paid receipts, or copies thereof, within 30 days from the date the statement showing estimated cost was furnished to the lessee, as required by this Section. If no such statement and receipts, or copies thereof, are furnished to the lessee as required by this Section, the lessor shall return the security deposit in full within 45 days of the date that the lessee vacated the premises.

Upon a finding by a circuit court that a lessor has refused to supply the itemized statement required by this Section, or has supplied such statement in bad faith, and has failed or refused to return the amount of the security deposit due within the time limits provided, the lessor shall be liable for an amount equal to twice the amount of the security deposit due, together with court costs and reasonable attorney's fees.

710/1.1 Transferee Liability

In the event of a sale, lease, transfer or other direct or indirect disposition of residential real property, other than to the holder of a lien interest in such property, by a lessor who has received a security deposit or prepaid rent from a lessee, the transferee of such property shall be liable to that lessee for any security deposit, including statutory interest, or prepaid rent which the lessee has paid to the transferor. Transferor shall remain jointly and severally liable with the transferee to the lessee for such security deposit or prepaid rent.

Act 715

SECURITY DEPOSIT INTEREST ACT

715/1.   Interest to be paid by lessor on security deposits—Rate

A lessor of residential real property, containing 25 or more units in either a single building or a complex of buildings located on contiguous parcels of real property, who receives a security deposit from a lessee to secure the payment of rent or compensation for damage to property shall pay interest to the lessee computed from the date of the deposit at a rate equal to the interest paid by the largest commercial bank, as measured by total assets, having its main banking premises in this State on minimum deposit passbook savings accounts as of December 31 of the calendar year immediately preceding the inception of the rental agreement on any deposit held by the lessor for more than 6 months.

715/2.   Time for payment—Penalty for refusal to pay

The lessor shall, within 30 days after the end of each 12 month rental period, pay to the lessee any interest by cash or credit to be applied to rent due, except when the lessee is in default under the terms of the lease.

A lessor who willfully fails or refuses to pay the interest required by this Act shall, upon a finding by a circuit court that he has willfully failed or refused to pay, be liable for an amount equal to the amount of the security deposit, together with court costs and reasonable attorney's fees.

715/3.   This Act does not apply to any deposit made with respect to public housing.

Act 720

RETALIATORY EVICTION ACT

720/1.   It is declared to be against the public policy of the State for a landlord to terminate or refuse to renew a lease or tenancy of property used as a residence on the ground that the tenant has complained to any governmental authority of a bona fide viola-tion of any applicable building code, health ordinance, or similar regulation. Any provision in any lease, or any agreement or understanding, purporting to permit the landlord to terminate or refuse to renew a lease or tenancy for such reason is void.

Act 745

MOBILE HOME LANDLORD AND TENANT ACT

745/1.   Applicability

This Act shall regulate and determine legal rights, remedies and obligations of the parties to any lease of a mobile home or mobile home lot in a mobile home park containing five or more mobile homes within this State. Any lease, written or oral, shall be unenforceable insofar as any provision thereof conflicts with any provision of this Act.

745/2.   Jurisdiction

Any person whether or not a citizen or resident of this State, who owns, holds an ownership or beneficial interest in, uses, manages or possesses real estate situated in this State, submits himself or his personal representative to the jurisdiction of the courts of this State as to any action proceeding for the enforcement of an obligation arising under this Act.

745/3.   Definitions

Unless otherwise expressly defined, all terms in this Act shall be construed to have their ordinarily accepted meanings or such meaning as the context therein requires.

(a) "Person" means any legal entity, including but not limited to, an individual, firm, partnership, association, trust, joint stock company, corporation or successor of any of the foregoing.

(b) "Mobile Home" means a structure designed for permanent habitation and so constructed as to permit its transport on wheels, temporarily or permanently attached to its frame, from the place of its construction to the location or subsequent locations at which it is intended to be a permanent habitation and designed to permit the occupancy thereof as a dwelling place of one or more persons, provided that any such structure served by individual utilities and resting on a permanent foundation, with wheels, tongue and hitch permanently removed, shall not be construed as a "mobile home."

(c) "Mobile Home Park" or "Park" means an area of land or lands upon which five or more independent mobile homes are harbored for rent.

(d) "Park Owner" means the owner of a mobile home park and any person authorized to exercise any aspect of the management of the premises, including any person who directly or indirectly receives rents and has no obligation to deliver the whole of such receipts to another person.

(e) "Tenant" means any person who occupies a mobile home rental unit for dwelling purposes or a lot on which he parks a mobile home for an agreed upon consideration.

(f) "Rent" means any money or other consideration given for the right of use, possession and occupancy of property, be it a lot or mobile home.

(g) "Master antenna television service" means any and all services provided by or through the facilities of any closed circuit coaxial cable communication system, or any microwave or similar transmission services other than a community antenna television system as defined in Section 11-42-11 of the Illinois Municipal Code.

745/4. Requisites for Rental or Offer of Mobile Home or Lot for Rental

No person shall rent or offer for rent any mobile home which does not conform to the sanitation, housing and health codes of the State or of the county or municipality in which the mobile home is located.

No person shall rent or offer for rent any lot in a mobile home park which does not conform to subdivision ordinances of the county or municipality in which the mobile home park is located.

745/4a.

No park owner, after the effective date of this amendatory Act of 1987, may require a tenant to remove an outside conventional television antenna, or require that a tenant subscribe to and pay for master antenna television services rather than use an outside conventional television antenna. This Section shall not prohibit an owner from supplying free master antenna television services provided that the price of such services, is not made a part of the rent of the tenant. This Section also shall not prohibit a park owner from requiring a tenant to remove an outside conventional television antenna if such owner makes available master antenna television services at no charge above the rental stated in such tenant's lease.

745/5. Exemptions

No mobile home park operated by the State or the Federal Government, or park land owned by either, and no trailer park operated for the use of recreational campers or travel trailers shall be subject to the provisions of this Act.

745/6. Obligation of Park Owner to Offer Written Lease

No person shall offer a mobile home or lot for rent or sale in a mobile home park without having first exhibited to the prospective tenant or purchaser a copy of the lease applicable to the respective mobile home park.

(a) The park owner shall be required to offer to each present and future tenant a written lease for a term of not less than 12 months, unless the parties agree to a different term subject to existing leases which shall be continued pursuant to their terms.

(b) Tenants in possession on the effective date of this Act shall have 30 days after receipt of the offer for a written lease within which to accept or reject such offer; during which period, the rent may not be increased or any other terms and conditions changed, except as permitted under this Act; providing that if the tenant has not so elected he shall vacate within the 30 day period.

(c)	The park owner shall notify his tenants in writing not later than 30 days after the effective date of this Act, that a written lease shall be available to the tenant and that such lease is being offered in compliance with and will conform to the requirements of this Act.

### 745/7.	Effect of Unsigned Lease

If the tenant shall fail to sign a written lease which has been signed and tendered to him by the owner and shall further provide the owner with a rejection in writing of such offer, the tenant's continuation of possession and payment of rent without reservation shall constitute an acceptance of the lease with the same effect as if it had been signed by the tenant.

### 745/8.	Renewal of Lease

Every lease of a mobile home or lot in a mobile home park shall contain an option which automatically renews the lease; unless: (a) the tenant shall notify the owners 30 days prior to the expiration of the lease that he does not intend to renew the lease; or (b) the park owner shall notify the tenant 30 days prior to the expiration of the lease that the lease will not be renewed and specify in writing the reasons, such as violations of park rules, health and safety codes or irregular or non-payment of rent; or (c) the park owner elects to cease the operation of either all or a portion of the mobile home park. The tenants shall be entitled to at least 12 months notice of such ceasing of operations. If 12 months or more remain on the existing lease at the time of notice, the tenant is entitled to the balance of the term of his lease. If there is less than 12 months remaining in the term of his lease, the tenant is entitled to the balance of his lease plus a written month to month tenancy, at the expiring lease rate to provide him with a full 12 months notice.

All notices required under this Section shall be by certified mail or personal service. Certified mail shall be deemed to be effective upon the date of mailing.

### 745/9.	The Terms of Fees and Rents

The terms for payment of rent shall be clearly set forth and all charges for services, ground or lot rent, unit rent, or any other charges shall be specifically itemized in the lease and in all billings of the tenant by the park owner.

The owner shall not change the rental terms nor increase the cost of fees, except as provided herein.

The park owner shall not charge a transfer or selling fee as a condition of sale of a mobile home that is going to remain within the park unless a service is rendered.

Rents charged to a tenant by a park owner may be increased upon the renewal of a lease. Notification of an increase shall be delivered 60 days prior to expiration of the lease.

### 745/10.	Waiver of Provisions

Any provision of a lease whereby any provisions of this Act are waived is declared void.

### 745/11.	Provisions of Mobile Home Park Leases

Any lease hereafter executed or currently existing between an owner and tenant in a mobile home park in this State shall also contain, or shall be made to contain, the following covenants binding the owner at all times during the term of the lease to:

(a) identify to each tenant prior to his occupancy the lot area for which he will be responsible;

(b) keep all exterior property areas not in the possession of a tenant, but part of the mobile home park property, free from the species of weeds and plant growth which are generally noxious or detrimental to the health of the tenants;

(c) maintain all electrical, plumbing, gas or other utilities provided by him in good working condition with the exception of emergencies after which repairs must be completed within a reasonable period of time;

(d) maintain all subsurface water and sewage lines and connections in good working order;

(e) respect the privacy of the tenants and if only the lot is rented, agree not to enter the mobile home without the permission of the mobile home owner, and if the mobile home is the property of the park owner, to enter only after due notice to the tenant, provided, the park owner or his representative may enter without notice in emergencies;

(f) maintain all roads within the mobile home park in good condition;

(g) include a statement of all services and facilities which are to be provided by the park owner for the tenant, e.g. lawn maintenance, snow removal, garbage or solid waste disposal, recreation building, community hall, swimming pool, golf course, laundromat, etc.;

(h) disclose the full names and addresses of all individuals in whom all or part of the legal or equitable title to the mobile home park is vested, or the name and address of the owners' designated agent;

(i) provide a custodian's office and furnish each tenant with the name, address and telephone number of the custodian and designated office.

745/12. Lease Prohibitions

No lease hereafter executed or currently existing between a park owner and tenant in a mobile home park in this State shall contain any provision:

(a) Permitting the park owner to charge a penalty fee for late payment of rent without allowing a tenant a minimum of 5 days beyond the date the rent is due in which to remit such payment;

(b) Permitting the park owner to charge an amount in excess of one month's rent as a security deposit;

(c) Requiring the tenant to pay any fees not specified in the lease;

(d) Permitting the park owner to transfer, or move, a mobile home to a different lot, including a different lot in the same mobile home park, during the term of the lease.

745/12a.

No lease hereafter executed between a mobile home park owner and a tenant in such a park in this State shall contain any provision requiring the tenant to purchase a mobile home from the park owner, or requiring that if the tenant purchases any mobile home during the lease term that such mobile home must be purchased from the park owner, and no such requirement shall be made as a condition precedent to entering into a lease agreement with any such tenant.

745/13. Tenant's Duties

The tenant shall agree at all times during the tenancy to:

(a) Keep the mobile home unit, if he rents such, or the exterior premises if he rents a lot, in a clean and sanitary condition, free of garbage and rubbish;

(b) Refrain from the storage of any inoperable motor vehicle;

(c) Refrain from washing all vehicles except at an area designated by park management;

(d) Refrain from performing any major repairs of motor vehicles at any time;

(e) Refrain from the storage of any icebox, stove, building material, furniture or similar items on the exterior premises;

(f) Keep the supplied basic facilities, including plumbing fixtures, cooking and refrigeration equipment and electrical fixtures in a leased mobile home unit in a clean and sanitary condition and be responsible for the exercise of reasonable care in their proper use and operation;

(g) Not deliberately or negligently destroy, deface, damage, impair or remove any part of the premises or knowingly permit any person to do so;

(h) Conduct himself and require other persons on the premises with his consent to conduct themselves in a manner that will not effect or disturb his neighbors peaceful enjoyment of the premises;

(i) Abide by all the rules or regulations concerning the use, occupation and maintenance of the premises; and

(j) Abide by any reasonable rules for guest parking which are clearly stated.

745/14. Rules and Regulations of Park

Rules and regulations promulgated and adopted by the park owner are enforceable against a tenant only if:

(a) A copy of all rules and regulations was delivered by the park owner to the tenant prior to his signing the lease;

(b) The purpose of such rules and regulations is to promote the convenience, safety and welfare of the tenants, preserve park property from damage or to fairly distribute park services and facilities to the tenants;

(c) They are reasonably related to the purpose for which adopted;

(d) They apply to all tenants in a fair manner;

(e) They are sufficiently explicit in prohibition, direction or limitation of the tenant's conduct to fairly inform him of what he must or must not do to comply; and

(f) They are not for the purpose of evading the obligation of the park owner.

A rule or regulation adopted during the term of a lease is enforceable against the tenant only if 30 days written notice of its adoption is given the tenant and such rule or regulation is not in violation of the terms and conditions of the lease.

745/14-1.

The Department of Public Health shall produce and distribute a pamphlet setting forth clearly, and in detail, the tenant's and park operator's rights and obligations under this Act. The pamphlet shall be produced within 90 days of the effective date of this amendatory Act of 1992.

Each park owner shall make these pamphlets available to all current tenants within 60 days after receiving the pamphlets. This requirement may be satisfied by distributing or mailing the pamphlets to each tenant. All new tenants shall be offered a pamphlet at or before the time at which they are offered a written lease.

A violation of the provisions of this Section shall not render any lease void or voidable nor shall it constitute:

(1) A defense to any action or proceeding to enforce the lease.

(2) A defense to any action or proceeding for breach of the lease.

745/15. Statutory Grounds for Eviction

A park owner may terminate the lease and evict a tenant for any one or more of the following acts:

(a) Non-payment of rent due;

(b) Failure to comply with the park rules;

(c) Failure to comply with local ordinances and State laws regulating mobile homes.

745/16. Improper Grounds for Eviction

The following conduct by a tenant shall not constitute grounds for eviction or termination of the lease, nor shall a judgment for possession of the premises be entered against a tenant:

(a) As a reprisal for the tenant's effort to secure or enforce any rights under the lease or the laws of the State of Illinois, or its governmental subdivisions of the United States;

(b) As a reprisal for the tenant's good faith complaint to a governmental authority of the park owner's alleged violation of any health or safety law, regulation, code or ordinance, or State law or regulation which has as its objective the regulation of premises used for dwelling purposes;

(c) As a reprisal for the tenant's being an organizer or member of, or involved in any activities relative to a home owners association.

745/17. Notice Required by Law

The following notice shall be printed verbatim in a clear and conspicuous manner in each lease or rental agreement of a mobile home or lot:

"IMPORTANT NOTICE REQUIRED BY LAW:

The rules set forth below govern the terms of your lease of occupancy arrangement with this mobile home park. The law requires all of these rules and regulations to be fair and reasonable, and if not, such rules and regulations cannot be enforced against you.

You may continue to reside in the park as long as you pay your rent and abide by the rules and regulations of the park. You may only be evicted for non-payment of rent, violation of laws, or for violation of the rules and regulations of the park and the terms of the lease.

If this park requires you to deal exclusively with a certain fuel dealer or other merchant for goods or service in connection with the use or occupancy of your mobile home or on your mobile home lot, the price you pay for such goods or services may not be more than the prevailing price in this locality for similar goods and services.

You may not be evicted for reporting any violations of law or health and building codes to boards of health, building commissioners, the department of the Attorney General or any other appropriate government agency."

745/18. Security Deposit; Interest

(a) If the lease requires the tenant to provide any deposit with the park owner for the term of the lease, or any part thereof, said deposit shall be considered a Security Deposit. Security Deposits shall be returned in full to the tenant, provided that the tenant has paid all rent due in full for the term of the lease and has caused no actual damage to the premises.

The park owner shall furnish the tenant, within 15 days after termination or expiration of the lease, an itemized list of the damages incurred upon the premises and the estimated cost for the repair of each item. The tenant's failure to object to the itemized list within 15 days shall constitute an agreement upon the amount of damages specified therein. The park owner's failure to furnish such itemized list of damages shall constitute an agreement that no damages have been incurred upon the premises and the entire security deposit shall become immediately due and owing to the tenant.

The tenant's failure to furnish the park owner a forwarding address shall excuse the park owner from furnishing the list required by this Section.

(b) A park owner of any park regularly containing 25 or more mobile homes shall pay interest to the tenant, on any deposit held by the park owner, computed from the date of the deposit at a rate equal to the interest paid by the largest commercial bank, as measured by total assets, having its main banking premises in this State on minimum deposit passbook savings accounts as of December 31 of the preceding year on any such deposit held by the park owner for more than 6 months.

However, in the event that any portion of the amount deposited is utilized during the period for which it is deposited in order to compensate the owner for non-payment of rent or to make a good faith reimbursement to the owner for damage caused by the tenant, the principal on which the interest accrues may be recomputed to reflect the reduction for the period commencing on the first day of the calendar month following the reduction.

The park owner shall, within 30 days after the end of each 12-month period, pay to the tenant any interest owed under this Section in cash, provided, however, that the amount owed may be applied to rent due if the owner and tenant agree thereto.

A park owner who willfully fails or refuses to pay the interest required by this Act shall, upon a finding by a circuit court that he willfully failed or refused to pay, be liable for an amount equal to the amount of the security deposit, together with court costs and a reasonable attorney's fee.

745/19. Purchase of Goods and Services

(a) No park owner shall restrict a tenant in his choice of a seller of fuel, furnishings, accessories or goods or services connected with a mobile home unless such restriction is necessary to protect the health or safety of the park residents. The park owner may determine by rule or regulation the style or quality of exterior equipment to be purchased by the tenant from a vendor of the tenant's choosing.

Provided that no park owner shall be required to permit service vehicles in the park in such numbers and with such frequency that a danger is created for pedestrian traffic in the park.

(b) No park owner shall require as a condition of tenancy or continued tenancy for a tenant to purchase fuel oil or bottled gas from any particular fuel oil or bottled gas dealer or distributor.

Provided that this Section shall not apply to a park owner who provides a centralized distribution system for fuel oil or bottled gas, or both, for residents therein. No park owner providing a centralized distribution system shall charge residents more than a reasonable retail price.

745/20. Gifts, Donations, Bonus, Gratuity, Etc.

(a) Any park owner who, directly or indirectly, receives, collects or accepts from any person any donation, gratuity, bonus or gift, in addition to lawful charges, upon the representation that compliance with the request or demand will facilitate, influence or procure an advantage in entering into an agreement, either oral or written, for the lease or rental of real property, or contract of sale of a mobile home, or any park owner or his representative, who refuses to enter into such lease or contract of sale unless he receives, directly or indirectly, a donation, gratuity, bonus or gift, or any park owner or his representative who directly or indirectly aids, abets, requests or authorizes any other person to violate any provision of this Section, commits a violation of this Act.

(b) Any person who pays such donation, gratuity, bonus or gift may recover twice its value, together with costs of the action, against any such person in violation of this Section.

745/21. Remedies, Tenants

If the park owner fails to substantially conform to the lease agreement or fails to substantially comply with any code, statute, ordinance or regulation governing the operation of a mobile home park or the maintenance of the premises, the tenant may, on written notice to the park owner, terminate the lease and vacate the premises at any time during the first 30 days of occupancy.

After the expiration of said 30 days the tenant may terminate the lease only if he has remained in possession in reliance upon the park owner's written promise to correct all or any part of the condition which would justify termination by the tenant under this Section.

Any condition which deprives the tenant of substantial benefit and enjoyment which the park owner shall fail to remedy within 30 days after having received notice in writing of such condition shall constitute grounds for the tenant to terminate the lease and vacate the premises.

No such notice shall be required where the condition renders the mobile home uninhabitable or poses an imminent threat to the health, welfare and safety of any occupant.

If such condition was proximately caused by the willful or negligent act or omission of the park owner, the tenant may recover any damages sustained as a result of the condition including, but not limited to, reasonable expenditures necessary to obtain adequate substitute housing while the mobile home is uninhabitable.

The tenant may sue to enforce all Sections of this Act and the court may award damages or grant any injunctive or other relief.

745/22. Remedies, Park Owner

A park owner may, any time rent is overdue, notify the tenant in writing that unless payment is made within the time specified in the notice, not less than 5 days after receipt thereof, the lease will be terminated. If the tenant remains in default, the park owner may institute legal action for recovery of possession, rent due and any damages.

If the tenant breaches any provision of the lease or rules and regulations of the mobile home park, the park owner shall notify the tenant in writing of his breach. Such notice shall specify the violation and advise the tenant that if the violation shall continue for more than 24 hours after receipt of such notice the park owner may terminate the lease.

745/23. Termination of Lease

If a tenant shall remain in possession of the premises after the expiration of his lease without having notified the park owner of his acceptance or rejection of a renewal of the lease and without the park owner's consent, the tenant shall pay to the park owner a sum, not to exceed twice the monthly rental under the previous lease, computed and pro-rated daily for each day he shall remain in possession.

745/24. Sale of Mobile Home

The park owner shall be enjoined and restrained from prohibiting, limiting, restricting, obstructing or in any manner interfering with the freedom of any mobile home owner to:

(a) Sell his mobile home to a purchaser of his choice, provided that the park owner shall be allowed to promulgate any general qualifications or lawful restrictions on park residents which limit or define the admission of entrants to the park. The purchaser, prior to closing, must obtain a written and signed lease;

(b) Employ or secure the services of an independent salesperson in connection with the sale of said mobile home, providing that said salesperson collects and remits all governmental taxes.

The park owner is prohibited from imposing any fee, charge or commission for the sale of a mobile home, except when a mobile home owner requests the park owner or his agent to assist in securing a purchaser for his mobile home. A commission may be accepted for such service subject only to the following conditions:

(1) That the exact amount of commission or fee shall be a percentage of the actual sales price of the mobile home; and

(2) That the maximum percentage figure for the services in the resale of the mobile home by park owner or his agent shall be set forth in writing prior to the sale.

The park owner is prohibited from requiring, upon the sale by a tenant of a mobile home to a qualified purchaser, the removal from the park of such mobile home unless the mobile home is less than 12 feet wide or is significantly deteriorated and in substantial disrepair, in which case the park owner shall bear the burden of demonstrating such fact and must, prior to sale, have given the tenant written notice thereof, and that unless first corrected, removal will be required upon sale.

745/25.　Meetings of Tenants

Meetings by tenants relating to mobile home living shall not be subject to prohibition by the park owner if such meetings are held at reasonable hours and when facilities are available and not otherwise in use.

745/26.

This Act shall be cited as the "Mobile Home Landlord and Tenant Rights Act."

City of Chicago Residential Landlord and Tenant Ordinance

Municipal Code Title 5, Chapter 12

5-12-010　Title, Purpose and Scope

This chapter shall be known and may be cited as the "Residential Landlord and Tenant Ordinance," and shall be liberally construed and applied to promote its purposes and policies.

* * * * *

This chapter applies to, regulates and determines rights, obligations and remedies under every rental agreement entered into or to be performed after the effective date of is chapter for a dwelling unit located within the City of Chicago, regardless of where the unit is made, subject only to the limitations contained in Section 5-12-020. This chapter applies specifically to rental agreements for dwelling units operated under subsidy programs of agencies of the United States and or the State of Illinois, including specifically, programs operated or subsidized by the Chicago Housing Authority an or the Illinois Housing Development Authority to the extent that this chapter is not in direct conflict with statutory or regulatory provision governing such programs.

5-12-020　Exclusions

Rental of the following dwelling units shall not be governed by this chapter, unless the rental agreement thereof is created to avoid the application of this chapter:

(a) Dwelling units in owner-occupied building containing six units or less; provided, however, that the provisions of section 5-12-160 shall apply to every rented dwelling unit in such buildings within the City of Chicago.

(b) Dwelling units in hotels, motels, inns, tourist houses, rooming houses and boarding houses, but only until such time as the dwelling unit has been occupied by a tenant for 32 or more continuous days and tenant pays a monthly rent, exclusive of any period of wrongful occupancy contrary to agreement with an owner. Notwithstanding the above, the prohibition against interruption of tenant occupancy set forth in Section 5-12-160 shall apply to every rented dwelling unit in such buildings within the City of Chicago. No landlord shall bring an action to recover possession of such unit, or avoid renting monthly in order to avoid the application of this chapter. Any willful attempt to avoid application of this chapter by an owner may be punishable by criminal or civil action.

(c) Housing accommodations in any hospital, convent, monastery, extended care facility, asylum or not-for-profit home for the aged, temporary overnight shelter, transitional shelter, or in a dormitory owned and operated by an elementary school, high school or institution of higher learning.

(d) A dwelling unit that is occupied by a purchaser pursuant to a real estate purchase contract prior to e transfer of title to such property to such purchaser, or by a seller of property pursuant to a real estate purchase contract subsequent to the transfer of title from such seller.

(e) A dwelling unit occupied by an employee of a landlord whose right to occupancy is conditional upon employment in or about the premises; and

(f) A dwelling unit in a cooperative occupied by a holder of a proprietary lease.

5-12-030 Definitions

Whenever used in this chapter, the following words and phrases shall have the following meanings:

(a) "Dwelling unit" means a structure or the part of a structure that is used as a home, residence or sleeping place by one or more persons who maintain a household, together with common areas, land and appurtenant buildings thereto, and all housing services, privileges, furnishings and facilities supplied in connection with the use or occupancy thereof, including garage and parking facilities.

(b) "Landlord" means the owner, agent, lessor or sublessor, or the successor In interest of any of them, of a dwelling unit or the building of which it is part.

(c) "Owner" means one or more persons, jointly or severally, in whom is vested all or part of the legal title to property, or all or part of the beneficial ownership and a right to present use and enjoyment of the premises, including a mortgagee in possession.

(d) "Person" means an individual, corporation, government, governmental subdivision or agency, business trust, estate, trust, partnership or association or any other legal or commercial entity.

(e) "Premises" means the dwelling unit and the structure of which it is a part, and facilities and appurtenances therein, and grounds, areas and facilities held out for the use of tenants.

(f) "Rent" means any consideration, including any payment, bonus, benefits or gratuity, demanded or received by a landlord for or in connection with the use or occupancy of a dwelling unit.

(g) "Rental agreement" means all written or oral agreements embodying the terms and conditions concerning the use and occupancy of a dwelling unit.

(h) "Tenant" means a person entitled by written or oral agreement, subtenancy approved by the landlord or by sufferance, to occupy a dwelling unit to the exclusion of others.

5-12-040 Tenant Responsibilities

Every tenant must:

(a) Comply with all obligations imposed specifically upon tenants by provisions of the municipal code applicable to dwelling units;

(b) Keep that part of the premises that he occupies and uses as safe as the condition of the premises permits;

(c) Dispose of all ashes, rubbish, garbage and other waste from his dwelling unit in a clean and safe manner;

(d) Keep all plumbing fixtures in the dwelling unit or used by the tenants as clean as their condition permits;

(e) Use in a reasonable manner all electrical, plumbing, sanitary, heating, ventilating, air conditioning and other facilities and appliances, including elevators, in the premises;

(f) Not deliberately or negligently destroy, deface, damage, impair or remove any part of the premises or knowingly permit any person on the premises with his consent to do so; and

(g) Conduct himself and require other persons on the premises with his consent to conduct themselves in a manner that will not disturb his neighbor's peaceful enjoyment of the premises.

5-12-050 Landlord's Right of Access

A tenant shall not unreasonably withhold consent to the landlord to enter the dwelling unit:

(a) To make necessary or agreed repairs, decorations, alterations or improvements;

(b) To supply necessary or agreed services;

(c) To conduct inspections authorized or required by any government agency;

(d) To exhibit the dwelling unit to prospective or actual purchasers, mortgagees, workmen or contractors;

(e) To exhibit the dwelling unit to prospective tenants 60 days or less prior to the expiration of the existing rental agreement;

(f) For practical necessity where repairs or maintenance elsewhere in the building unexpectedly require such access;

(g) To determine a tenant's compliance with provisions in the rental agreement; and

(h) In case of emergency-

The landlord shall not abuse the right of access or use it to harass the tenant. Except in cases where access is authorized by subsection (f) or (h) of this section, the landlord shall give the tenant notice of the landlord's intent to enter of no loss than two days. Such notice shall be provided directly to each dwelling unit by mail, telephone, written notice to the dwelling unit or by other reasonable means designed in good faith to provide notice to the tenant. If access is required because of repair work or common facilities or other apartments, a general notice may be given by the landlord to all potentially affected tenants that entry ma be required. In cases where access is authorized by subsection (f) or (h) of this section. the landlord may enter the dwelling unit without notice or consent of the tenant. The landlord shall give the tenant notice of such entry within two days after such entry.

The landlord may enter only at reasonable times except in case of an emergency. An entry between 8:00 A.M. and 8:00 P.M. or at any other time expressly requested by the tenant shall be presumed reasonable.

5-12-060   Remedies for Improper Denial of Access

If the tenant refuses to allow lawful access, the landlord may obtain injunctive relief to compel access or terminate the rental agreement pursuant to Section 5-12-130(b) of this chapter. In either case, the landlord may recover damages.

If the landlord makes an unlawful entry or a lawful entry in an unreasonable manner or makes repeated unreasonable demands for entry otherwise lawful, but which have the effect of harassing the tenant, the tenant may obtain injunctive relief to prevent the recurrence of the conduct, or terminate the rental agreement pursuant to the notice provisions of Section 5-12-110(a). In each case, tenant may recover an amount equal to not more than one month's rent or twice the damage sustained him, whichever is greater.

5-12-070   Landlord's Responsibility to Maintain

The landlord shall maintain the premises in compliance with all applicable provisions of the municipal code and shall promptly make any and all repairs necessary to fulfill this obligation.

5-12-080   Security Deposits

(a) A landlord shall hold all security deposits received by him in a federally insured interest-bearing account in a bank, savings and loan association or other financial institution located in the State of Illinois. A security deposit and interest due thereon shall continue to be the property of the tenant making such deposit, shall not be commingled with the assets of the landlord, and shall not be subject to the claims of any creditor of the landlord or of the landlord's successors in interest, including a foreclosing mortgagee or trustee in bankruptcy.

(b) Any landlord or landlord's agent who receives a security deposit from a tenant or prospective tenant shalt give said tenant or prospective tenant at the time of receiving such security deposit a receipt indicating the amount of such security deposit, the name of the person receiving it and, in the case of the agent, the name of the landlord for whom such security deposit is received, the date on which it is received, and a description of the dwelling unit. The receipt shall be signed by the person receiving the security deposit. Failure to comply with this subsection shall entitle the tenant to immediate return of security deposit

(c) A landlord who holds a security deposit or prepaid rent pursuant to this section for more than six months, after the effective date of this chapter shall pay interest to the tenant accruing from the beginning date of the rental term specified in the rental agreement at the rate determined in accordance with Section 5-12-081. The landlord shall, within 30 days after the end of each 12 month rental period, pay to the tenant any interest, by cash or credit to be applied to the rent due.

(d) The landlord shall, within 45 days after the date that the tenant vacates the dwelling unit or within 7 days after the date that the tenant provides notice of termination of the rental agreement pursuant to Section 5-12-110(g), return to the tenant the security deposit or any balance thereof and the required interest thereon; provided, however, that the landlord may deduct from such security deposit or interest due thereon for the following:

(1) Any unpaid rent which has not been validly withheld or deducted pursuant to state or federal law or local ordinance; and

(2) A reasonable amount necessary to repair any damage caused to the premises by the tenant or any person under the tenant's control or on premises with the tenant's consent,

reasonable wear and tear excluded. In case of such damage, the landlord shall deliver or mail to the last known address of the tenant within 30 days an itemized statement of the damages allegedly caused to the premises and the estimated or actual cost for repairing or replacing each item on that statement, or actual copies of the paid receipts for the repair or replacement. If estimated cost is given, the landlord shall furnish the tenant with copies of paid receipts or a certification of actual costs of repairs of damage if the work was performed by the landlord's employees within 30 days from the ate the statement showing estimated cost was furnished to the tenant.

(e) In the event of a sale, lease, transfer or other direct or indirect disposition of residential real property, other than to the holder of a lien interest in such property, by a landlord who has received a security deposit or pre aid rent row a tenant, the successor landlord of such property shall be liable to that tenant for any security deposit, including statutory interest, or prepaid rent which the tenant as paid to the transferor.

The successor landlord shall, within 10 days from the date of such transfer, notify the tenant who made such security deposit by delivering or mailing to the tenant's last known address that such security deposit was transferred to the successor landlord and that the successor landlord is holding said security deposit. Such notice shall also contain the successor landlord's name, business address, and business telephone number of the successor landlord's agent, if any. The notice shall be in writing.

The transferor shall remain jointly and severally liable with the successor landlord to the tenant or such security deposit or prepaid rent, unless and until such transferor transfers said security deposit or prepaid rent to the successor landlord and provides notice, in writing, to the tenant of such transfer of said security deposit or prepaid rent, specifying the name, business address and business telephone number of the successor landlord or his agent within 10 days of transfer.

(f) If the landlord or landlord's agent fails to comply with any provision of Section 5-12-080 (a)—(e), the tenant shall be awarded damages in an amount equal to two times the security deposit plus interest at a rate determined in accordance with Section 5-12-081 (Amended February 7, 1997). This subsection does not preclude the tenant from recovering other damages to which he may be entitled under this chapter.

5-12-081   Interest Rate on Security Deposits

During June of 1997 and thereafter during December of each year, the city comptroller shall review the status of banks within the city and interest rates on passbook savings accounts, insured money market accounts and six-month certificates of deposit at commercial banks located within the city. On the first business day of July of 1997, and thereafter on the first business day of each year, the city comptroller shall announce the rates of interest as of the last business day of the prior month, on passbook savings accounts, insured money market accounts and six month certificates of deposit at the commercial bank having its main branch located in the city and having the largest total asset value. The rates for money market account shall be based on the minimum deposits for such investments. The rates for certificates of deposit shall be based on a deposit of $1000. The comptroller shall calculate and announce the average of all three rates. The average of these rates so announced by the city comptroller shall be the rate of interest on security deposits under rental agreements governed by this chapter and made or renewed after the most recent announcement.

5-12-082   Interest Rate Notification

The city comptroller, after computing the rate of interest on security deposit governed by this chapter, shall cause the new rate of security deposit interest to be published for five consecutive business days in two or more newspapers of general circulation in the city. The mayor shall direct the appropriate city department to prepare and publish for free public distribution at government offices, libraries, schools and community organizations, a pamphlet or brochure describing the respective rights, obligations and interest rate as well as the interest rate of each of the prior two years. The commissioner shall also distribute the new rate of security deposit interest, as well as the interest rate for each of the prior two years, through public service announcements to all radio and television outlets broadcasting in the city.

5-12-090 Identification of Owners and Agents

A landlord or any person authorized to enter into an oral or written rental agreement on the landlord's behalf shall disclose to the tenant in writing or before the commencement of the tenancy the name, address, and telephone number of:

(a) The owner or person authorized to manage the premises; and

(b) A person authorized to act for and on behalf of the owner for the purpose of service of process and for the purpose of receiving and receipting for notices and demands. A person who enters into a rental agreement and fails to comply with the requirements of this section becomes an agent of the landlord or the purpose of (i) service of process and receiving and receipting for notices and demands and (ii) performing the obligations of the landlord under this chapter under the rental agreement.

The information required to be furnished by this section shall be kept current and this section extends to and is enforceable against any successor landlord, owner, or manager.

If the landlord fails to comply with this section, the tenant may terminate the rental agreement pursuant to the notice provisions of Section 5-12-110(a). If landlord fails to comply with the requirements of this section after receipt of written notice pursuant to Section 5-12-110(a), the tenant shall recover one month's rent or actual damages whichever is greater.

5-12-100 Notice of Conditions Affecting Habitability

Before a tenant initially enters into or renews a rental agreement for a dwelling unit, the landlord or any person authorized to enter into a rental agreement on his behalf shall disclose to the tenant in writing:

(a) Any code violations which have been cited by the City of Chicago during the previous 12 months for the dwelling unit and common areas and provide notice of the pendency of any code enforcement litigation or compliance board proceeding pursuant to Chapter 13-8-070 of the municipal code affecting the dwelling unit or common area. The notice shall provide the case number of the litigation landlord the identification number of the compliance board preceding and a listing of any code violations cited.

(b) Any notice of intent by the City of Chicago or any utility provider to terminate water, gas, electrical or other utility service to the welling unit or common areas. The disclosure shall state the type of service to be terminated, the intended date of termination, an whether the termination will affect the dwelling unit, the common area or both. A landlord shall be under a continuing obligation to provide disclosure of the information described in this subsection (b) throughout a tenancy. If a landlord violates this section, the tenant or prospective tenant shall be entitled to remedies described in Section 5-1-090.

5-12-110 Tenants Remedies

In addition to any remedies provided under federal law, a tenant shall have the remedies specified in is section under the circumstances herein set forth.

For purposes of this section, material noncompliance with Section 5-12-070 shall include, but is not limited to, any of the following circumstances:

- Failure to maintain the structural integrity of the building or structure or parts thereof;
- Failure to maintain floors in compliance with the safe load-bearing requirements of the municipal code;
- Failure to comply with applicable requirements of the municipal code for the number, width, construction, location or accessibility of exits;
- Failure to maintain exit, stairway, fire escape or directional signs where required by the municipal code;
- Failure to provide smoke detectors, sprinkler systems, standpipe systems, fire alarm systems, automatic fire detectors or fire extinguishers where required by the municipal code;
- Failure to maintain elevators in compliance with applicable provisions of the municipal code;
- Failure to provide and maintain in good working order a flush water closet, lavatory basin, bathtub or shower, or kitchen sink;
- Failure to maintain heating facilities or gas-fired appliances in compliance with the requirements of the municipal code;

- Failure to provide heat or hot water in such amounts and at such levels and times as required by the municipal code;

- Failure to provide hot and cold running water as required by the municipal code;

- Failure to provide adequate hall or stairway lighting as required by the municipal code;

- Failure to maintain the foundation, exterior walls or exterior roof in sound condition and repair. substantially watertight and protected against rodents;

- Failure to maintain floors, interior walls or - ceilings in sound condition and good repair;

- Failure to maintain windows, exterior doors or basement hatchways in sound condition and repair and substantially tight and to provide locks or security devices as required by the municipal code, including dead latch locks, deadbolt locks, sash or ventilation locks, and front door windows or peep holes;

- Failure to supply screens where required by the municipal code;

- Failure to maintain stairways or porches in safe condition and sound repair;

- Failure to maintain the basement or cellar in a safe and sanitary condition;

- Failure to maintain facilities, equipment or chimneys in safe and sound working conditions;

- Failure to prevent the accumulation of stagnant water;

- Failure to exterminate insects. rodents or other pests;

- Failure to supply or maintain facilities for refuse disposal;

- Failure to prevent the accumulation of garbage, trash, refuse or debris as required by the municipal code;

- Failure to provide adequate light or ventilation as required by the municipal e;

- Failure to maintain plumbing facilities, piping. fixtures, appurtenances and appliances in go operating condition and repair;

- Failure to provide or maintain electrical 5 stems, circuits, receptacles and devices as required by the municipal code;

- Failure to maintain and repair any equip-

ment which the landlord supplies or is required to supply; or

- Failure to maintain the dwelling unit and common areas in a fit and habitable condition.

(a) **Noncompliance by Landlord.** If there is material noncompliance by the landlord with a rental agreement or with Section 5-12-070 either of which renders the premises not reasonably fit and habitable, the tenant under the rental agreement may deliver a written notice to the landlord specifying the acts landlord omissions constituting the material noncompliance and specifying that the rental agreement will terminate on a date not less an 14 days after receipt of the notice by the landlord, unless the material noncompliance is remedied by the landlord within the time period specified in the notice. If the material noncompliance is not remedied within the time period so specified in the notice, the rental agreement shall terminate, and the tenant shall deliver possession of the dwelling unit to the landlord within 30 days after the expiration of the time period specified in the notice. If possession shall not be so delivered, then the tenant's notice shall be deemed withdrawn and the lease shall remain in full force and effect. If the rental agreement is terminated, the landlord shall return all pre aid rent. security and interest recoverable by the tenant under section 5-12-080.

(b) **Failure to Deliver Possession.** If the landlord fails to deliver possession of the dwelling unit to the tenant in compliance with the residential rental agreement or Section 5-12-070, rent for the dwelling unit shall abate until possession is delivered, and the tenant may;

(1) Upon written notice to the landlord, terminate the rental agreement and upon termination the landlord shall return all prepaid rent and security; or

(2) Demand performance of the rental agreement by the landlord and, if the tenant elects, maintain an action for possession of the dwelling unit against the landlord or any person wrongfully in possession and recover the damages substantiated by him. If a person's failure to deliver possession is wilful, an aggrieved person may recover from the

person withholding possession an amount not more than two months' rent or twice the actual damages sustained by him, whichever is greater.

(c) **Minor Defects.** If there is material noncompliance by the landlord with the rental agreement or with Section 5-2-070, and the reasonable cost of compliance does not exceed the greater of $500.00 or one-half of the monthly rent, the tenant ma recover damages for the material noncompliance or ma notify the landlord in writing of his intention to correct the condition at the landlord's expense; provided, however, that this subsection shall not be applicable if the reasonable cost of compliance exceeds one month's rent. If the landlord fails to correct the defect within 14 days after being notified by the tenant in writing or promptly as conditions require in case of emergency, the tenant may have the work done in a workmanlike manner and in compliance with existing law and building regulations and, after submitting to the landlord a paid bill from an appropriate tradesman or supplier, deduct from his or her rent the amount thereof, not to exceed the limits specified by this subsection and not to exceed the reasonable price then customarily charged for such work. A tenant shall not repair at the landlord's expense if the condition was caused by the deliberate or negligent act or omission of the tenant, a member of the tenant's family, or other person on the premises with the tenant's consent.

Before correcting a condition affecting facilities shared by more than one dwelling unit, the tenant shall notify all other affected tenants and shall-cause the work to be done so as to create the least practical inconvenience to the other tenants. Nothing herein shall be deemed to grant any tenant any right to repair any common element or dwelling unit in a building subject to a condominium regime other than in accordance with the declaration and bylaws of such condominium building; provided, that the declaration and bylaws have not been created to avoid the application of this chapter.

For purposes of mechanics' lien laws, repairs performed or materials furnished pursuant to this subsection shall not be construed as having been performed or furnished pursuant to authority of or with permission of the landlord.

(d) **Failure to Maintain.** If there is material noncompliance by the landlord with the rental agreement or with Section 5-12-070, the tenant may notify the landlord in writing of the tenant's intention to withhold from the monthly rent an amount which reasonably reflects the reduced value of the premises due to the material noncompliance. If the landlord fails to correct the condition within 14 days after being notified by the tenant in writing, the tenant may, during the time such failure continues, deduct from the rent the stated amount. A tenant shall not withhold rent under this subsection if the condition was caused by the deliberate or negligent act or omission of the tenant, a member of the tenant's family, or other person on the premises with the tenant's consent.

(e) **Damages and Injunctive Relief.** If there is material noncompliance by the landlord with the rental agreement or with Section 5-12-070, the tenant may obtain injunctive relief, and/or recover damages by claim or defense. This subsection does not preclude the tenant from obtaining other relief to which he may be entitled under this chapter.

(f) **Failure to Provide Essential Services.** If there is material noncompliance by the landlord with the rental agreement or with Section 5-12-070, either of which constitutes an immediate danger to the health and safety of the tenant or if, contrary to the rental agreement or Section 5-12-070, the landlord fails to supply heat, running water, hot water, electricity, gas or plumbing, the tenant may give written notice to the landlord specifying the material noncompliance or failure. If the landlord has, pursuant to this ordinance or in the rental agreement, informed the tenant of an address at which notices to the landlord are to be received, the tenant shall mail or deliver the written notice required in this section to such address. If the landlord has not informed the tenant of an address at which notices to the landlord are to be received, the written notice required in this section shall be delivered by mail to the last known address of the landlord or by other reasonable means designed in good faith to provide written notice to the landlord. After such notice, the tenant may during the period of the landlord's non-compliance or failure:

(1) Procure reasonable amounts of heat, running water, hot water, electricity, gas or plumbing service, as the case may be and upon presentation to the landlord of paid receipts deduct their cost from the rent; or

(2) Recover damages based on the reduction in the fair rental value of the dwelling unit; or

(3) Procure substitute housing, in which case the tenant is excused from paying rent for the period of the landlord's noncompliance. The tenant may recover the cost of the reasonable value of the substitute housing up to an amount equal to the monthly rent for each month or portion thereof of noncompliance as prorated.

In addition to the remedies set forth in Section 5-12-110 (f)(1)-(3), the tenant may:

(4) Withhold from the monthly rent an amount that reasonably reflects the reduced value of the premises due to the material noncompliance or failure if the landlord fails to correct the condition within 24 hours after being notified by the tenant; provided, however, that no rent shall be withheld if the failure is due to the inability of the utility provider to provide service; or

(5) Terminate the rental agreement by written notice to the landlord if the material non-compliance or failure persists for more than 72 hours after the tenant has notified the landlord of the material noncompliance or failure; provided, however, that no termination shall be allowed if the failure is due to the inability of the utility provider to provide service. If the rental agreement is terminated, the landlord shall return all prepaid rent, security deposits and interest thereon in accordance with Section 5-12-080 and tenant shall deliver possession of the dwelling unit to the landlord within 30 days after the expiration of the 72 hour time period specified in the notice. If possession shall not be so delivered, then the tenant's notice shall be deemed withdrawn and the lease shall remain in full force and effect.

If the tenant proceeds under this subsection (f),

he may not proceed under subsection (c) or (d). The tenant may not exercise his rights under this subsection if the condition was caused by the deliberate or negligent act or omission of the tenant, a member of his family, or other person on the premises with his consent. Before correcting a condition, the repair of which will affect more than his own d-welling unit, the tenant shall notify all other tenants affected and shall cause the work to be done so as to result in the least practical inconvenience to other tenants.

(g) **Fire or Casualty Damage.** If the dwelling unit or common area are damaged or destroyed by fire or casualty to an extent that the dwelling unit is in material noncompliance with the rental agreement or with section 5-12-070, the tenant may:

(1) Immediately vacate the premises and notify the landlord in writing within 14 days thereafter of the tenant's intention to terminate the rental agreement, in which case the rental agreement terminates as of the date of the fire or casualty; or

(2) If continued occupancy is lawful, vacate any part of the dwelling unit rendered unusable by the fire or casualty, in which case the tenant's liability for rent is reduced in proportion to the reduction in the fair rental value of the dwelling unit; or

(3) If the tenant desires to continue the tenancy, and if the landlord has promised or begun work to repair the damage or destruction but fails to carry out the work to restore the dwelling unit or common area diligently and within a reasonable time, notify the landlord in writing within 14 days after the tenant becomes aware that the work is not being carried out diligently or within a reasonable time of the tenant's intention to terminate the rental agreement, in which case the rental agreement terminates as of the date of the fire or casualty.

If the rental agreement is terminated under this subsection (g) the landlord shall return all security and all prepaid rent in accordance with Section 5-12-080(d). Accounting for rent in the event of termination or apportionment shall be made as of the date of the fire or casualty. A tenant may not exercise remedies in this subsection if the fire or casualty damage was caused by the deliberate or negligent act or omission of the tenant, a member of his family or a person on the premises with his consent.

5-12-120   Subleases

If the tenant terminates the rental agreement prior to its expiration date, except for cause authorized by this chapter, the landlord shall make a good faith effort to re-rent the tenant's dwelling unit at a fair rental, which shall be the rent charged for comparable dwelling units in the premises or in the same neighborhood. The landlord shall accept a reasonable sublease proposed by the tenant without an assessment of additional fees or charges.

If the landlord succeeds in re-renting the dwelling unit at a fair rental, the tenant shall be liable for the amount by which the rent due from the date of premature termination to the termination of the initial rental agreement exceeds the fair rental subsequently received by the landlord from the date of premature termination to the termination of the initial rental agreement.

If the landlord makes a good faith effort to re-rent the dwelling unit at a fair rental and is unsuccessful, the tenant shall be liable for the rent due for the period of the rental agreement. The tenant shall also be liable for the reasonable advertising costs incurred by the landlord in seeking to re-rent the dwelling unit.

5-12-130   Landlord Remedies

Every landlord shall have the remedies specified in this section for the following circumstances:

(a) **Failure to Pay Rent.** If all or any portion of rent is unpaid when due and the tenant fails to pay the unpaid rent within five days after written notice by the landlord of his intention to terminate the rental agreement if rent is not so paid, the landlord may terminate the rental agreement. Nothing in this subsection shall affect a landlord's obligation to provide notice of termination of tenancy in subsidized housing as required under federal law or regulations. A landlord may also maintain an action for rent and/or damages without terminating the rental agreement.

(b) **Noncompliance by Tenant.** If there is material noncompliance by a tenant with a rental agreement or with Section 5-12-040, the landlord of such tenant's dwelling unit may deliver written notice to the tenant specifying the acts and/or omissions constituting the breach and that the rental agreement will terminate upon a date not less than 10 days after receipt of the notice, unless the breach is remedied by the tenant within that period of time. If the breach is not remedied within the 10 day period, the residential rental agreement shall terminate as provided in the notice. The landlord may recover damages and obtain injunctive relief for any material noncompliance by the tenant with the rental agreement or with Section 5-12-040. If the tenant's noncompliance is wilful, the landlord may also recover reasonable attorney's fees.

(c) **Failure to Maintain.** If there is material noncompliance by the tenant with Section 5-12-040 (other than subsection (g) thereof), and the tenant fails to comply as promptly as conditions permit in case of emergency or in cases other than emergencies within 14 days of receipt of written notice by the landlord specifying the breach and requesting that the tenant remedy it within that period of time, the landlord may enter the dwelling unit and have the necessary work done in the manner required by law. The landlord shall be entitled to reimbursement from the tenant of the costs of repairs under this section.

(d) **Disturbance of Others.** If the tenant violates Section 5-12-040(g) within 60 days all receipt of a written notice as provided in subsection (b), the landlord may obtain injunctive relief against the conduct constituting the violation, or may terminate the rental agreement on 10 days' written notice to the tenant.

(e) **Abandonment.** Abandonment of the dwelling unit shall be deemed to have occurred when:

(1) Actual notice has been provided to the landlord by the tenant indicating the tenant's intention not to return to the dwelling unit; or

(2) All persons entitled under a rental agreement to occupy the dwelling unit have been absent from the unit for a period of 21 days or for one rental period when the rental agreement is for less than a month, and such persons have removed their personal prop-

erty from the premises, and rent for that period is unpaid; or

(3) All persons entitled under a rental agreement to occupy the dwelling unit have been absent from the unit for a period of 32 days, and rent for that period is unpaid.

Notwithstanding the above, abandonment of the dwelling unit shall not be deemed to have occurred if any person entitled to occupancy has provided the landlord a written notice indicating that he still intends to occupy the unit and makes full payment of all amounts due to the landlord.

If the tenant abandons the dwelling unit, the landlord shall make a good faith effort to re-rent it at a fair rental, which shall be the rent charged for comparable dwelling units in the premises or in the same neighborhood. If the landlord succeeds in re-renting the dwelling unit at a: air rental, the tenant shall be liable for the amount by which the rent due from the date of abandonment to the termination of the initial rental agreement exceeds the fair rental subsequently received by the landlord from the date of abandonment to the termination of the initial rental agreement. If the landlord makes a good faith effort to re-rent the dwelling unit at a fair rental and is unsuccessful, the tenant shall be liable for the rent due for the period of the rental agreement. The tenant shall also be liable for the reasonable advertising expenses and reasonable redecoration costs incurred by the landlord pursuant to this subsection.

(f) **Disposition of Abandoned Property.** If the tenant abandons the dwelling unit as described in subsection (e) hereof, or fails to remove his personal property from the premises after termination of a rental agreement, the landlord shall leave the property in the dwelling unit or remove and store all abandoned property from the dwelling unit and may dispose of the property after seven days. Notwithstanding the foregoing, if the landlord reasonably believes such abandoned property to be valueless or of such little value that the cost of storage would exceed the amount that would be realized from sale, or if such property is subject to spoilage, the landlord may immediately dispose of such property.

(g) **Waiver of Landlord's Right to Terminate.** If the

landlord accepts the rent due knowing that them is a default in payment of rent by the tenant he thereby waives his right to terminate the rental agreement for that breach.

(h) **Remedy After Termination.** If the rental agreement is terminated, the landlord shall have a claim for possession and/or for rent.

(i) **Notice of Renewal of Rental Agreement.** No tenant shall be required to renew a rental agreement more than ninety (90) days prior to the termination date of the rental agreement. If the landlord violates this subsection, the tenant shall recover one month's rent or actual damages, whichever is greater.

(j) **Notice of Refusal to Renew.** Rental Agreement. Provided that the landlord has not exercised, or is not in the process of exercising, any of on 5-12-130 (a)—(h) hereof, the landlord shall notify the tenant in writing at least thirty (30) days prior to the stated termination date of the rental agreement of the landlord's intent either to terminate a month to month tenancy or not to renew an existing rental agreement. If the landlord fails to give the required written notice, the tenant may remain in the dwelling unit for up to sixty (60) days after the date on which such required written notice is given to the tenant, regardless of the termination date specified in the existing rental agreement. During such occupancy, the terms and conditions of the tenancy (including, without limitation, the rental rate) shall be the same as the terms and conditions during the month of tenancy immediately preceding the notice; provided, however, that if rent was waived or abated in the preceding month or months as part of the original rental agreement, the rental amount during such sixty (60) day period shall be at the rate established on the last date that a full rent payment was made.

5-12-140   Rental Agreement

Except as otherwise specifically provided by this chapter, no rental agreement may provide that the landlord or tenant:

(a) Agrees to waive or forego rights, remedies or obligations provided under this chapter;

(b) Authorizes any person to confess judgment on a claim arising out of the rental agreement;

(c) Agrees to the limitation of any liability of the

landlord or tenant arising under law;

(d) Agrees to waive any written termination of tenancy notice or manner of service thereof provided under state law or this chapter;

(e) Agrees to waive the right of any party to a trial by jury;

(f) Agrees that in the event of a lawsuit arising out of the tenancy the tenant will pay the landlord's attorney's fees except as provided for by court rules, statute, or ordinance;

(g) Agrees that either party may cancel or terminate a rental agreement at a different time or within a shorter time period than the other party, unless such provision is disclosed in a separate written notice;

(h) Agrees that a tenant shall pay a charge, fee or penalty in excess of $10.00 per month for the first $500.00 in monthly rent plus 5% per month for any amount in excess of $500.00 in monthly rent for the late payment of rent;

(i) Agrees that, if a tenant pays rent before a specified date or within a specified time period in the month, the tenant shall receive a discount or reduction in the rental amount in excess of $10-00 per month for the first $500.00 in monthly rent plus 5% per month for any amount in excess of $500.00 in monthly rent.

A provision prohibited by this section included in a rental agreement is unenforceable.

The tenant may recover actual damages sustained by the tenant because of the enforcement of a prohibited provision. If the landlord attempts to enforce a provision in a rental agreement prohibited by this section the tenant may recover two months' rent.

5-12-150 Prohibition On Retaliatory Conduct By Landlord

It is declared to be against public policy of the City of Chicago for a landlord to take retaliatory action against a tenant, except for violation of a rental agreement or violation of a law or ordinance. A landlord may not knowingly terminate a tenancy, increase rent, decrease services, bring or threaten to bring a lawsuit against a tenant for possession or refuse to renew a lease or tenancy because the tenant has in good faith:

(a) Complained of code violations applicable to the premises to a competent governmental agency, elected representative or public official charged

with responsibility for enforcement of a building, housing, health or similar code; or

(b) Complained of a building, housing, health or similar code violation or an illegal landlord practice to a community organization or the news media; or

(c) Sought the assistance of a community organization or the news media to remedy a code violation or illegal landlord practice; or

d) Requested the landlord to make repairs to the premises as required by a building code, health ordinance, other regulation, or the residential rental agreement; or

(e) Becomes a member of a tenant's union or similar organization; or

(f) Testified in any court or administrative proceeding concerning the condition of the premises; or

(g) Exercised any right or remedy provided by law. If the landlord acts in violation of this section, the tenant has a defense in any retaliatory action against him for possession and is entitled to the following remedies: he shall recover possession or terminate the rental agreement and, in either case, recover an amount equal to and not more than two months' rent or twice the damages sustained by him, whichever is greater, and reasonable attorney's fees. If the rental agreement is terminated, the landlord shall return all security and interest recoverable under Section 5-12-080 and all prepaid rent. In an action by or against the tenant, if there is evidence of tenant conduct protected herein within one year prior to the alleged act of retaliation, that evidence shall create a rebuttable presumption that the landlord's conduct was retaliatory. The presumption shall not arise if the protected tenant activity was initiated for the alleged act of retaliation.

5-12-160 Prohibition On Interruption Of Tenant Occupancy By Landlord

It is unlawful for any landlord or any person acting at his direction knowingly to oust or dispossess or threaten or attempt to oust or dispossess any tenant from a dwelling unit without authority of law, by plugging, changing, adding or removing any lock or latching device; or by blocking any entrance into said unit; or by removing any door or window from said unit; or by interfering with the services to said unit; including but not limited to electricity, gas, hot or cold water, plumbing, heat or telephone service; or by removing a tenant's personal property from said unit; or by the removal or incapacitating of appliances or fixtures, except for the purpose of making necessary repairs; or by the use or threat of force, violence or injury to a tenant's person or property; or by any act rendering a dwelling unit or any part thereof or any personal property located therein inaccessible or uninhabitable. The foregoing shall not apply where:

(a) A landlord acts in compliance with the laws of Illinois pertaining to forcible entry and detainer and engages the sheriff of Cook County to forcibly evict a tenant or his personal property; or

(b) A landlord acts in compliance with the laws of Illinois pertaining to distress for rent; or

(c) A landlord interferes temporarily with possession only as necessary to make needed repairs or inspection and only as provided by law; or

(d) The tenant has abandoned the dwelling unit, as defined in Section 5-12-130(e). Whenever a complaint of violation of this provision is received by the Chicago Police Department, the department shall investigate and determine whether a violation has occurred. Any person found guilty of violating this section shall be fined not less than $200.00 nor more than $500.00, and each day that such violation shall occur or continue shall constitute a separate and distinct offense for which a fine as herein provided shall be imposed. If a tenant in a civil legal proceeding against his landlord establishes that a violation of this section has occurred he shall be entitled to recover possession of his dwelling unit or personal property and shall recover an amount equal to not more than two months' rent or twice the actual damages sustained by him, whichever is greater. A tenant may pursue any civil remedy for violation of this section regardless of whether a fine has been entered against the landlord pursuant to this section.

5-12-170   Summary Of Ordinance Attached To Rental Agreement

The commissioner of the department of housing shall prepare a summary of this chapter, describing the respective rights, obligations and remedies of landlords and tenants hereunder, and shall make such summary available for public inspection and copying. The commission shall also, after the city comptroller

has announced the rate of interest on security deposits on the first business day of the year, prepare a separate summary describing the rights, obligations, and remedies of landlords and tenants with respect to security deposits, including the interest rate as well as the rate for each of the prior two years through public service announcements to all radio and television outlets broadcasting in the city. A copy of such summary shall be attached to each written renal agreement when any such agreement is initially offered to any tenant or prospective tenant by or on behalf of a landlord and whether such agreement is for a new rental or a renewal thereof. Where there is an oral agreement, the landlord shall give to the tenant a copy of the summary.

If the landlord acts in violation of this section, the tenant m terminate the rental agreement by written notice. The written notice shall specify the date of termination no later than 30 days from the date of the written notice. If a tenant in a civil legal proceeding against his landlord establishes that a violation of this section has occurred, he shall be entitled to recover $100.00 in damages.

5-12-180   Attorney's Fees

Except in cases of forcible entry and detainer actions, the prevailing plaintiff in any action arising out of a landlord's or tenant's application of the rights or remedies made available in this ordinance shall be entitled to all court costs and reasonable attorney's fees; provided, however, that nothing herein shall be deemed or interpreted as precluding the awarding of attorney's fees in forcible entry and detainer actions in accordance with applicable law or as expressly provided in this ordinance.

Appendix D
Forms

Use of the forms in this appendix is either described in the text or should be self-explanatory. You may be able to use some of these forms "as is," but in most situations they will require some modification in order to fit your situation, to comply with local ordinances, or to comply with changes in the law.

The lease forms in this appendix are designed to comply with the current basic requirements of federal law and Illinois state law, and to cover the most common rental situations. However, these forms may not comply with your local ordinances, therefore, you will need to check your local ordinances and modify the lease forms as necessary to comply with local requirements.

MUNICIPAL
ORDINANCES

Some municipal ordinances require certain paragraphs to be in all leases. If this is the case in the municipality where your property is located, you may either re-type the lease form in this appendix and add the required language, or simply attach a separate use the ADDENDUM TO LEASE/RENTAL AGREEMENT (form 38) to add the required provisions. In other municipalities, you may be able to obtain the required provisions from the local government office that regulates rental property.

If you are not certain about what is required in the municipality where your property is located, or are not certain about whether a lease form you intend to use complies with that municipality's requirements, you should consult an attorney who handles landlord/tenant matters in that municipality.

COURT FORMS

Court forms are available free from most Circuit Courts, and should be obtained and used. The court forms in this appendix are offered as samples to aid in the understanding of this book, and to use in the event that a particular form is not available from the court. If you do need to use a court form from this appendix, be aware that you may need to modify the form to make it acceptable to the court in your area. Changes in the law, or unique requirements of your judge or judicial circuit, may require you to make such changes.

Each circuit has its own forms which may differ in both title and content from what is presented here. Some Illinois county court systems are on the internet and allow you to download forms from their internet site. If you are confused as to what court form to use, the clerk of the court in your county may be able to assist you; or you can consult with an attorney.

TABLE OF FORMS

The following basic forms are included in this appendix:

TENANT APPLICATION

Name_____ Date of Birth _____

Name_____ Date of Birth _____

Soc. Sec. Nos._____

Drivers' License Nos._____

Children & Ages_____

Present Landlord_____ Phone_____

Address _____ How Long?_____

Previous Landlord_____ Phone_____

Address_____

Second Previous Landlord_____ Phone_____

Address_____

Nearest Relative_____ Phone_____

Address_____

Employer_____ Phone_____

Address_____

Second Applicant's Employer_____Phone_____

Address_____

Pets_____

Other persons who will stay at premises for more than one week_____

_____

Bank Name_____Acct. #_____

Bank Name_____Acct. #_____

Have you ever been evicted?_____

Have you ever been in litigation with a landlord?_____

The undersigned hereby attest(s) that the above information is true.

_____

_____

INSPECTION REPORT

Date: _____

Unit: _____

AREA	CONDITION			
	Move-In		Move-out	
	Good	Poor	Good	Poor
Yard/garden				
Driveway				
Patio/porch				
Exterior				
Entry light/bell				
Living room/Dining room/Halls:				
Floors/carpets				
Walls/ceiling				
Doors/locks				
Fixtures/lights				
Outlets/switches				
Other				
Bedrooms:				
Floors/carpets				
Walls/ceiling				
Doors/locks				
Fixtures/lights				
Outlets/switches				
Other				
Bathrooms:				
Faucet(s)				
Toilet				
Sink/tub				
Floors/carpet				
Walls/ceiling				
Doors/locks				
Fixtures/lights				
Outlets/switches				
Other				
Kitchen:				
Refrigerator				
Range				
Oven				
Dishwasher				
Sink/disposal				
Cabinets/counters				
Floors/carpets				
Walls/ceiling				
Doors/locks				
Fixtures/lights				
Outlets/switches				
Other				
Misc.				
Closets/pantry				
Garage				
Keys				
Other				

PET REFERENCE

Date: _____

Tenant Information:

Name: _____

Address: _____

_____

Telephone: Home: _____ Work: _____

Pet Information:

1. List pet(s):

Name	Type	Age
_____	_____	_____
_____	_____	_____
_____	_____	_____
_____	_____	_____

2. Veterinarian: _____

3. Are pets permitted where you currently live? _____

4. Can we call your current landlord for a pet reference? _____
    Landlord: _____ Telephone No. _____
    How long did your pet(s) live there? From _____ to _____.

5. Can we call any former landlords for pet references? _____

Landlord	Telephone No.
_____	_____
_____	_____

6. Please list references who know you and your pet(s), and who will be willing to discuss your pet(s).

Name	Position (e.g., neighbor, veterinarian, pet trainer)	Telephone No.
_____	_____	_____
_____	_____	_____
_____	_____	_____
_____	_____	_____

PET AGREEMENT

THIS AGREEMENT is made pursuant to that certain Lease/Rental Agreement dated _____, between _____ as Landlord and _____as Tenant.

In consideration of $_____ as non-refundable cleaning payment and $_____ as additional security deposit paid by Tenant to Landlord, Tenant is allowed to keep the following pet(s): _____ on the premises _____ under the following conditions:

1.   No pets other than those listed above shall be kept on the premises without the further written permission of the Landlord.

2.   Tenant agrees at all times to keep the pet(s) from becoming a nuisance to neighbors and/or other tenants. This includes cleaning any animal waste on and about the premises; and, if any pet is a dog, controlling barking.

3.   Tenant agrees to be responsible for keeping all areas where any pets are housed clean, safe, and free of parasites, including fleas.

4.   Tenant agrees that all pets will receive proper veterinary care, including all legally required inoculations; will be kept clean and well-groomed; will be properly fed and exercised; and will be maintained in accordance with any applicable state and local laws, including the wearing of identification tags.

5.   No pet is to be left alone for a period longer than that which is appropriate according to the needs of the individual pet. Although this period may vary depending upon the particular pet, it is agreed that, in general, dogs should not be left for more than 10 hours, and other pets for more than 24 hours, on a regular basis.

6.   When the Landlord has reasonable cause to believe that a pet has been left alone and either the pet is creating a disturbance or an emergency situation appears to exist with respect to the pet, the Landlord will attempt to contact the Tenant to remedy the situation. If the Landlord is unable to contact the Tenant within a reasonable time under the circumstances, the Landlord may enter the Tenant's premises and make any necessary arrangements for the pet's care, including obtaining emergency veterinary services and removing the pet and placing it in a temporary home, such as a boarding kennel. Any costs incurred will be the responsibility of the Tenant.

7.   Tenant shall not engage in any commercial pet-raising activities.

8.   In the event any pet produces a litter, Tenant may keep them at the premises no longer than one month past weaning.

9.   In the event any pet causes destruction of the property or becomes a nuisance, or the Tenant otherwise violates any provision of this Pet Agreement, it will be considered a material breach of the Lease/Rental Agreement and the Landlord may terminate the Lease/Rental Agreement according to Illinois law.

Date: _____

Landlord: Tenant:

_____   _____

_____   _____

Disclosure of Information on Lead-Based Paint and/or Lead-Based Paint Hazards

Lead Warning Statement
Housing built before 1978 may contain lead-based paint. Lead from paint, paint chips, and dust can pose health hazards if not managed properly. Lead exposure is especially harmful to young children and pregnant women. Before renting pre-1978 housing, lessors must disclose the presence of known lead-based paint and/or lead-based paint hazards in the dwelling. Lessees must also receive a federally approved pamphlet on lead poisoning prevention.

Lessor's Disclosure
(a) Presence of lead-based paint and/or lead-based paint hazards (Check (i) or (ii) below):

    (i)_____ Known lead-based paint and/or lead-based paint hazards are present in the housing (explain).

_____

    (ii)_____ Lessor has no knowledge of lead-based paint and/or lead-based paint hazards in the housing.

(b) Records and reports available to the lessor (Check (i) or (ii) below):

    (i)_____ Lessor has provided the lessee with all available records and reports pertaining to lead-based paint and/or lead-based paint hazards in the housing (list documents below).

_____

    (ii)_____ Lessor has no reports or records pertaining to lead-based paint and/or lead-based paint hazards in the housing.

Lessee's Acknowledgment (initial)
(c)_____ Lessee has received copies of all information listed above.
(d)_____ Lessee has received the pamphlet Protect Your Family from Lead in Your Home.

Agent's Acknowledgment (initial)
(e)_____ Agent has informed the lessor of the lessor's obligations under 42 U.S.C. 4852d and is aware of his/her responsibility to ensure compliance.

Certification of Accuracy
The following parties have reviewed the information above and certify, to the best of their knowledge, that the information they have provided is true and accurate.

Lessor	Date	Lessor	Date
Lessee	Date	Lessee	Date
Agent	Date	Agent	Date

House or Duplex Lease

LANDLORD: _____   TENANT: _____

_____   _____

PROPERTY:_____

IN CONSIDERATION of the mutual covenants and agreements herein contained, Landlord hereby leases to Tenant and Tenant hereby leases from Landlord the above-described property under the following terms:

1.   TERM. This lease shall be for a term of _____, beginning _____, _____ and ending _____, _____.

2.   RENT. The rent shall be $_____ per _____ and shall be due on or before the _____ day of each _____. In the event the rent is received more than three (3) days late, a late charge of $_____ shall be due. In the event a check bounces or an eviction notice must be posted, Tenant agrees to pay a $15.00 charge.

3.   PAYMENT. Payment must be received by Landlord on or before the due date at the following address: _____ or such place as designated by Landlord in writing. Tenant understands that this may require early mailing. In the event a check bounces, Landlord may require cash or certified funds.

4.   DEFAULT. In the event Tenant defaults under any terms of this lease, Landlord may recover possession as provided by law and seek monetary damages.

5.   SECURITY. Landlord acknowledges receipt of the sum of $_____ as the last month's rent under this lease, plus $_____ as security deposit. In the event Tenant terminates the lease prior to its expiration date, said amounts are non-refundable as a charge for Landlord's trouble in securing a new tenant, but Landlord reserves the right to seek additional damages if they exceed the above amounts. Security deposit may not be used by Tenant as rent.

6.   UTILITIES. Tenant agrees to pay all utility charges on the property except: _____ _____.

7.   MAINTENANCE. Tenant has examined the property, acknowledges it to be in good repair, and in consideration of the reduced rental rate, Tenant agrees to keep the premises in good repair and to do all minor maintenance promptly (under $_____ excluding labor) and provide extermination service.

8.   LOCKS. If Tenant adds or changes locks on the premises, Landlord shall be given copies of the keys. Landlord shall at all times have keys for access to the premises in case of emergencies.

9.   ASSIGNMENT. This lease may not be assigned by Tenant without the written consent of the Landlord.

10. USE. Tenant shall not use the premises for any illegal purpose or any purpose which will increase the rate of insurance; and shall not cause a nuisance for Landlord or neighbors. Tenant shall not create any environmental hazards on the premises and shall comply with all applicable laws.

11. LAWN. Tenant agrees to maintain the lawn and shrubbery on the premises at Tenant's expense.

12. LIABILITY. Tenant shall be responsible for insurance on his own property and agrees not to hold Landlord liable for any damages to Tenant's property on the premises.

13. ACCESS. Landlord reserves the right to enter the premises for the purposes of inspection and to show to prospective purchasers.

14. PETS. No pets shall be allowed on the premises except: _____ _____, and there shall be a $_____ non-refundable pet deposit.

15. OCCUPANCY. The premises shall not be occupied by more than _____ adults and _____ children.

16. TENANT'S APPLIANCES. Tenant agrees not to use any heaters, fixtures, or appliances drawing excessive electrical current without consent of the Landlord.

17. PARKING. Tenant agrees that no parking is allowed on the premises except: _____

_____.

No boats, recreation vehicles, or disassembled automobiles may be stored on the premises.

18. FURNISHINGS. Any articles provided to Tenant and listed on attached schedule are to be returned in good condition at the termination of this lease.

19. ALTERATIONS AND IMPROVEMENTS. Tenant shall make no alterations to the property without the written consent of the Landlord; and any such alterations or improvements shall become the property of the Landlord.

20. ENTIRE AGREEMENT. This lease constitutes the entire agreement between the parties and may not be modified except in writing signed by both parties.

21. HARASSMENT. Tenant shall not do any acts to intentionally harass the Landlord or other tenants.

22. ATTORNEY'S FEES. In the event it becomes necessary to enforce this Agreement through the services of an attorney, Tenant shall be required to pay Landlord's attorney's fees.

23. SEVERABILITY. In the event any section of this Agreement shall be held to be invalid, all remaining provisions shall remain in full force and effect.

24. RECORDING. This lease shall not be recorded in any public records.

25. WAIVER. Any failure by Landlord to exercise any rights under this Agreement shall not constitute a waiver of Landlord's rights.

26. ABANDONMENT. In the event Tenant abandons the property prior to the expiration of the lease, Landlord may relet the premises and hold Tenant liable for any costs, lost rent or damage to the premises. Landlord may assume abandonment if Tenant has been away from premises for _____ days without notice.

27. SUBORDINATION. Tenant's interest in the premises shall be subordinate to any encumbrances now or hereafter placed on the premises, to any advances made under such encumbrances, and to any extensions or renewals thereof. Tenant agrees to sign any documents indicating such subordination which may be required by lenders.

28. SURRENDER OF PREMISES. At the expiration of the term of this lease, Tenant shall immediately surrender the premises in as good condition as at the start of this lease.

29. LIENS. The estate of Landlord shall not be subject to any liens for improvements contracted by Tenant.

30. SMOKE DETECTORS. Tenant shall be responsible for supplying smoke detectors, for keeping them operational, and for changing the battery when needed.

31. ABANDONED PROPERTY. By signing this Agreement the Tenant agrees that upon surrender or abandonment, the Landlord shall not be liable or responsible for storage or disposition of the Tenant's personal property.

32. MISCELLANEOUS PROVISIONS. _____

_____

_____.

WITNESS the hands and seals of the parties hereto as of this _____ day of _____, _____.

LANDLORD: TENANT:

_____   _____

_____   _____

APARTMENT LEASE

LANDLORD: _____ TENANT: _____

_____ _____

PROPERTY:_____

IN CONSIDERATION of the mutual covenants and agreements herein contained, Landlord hereby leases to Tenant and Tenant hereby leases from Landlord the above-described property under the following terms:

1. TERM. This lease shall be for a term of _____, beginning _____, _____ and ending _____, _____.

2. RENT. The rent shall be $_____ per _____ and shall be due on or before the _____ day of each _____. In the event the rent is received more than three (3) days late, a late charge of $_____ shall be due. In the event a check bounces or an eviction notice must be posted, Tenant agrees to pay a $15.00 charge.

3. PAYMENT. Payment must be received by Landlord on or before the due date at the following address: _____ or such place as designated by Landlord in writing. Tenant understands that this may require early mailing. In the event a check bounces, Landlord may require cash or certified funds.

4. DEFAULT. In the event Tenant defaults under any terms of this lease, Landlord may recover possession as provided by Law and seek monetary damages.

5. SECURITY. Landlord acknowledges receipt of the sum of $_____ as the last month's rent under this lease, plus $_____ as security deposit. In the event Tenant terminates the lease prior to its expiration date, said amounts are non-refundable as a charge for Landlord's trouble in securing a new tenant, but Landlord reserves the right to seek additional damages if they exceed the above amounts. Security deposit may not be used by Tenant as rent.

6. UTILITIES. Tenant agrees to pay all utility charges on the property except: _____ _____.

7. MAINTENANCE. Tenant has examined the property, acknowledges it to be in good repair. Tenant shall immediately repair any and all damage to the premises caused by Tenant or Tenant's guests. In the event of maintenance problems not caused by Tenant, they shall be immediately reported to Landlord or Landlord's agent.

8. LOCKS. If Tenant adds or changes locks on the premises, Landlord shall be given copies of the keys. Landlord shall at all times have keys for access to the premises in case of emergencies.

9. ASSIGNMENT. This lease may not be assigned by Tenant without the written consent of the Landlord.

10. USE. Tenant shall not use the premises for any illegal purpose or any purpose which will increase the rate of insurance, and shall not cause a nuisance for Landlord or neighbors. Tenant shall not create any environmental hazards on the premises and shall comply with all applicable laws.

11. CONDOMINIUM. In the event the premises are a condominium unit, Tenant agrees to abide by all rules, regulations and the declaration of condominium. Maintenance and recreation fees are to be paid by _____. This lease is subject to approval by the condominium association and Tenant agrees to pay any fees necessary for such approval.

12. LIABILITY. Tenant shall be responsible for insurance on his own property and agrees not to hold Landlord liable for any damages to Tenant's property on the premises.

13. ACCESS. Landlord reserves the right to enter the premises for the purposes of inspection and to show to prospective purchasers.

14. PETS. No pets shall be allowed on the premises except: _____ _____ and there shall be a $_____ non-refundable pet deposit.

15. OCCUPANCY. The premises shall not be occupied by more than _____ adults and _____ children.

16. TENANT'S APPLIANCES. Tenant agrees not to use any heaters, fixtures, or appliances drawing excessive electrical current without consent of the Landlord.

17. PARKING. Tenant agrees that no parking is allowed on the premises except: _____.
No boats, recreation vehicles or disassembled automobiles may be stored on the premises.

18. FURNISHINGS. Any articles provided to Tenant and listed on attached schedule are to be returned in good condition at the termination of this lease.

19. ALTERATIONS AND IMPROVEMENTS. Tenant shall make no alterations to the property without the written consent of the Landlord and any such alterations or improvements shall become the property of the Landlord.

20. ENTIRE AGREEMENT. This lease constitutes the entire agreement between the parties and may not be modified except in writing signed by both parties.

21. HARASSMENT. Tenant shall not do any acts to intentionally harass the Landlord or other tenants.

22. ATTORNEY'S FEES. In the event it becomes necessary to enforce this Agreement through the services of an attorney, Tenant shall be required to pay Landlord's attorney's fees.

23. SEVERABILITY. In the event any section of this Agreement shall be held to be invalid, all remaining provisions shall remain in full force and effect.

24. RECORDING. This lease shall not be recorded in any public records.

25. WAIVER. Any failure by Landlord to exercise any rights under this Agreement shall not constitute a waiver of Landlord's rights.

26. ABANDONMENT. In the event Tenant abandons the property prior to the expiration of the lease, Landlord may relet the premises and hold Tenant liable for any costs, lost rent, or damage to the premises. Landlord may assume abandonment if Tenant has been away from premises for _____ days without notice.

27. SUBORDINATION. Tenants interest in the premises shall be subordinate to any encumbrances now or hereafter placed on the premises, to any advances made under such encumbrances, and to any extensions or renewals thereof. Tenant agrees to sign any documents indicating such subordination which may be required by lenders.

28. SURRENDER OF PREMISES. At the expiration of the term of this lease, Tenant shall immediately surrender the premises in as good condition as at the start of this lease.

29. LIENS. The estate of Landlord shall not be subject to any liens for improvements contracted by Tenant.

30. SMOKE DETECTORS. Tenant shall be responsible for keeping smoke detectors operational and for changing battery when needed.

31. ABANDONED PROPERTY. By signing this Agreement the Tenant agrees that upon surrender or abandonment, the Landlord shall not be liable or responsible for storage or disposition of the Tenant's personal property.

32. MISCELLANEOUS PROVISIONS. _____
_____
_____.

WITNESS the hands and seals of the parties hereto as of this _____ day of _____, _____.

LANDLORD: TENANT:

_____   _____

_____   _____

RENTAL AGREEMENT

LANDLORD: _____ TENANT: _____

_____   _____

PROPERTY:_____

IN CONSIDERATION of the mutual covenants and agreements herein contained, Landlord hereby rents to Tenant and Tenant hereby rents from Landlord the above-described property under the following terms:

1.   TERM. This Rental Agreement shall be for a month-to-month tenancy which may be cancelled by either party upon giving notice to the other party at least 30 days prior to the end of a month

2.   RENT. The rent shall be $_____ per month and shall be due on or before the _____ day of each month. In the event the rent is received more than three (3) days late, a late charge of $_____ shall be due. In the event a check bounces or an eviction notice must be posted, Tenant agrees to pay a $15.00 charge.

3.   PAYMENT. Payment must be received by Landlord on or before the due date at the following address: _____ or such place as designated by Landlord in writing. Tenant understands that this may require early mailing. In the event a check bounces, Landlord may require cash or certified funds.

4.   DEFAULT. In the event Tenant defaults under any terms of this agreement, Landlord may recover possession as provided by Law and seek monetary damages.

5.   SECURITY. Landlord acknowledges receipt of the sum of $_____ as the last month's rent under this lease, plus $_____ as security deposit against rent or damages. In the event Tenant vacates the premises without giving proper notice, said amounts are non-refundable as a charge for Landlord's trouble in securing a new tenant, but Landlord reserves the right to seek additional payment for any damages to the premises. Security deposit may not be used by Tenant as rent.

6.   UTILITIES. Tenant agrees to pay all utility charges on the property except: _____ _____.

7.   MAINTENANCE. Tenant has examined the property, acknowledges it to be in good repair; and in consideration of the reduced rental rate, Tenant agrees to keep the premises in good repair, to do all minor maintenance promptly (under $_____ excluding labor), and provide extermination service.

8.   LOCKS. If Tenant adds or changes locks on the premises, Landlord shall be given copies of the keys. Landlord shall at all times have keys for access to the premises in case of emergencies.

9.   ASSIGNMENT. This agreement may not be assigned by Tenant without the written consent of the Landlord.

10. USE. Tenant shall not use the premises for any illegal purpose or any purpose which will increase the rate of insurance; and shall not cause a nuisance for Landlord or neighbors. Tenant shall not create any environmental hazards on the premises and shall comply with all applicable laws.

11. LAWN. Tenant agrees to maintain the lawn and shrubbery on the premises at his expense.

12. LIABILITY. Tenant shall be responsible for insurance on his own property and agrees not to hold Landlord liable for any damages to Tenant's property on the premises.

13. ACCESS. Landlord reserves the right to enter the premises for the purposes of inspection and to show to prospective purchasers.

14. PETS. No pets shall be allowed on the premises except: _____ and there shall be a $_____ non-refundable pet deposit.

15. OCCUPANCY. The premises shall not be occupied by more than _____ adults and _____ children.

16. TENANT'S APPLIANCES. Tenant agrees not to use any heaters, fixtures, or appliances drawing excessive electrical current without consent of the Landlord.

17. PARKING. Tenant agrees that no parking is allowed on the premises except: _____

_____.

No boats, recreation vehicles, or disassembled automobiles may be stored on the premises.

18. FURNISHINGS. Any articles provided to tenant and listed on attached schedule are to be returned in good condition at the termination of this agreement.

19. ALTERATIONS AND IMPROVEMENTS. Tenant shall make no alterations to the property without the written consent of the Landlord; and any such alterations or improvements shall become the property of the Landlord.

20. ENTIRE AGREEMENT. This rental agreement constitutes the entire agreement between the parties and may not be modified except in writing signed by both parties.

21. HARASSMENT. Tenant shall not do any acts to intentionally harass the Landlord or other tenants.

22. ATTORNEY'S FEES. In the event it becomes necessary to enforce this agreement through the services of an attorney, Tenant shall be required to pay Landlord's attorney's fees.

23. SEVERABILITY. In the event any section of this agreement shall be held to be invalid, all remaining provisions shall remain in full force and effect.

24. RECORDING. This agreement shall not be recorded in any public records.

25. WAIVER. Any failure by Landlord to exercise any rights under this agreement shall not constitute a waiver of Landlord's rights.

26. ABANDONMENT. In the event Tenant abandons the property prior to the expiration of the lease, Landlord may relet the premises and hold Tenant liable for any costs, lost rent or damages to the premises. Landlord may assume abandonment if Tenant has been away from premises for _____ days without notice.

27. SUBORDINATION. Tenants interest in the premises shall be subordinate to any encumbrances now or hereafter placed on the premises, to any advances made under such encumbrances, and to any extensions or renewals thereof. Tenant agrees to sign any documents indicating such subordination which may be required by lenders.

28. SURRENDER OF PREMISES. At the expiration of the term of this agreement, Tenant shall immediately surrender the premises in as good condition as at the start of this agreement.

29. LIENS. The estate of Landlord shall not be subject to any liens for improvements contracted by Tenant.

30. SMOKE DETECTORS. Tenant shall be responsible for keeping smoke detectors operational and for changing battery when needed.

31. ABANDONED PROPERTY. By signing this Agreement the Tenant agrees that upon surrender or abandonment, the Landlord shall not be liable or responsible for storage or disposition of the Tenant's personal property.

32. MISCELLANEOUS PROVISIONS. _____

_____.

WITNESS the hands and seals of the parties hereto as of this _____ day of _____, _____.

LANDLORD: TENANT:

_____   _____

_____   _____

Addendum to Lease—Chicago

RESIDENTIAL LANDLORD AND TENANT ORDINANCE SUMMARY

This Summary of the ordinance must be attached to every written rental agreement or be given to the tenant who has an oral rental agreement. Unless otherwise noted, all provisions are effective as of November 6, 1986. {Mun. Code ch. 5-12-170}

IMPORTANT: IF YOU SEEK TO EXERCISE RIGHTS UNDER THE ORDINANCE, OBTAIN A COPY OF THE ORDINANCE TO DETERMINE APPROPRIATE REMEDIES AND PROCEDURES. CONSULTING AN ATTORNEY WOULD ALSO BE ADVISABLE.

WHAT RENTAL UNITS ARE COVERED BY THE ORDINANCE? {MUN. CODE CH 5-12-010}

- All rental units with written or oral leases (including all subsidized units such as CHA, IHDA, Sect. 8, etc.)

WHAT RENTAL UNITS ARE NOT COVERED BY THE ORDINANCE? {MUN. CODE CH. 5-12-020}

- Owner-occupied buildings with six or fewer units.
- Units in hotels, motels, rooming houses, unless rented on a monthly basis and occupied for more than 32 days.
- School dormitory rooms, shelters, employee's quarters, non-residential rental properties.
- Co-ops and condominiums unless rented.

WHAT ARE THE TENANT'S GENERAL DUTIES UNDER THE ORDINANCE? {MUN. CODE CH. 5-12-040}

The tenant, the tenant's family and guests must:
- Comply with all obligations imposed specifically upon tenants by the Municipal Code, including maintaining smoke detector batteries with tenant's apartment.
- Keep the unit safe and clean.
- Use all equipment and facilities in a reasonable manner.
- Not damage the unit.
- Not disturb other residents.

LANDLORD'S RIGHT OF ACCESS {MUN. CODE CH. 5-12-050}

- A tenant shall permit reasonable access to a landlord upon receiving two days notice by mail, telephone, written notice or other means designed in good faith to provide notice. A general notice to all affected tenants may be given in the event repair work on common areas or other units may require such access.
- In the event of emergency or where repairs elsewhere unexpectedly require such access, the landlord must provide notice two days after entry.

SECURITY DEPOSITS AND PREPAID RENT {MUN. CODE CH. 5-12-080 AND 5-12-081}

- A landlord must give a tenant a receipt for a security deposit including the owner's name, the date it was received and a description of the dwelling unit. The receipt must be signed by the person accepting the security deposit.
- A landlord must pay interest each year at the rate set by the City Comptroller for security deposits held more than six months. (eff. 7-1-97)
- A landlord must pay interest each year at the rate set by the City Comptroller for prepaid rent held more than six months. (eff. 7-1-97)
- A landlord must return all security deposit and interest minus unpaid rent and money for damages within 45 days from the date the tenant vacates the dwelling unit.
- In the event of fire, a landlord must return all security deposit and interest, minus unpaid rent and money for damages, within seven days from the date that the tenant provides notice of termination of the rental agreement. (eff. 1-1-92)

Note: This addendum should be used with all Chicago residential leases except in owner-occupied buildings of six units or less

WHAT ARE THE LANDLORD'S GENERAL DUTIES UNDER THE ORDINANCE?

- To give tenant written notice of the owner's or manager's name, address and telephone number. {Mun. Code ch. 5-12-090}
- To give new tenants or tenants renewing a rental agreement, notice of building code citations issued by the City in the past 12 months; notice of pending Housing Court, Code Enforcement Bureau or Compliance Board actions; and notice of termination of water, electrical or gas service to the building. {Mun. Code ch. 5-12-100}
- To maintain the property in compliance with all applicable provisions of the Municipal Code. {Mun. Code ch. 5-12-070}
- Not force a tenant to renew an agreement more than 90 days before the existing agreement terminates. (eff. 1-1-92) {Mun. Code ch. 5-12-130(j)}
- Provide a tenant with at least 30 days written notice of his intention not to renew a rental agreement. If the landlord fails to give the required written notice, the tenant may remain in the dwelling unit for 60 days under the same terms and conditions as the last month of the existing agreement. (eff. 1-1-92) {Mun. Code ch. 5-12-140}
- To use a lease without prohibited provisions. {Mun. Code ch. 5-12-140}

TENANT REMEDIES {MUN. CODE CH. 5-12-110}

- If the landlord fails to maintain the property in compliance with the Code **AND such failure renders the premises not reasonably fit and habitable,** the tenant may:
  1) Request in writing that the landlord make repairs within 14 days or tenant may terminate vacate the premises within 30 days and if possession is not delivered, the tenant's notice is considered withdrawn. (eff. 1-1-92)
- If the landlord fails to maintain the property in material compliance with the Code and the tenant or tenant's family or guests are not responsible for the failure, the tenant may:
  1) Request in **writing** that the landlord make repairs within 14 days or tenant can withhold an amount of rent that reasonably reflects reduced value of the unit.
  2) Request in **writing** that the landlord make repairs within 14 days or tenant may have the repairs made and deduct up to $500 or 1/2 of the month's rent, whichever is more, but **not to exceed one month's rent**. The repairs must be done in compliance with existing law and building regulations. A receipt for the repairs must be given to the landlord and no more than the cost of the repairs can be deducted from the rent.
  3) File suit against the landlord for damages and injunctive relief.

FAILURE TO PROVIDE ESSENTIAL SERVICES (HEAT, RUNNING OR HOT WATER, ELECTRICITY, GAS OR PLUMBING) {MUN. CODE CH. 5-12-110 (F)}

- If, contrary to the lease, an essential service is not provided, or if the landlord fails to maintain the building in material compliance with the Code to such an extent that such failure constitutes an immediate danger to the health and safety of the tenant, and the tenant or tenant's family or guests are not responsible for such failure, the tenant may:
  1) Procure substitute service, and upon presenting paid receipts to the landlord, deduct the cost from the rent.
  2) File suit against the landlord and recover damages based on the reduced value of the dwelling unit.
  3) Procure substitute housing and be excused from paying rent for that period. The tenant also may recover from the landlord the cost of substitute housing up to an amount equal to the monthly rent for each month or portion thereof.
  4) Request that the landlord correct the failure within 24 hours and if the landlord fails to do so, withhold from the monthly rent an amount that reasonably reflects the reduced value of the premises. (eff. 1-1-92)
  5) Request that the landlord correct the failure within 72 hours and if the landlord fails to do so, terminate the rental agreement. If the rental agreement is terminated, the tenant must deliver possession within 30 days or the notice of termination is considered withdrawn. (eff. 1-1-92)

Note: **Remedies 4) and 5) may not be used if the failure is due to the utility provider's failure to provide service.** For the purposes of this section only, the notice a tenant provides must be in writing if the landlord has informed the tenant of an address to which notices should be sent. If the landlord does not inform the tenant of an address, the tenant may deliver written notice to the last known address of the landlord or by other reasonable means designed in good faith to provide written notice to the landlord. (eff. 1-1-92)

FIRE OR CASUALTY DAMAGE {MUN. CODE CH. 5-12-110 (G)}

- If the tenant, tenant's family or guests are **not** responsible for fire or accident, the tenant has three choices:
  1) The tenant may move out immediately, but if this is done, the tenant must provide written notice to the landlord of the intention to terminate within 14 days after moving out.
  2) The tenant may stay in the unit, **if it is legal,** but if the tenant stays and is denied use of a portion of the unit through damage, he may reduce his rent to reflect the reduced value of the unit.
  3) If the tenant stays and the landlord promises to begin work but fails to diligently carry out the work, the tenant may notify the landlord, in writing, within 14 days after the tenant becomes aware that the work is not being diligently carried out, of his intention to terminate the rental agreement.

SUBLEASES {MUN. CODE CH. 5-12-120}

- The landlord must accept a reasonable subtenant offered by the tenant without charging additional fees.
- If a tenant moves prior to the end of the rental agreement, the landlord must make a good faith effort to find a new tenant at a fair rent.
- If the landlord is unsuccessful in re-renting the unit, the tenant remains liable for the rent under the rental agreement, as well as the landlord's cost of advertising.

WHAT HAPPENS IF A TENANT PAYS RENT LATE?

- If the tenant fails to pay rent on time, the landlord may charge a $10.00 per month late fee on rents under $500.00 and a 5% per month late fee on that part of the rent that exceeds $500.00. (i.e., for a $450.00 monthly rent the late fee is $10.00, for a $700.00 monthly rent the late fee is $10.00 plus 5% of $200 or $20.00) (eff. 1-1-92) {Mun. Code ch. 5-12-140 (h)}
- The landlord cannot evict the tenant if he accepts full payment of the rent due. {Mun. Code ch. 5-12-130 (g)}

LANDLORD REMEDIES {MUN. CODE CH. 5-12-130}

- If the tenant fails to pay rent the landlord, after giving five 0days **written** notice to the tenant, may terminate the rental agreement.
- If the tenant fails to comply with the Code or the rental agreement, the landlord, after giving 10 days written notice to the tenant, may terminate the rental agreement if tenant fails to correct the violation.
- If the tenant fails to comply with the Code or the rental agreement, the landlord, after giving 14 days written notice to the tenant or in the case of emergency as promptly as conditions permit, may enter the dwelling unit and have the necessary work done. In this case, the tenant shall be responsible for the costs of repairs.

LOCKOUTS {MUN. CODE CH. 5-12-160}

- It is illegal for a landlord to lock out a tenant, or change the locks, or remove the doors of a rental unit, or to cut off heat, utility or water service, or to do anything which interferes with the tenant's use of the apartment.
- All lockouts are illegal and the Police Department is responsible for enforcement against such illegal activity. (eff. 1-1-92)
- The landlord shall be fined $200 to $500 for each day the lockout occurs or continues.
- The tenant may sue the landlord to recover possession of the unit and twice the actual damages sustained or two months' rent, whichever is greater.

PROHIBITION ON RETALIATORY CONDUCT BY LANDLORD {MUN. CODE CH. 5-12-150}

- A landlord **cannot** take retaliatory action against a tenant because a tenant complains or testifies **in good faith** to governmental agencies or officials, media, community groups, tenant unions or the landlord.

ATTORNEY'S FEES {MUN. CODE CH. 5-12-180}

- Except in eviction actions, the prevailing plaintiff in any action arising from the application of this Ordinance shall be entitled to recover all court costs and reasonable attorney's fees. (eff. 1-1-92)

WHERE CAN I GET A COPY OF THE ORDINANCE?

For a copy of the Ordinance, visit the Office of the City Clerk, Room 107, City Hall, 121 North LaSalle Street, Chicago, Illinois, or the Municipal Reference Library, Room 1002, City Hall.
Approved by the City of Chicago, January 1992

SECURITY DEPOSIT RECEIPT

Pursuant to that certain Lease/Rental Agreement dated _____,
between _____ as Landlord(s)
and _____ as Tenant(s);
this acknowledges receipt by the undersigned of a security deposit in the amount of
$_____, for the following premises:

_____

_____.

Date security deposit received: _____

Received by: _____
                        Signature

Name: _____

Title: _____

Security Deposit Bank Account Notice

To: _____

_____

_____

_____

_____

Pursuant to that certain Lease/Rental Agreement dated _____,
between _____ as Landlord
and _____ as Tenant; you are
hereby provided with the following information concerning the security deposit you posted:

Institution where funds are held: _____

_____

_____

_____

LANDLORD: _____

_____

INSPECTION REQUEST

Date:

To:

It will be necessary to enter your dwelling unit for the purpose of _____

_____

_____. If possible we would like

access on _____ at ____o'clock ___.m.

In the event this is not convenient, please call to arrange another time.

Sincerely,

_____

Address:

Phone:

STATEMENT FOR REPAIRS

Date:

To:

It has been necessary to repair damage to the premises which you occupy which was caused by you or your guests. The costs for repairs were as follows:

This amount is your responsibility under the terms of the lease and Illinois law and should be forwarded to us at the address below.

Sincerely,

_____

Address:

Phone:

Letter to Vacating Tenant

Date:

To:

Dear _____

This letter is to remind you that your lease will expire on _____. Please be advised that we do not intend to renew or extend the lease.

The keys should be delivered to us at the address below on or before the end of the lease along with your forwarding address. We will inspect the premises for damages, deduct any amounts necessary for repairs and refund any remaining balance as required by law.

Sincerely,

_____

Address:

Phone:

ANNUAL LETTER - CONTINUATION OF TENANCY

Date:

To:

Dear _____

    This letter is to remind you that your lease will expire on _____.
Please advise us within _____ days as to whether you intend to renew your lease. If so, we
will prepare a new lease for your signature(s).

    If you do not intend to renew your lease, the keys should be delivered to us at the
address below on or before the end of the lease along with your forwarding address. We will
inspect the premises for damages, deduct any amounts necessary for repairs and refund any
remaining balance as required by law.

    If we have not heard from you as specified above we will assume that you will be
vacating the premises and will arrange for a new tenant to move in at the end of your term.

                    Sincerely,

                    _____

                    Address:

                    Phone:

NOTICE OF TERMINATION OF AGENT

Date:

To:

    You are hereby advised that _____ is no longer our agent effective _____. On and after this date he or she is no longer authorized to collect rent, accept notices or to make any representations or agreements regarding the property.

    Rent should thereafter be paid to us directly unless you are instructed otherwise by in writing.

    If you have any questions you may contact us at the address or phone number below.

                    Sincerely,

                    _____

                    Address:

                    Phone:

Notice of Appointment of Agent

Date:

To:

You are hereby advised that effective _____,
our agent for collection of rent and other matters regarding the property will be
_____. However, no terms of the written lease may be modified
or waived without our written signature(s).

If you have any questions you may contact us at the address or phone number below.

Sincerely,

_____

Address:

Phone:

NOTICE OF NON-RENEWAL

(Tenant's Name and Address)

Dear _____:
        (Tenant's Name)

     You are notified that your tenancy will not be renewed at the end of the present term. You will be expected to vacate the premises on or before _____, _____. In the event that you do not vacate the premises by said date, legal action may be taken in which you may be held liable for double rent, court costs and attorney fees.

_____

Landlord's Name_____

Address _____

_____

Phone Number _____

Amendment to Lease/Rental Agreement

The undersigned parties to that certain agreement dated _____,
_____ on the premises known as _____,
hereby agree to amend said agreement as follows:

WITNESS the hands and seals of the parties hereto this _____ day of _____,
_____.

Landlord: Tenant:

_____   _____

_____   _____

THIRTY-DAY NOTICE OF TERMINATION

(OF MONTH-TO-MONTH TENANCY)

STATE OF ILLINOIS   )

)   SS.

COUNTY OF   )

To: _____

_____

_____

YOU ARE HEREBY NOTIFIED that your tenancy will not be renewed at the end of the present term. You will be expected to vacate the premises on or before _____, _____. In the event that you do not vacate the premises by said date, legal action may be taken in which you may be held liable for double rent, court costs and attorney fees.

Dated this _____ day of _____, _____.

Landlord's Name_____

Address _____

Phone Number _____

AFFIDAVIT OF SERVICE

I, _____, being duly sworn on oath, deposes and says that on the _____ day of _____, _____, (s)he served the foregoing notice on the tenant(s) named herein by delivering a copy hereof to _____

_____.

_____

Signature of person delivering notice

SUBSCRIBED AND SWORN to before me

this _____ day of _____, _____.

_____

NOTARY PUBLIC

SEVEN-DAY NOTICE OF TERMINATION
(OF WEEK-TO-WEEK TENANCY)

STATE OF ILLINOIS   )
)   SS.

COUNTY OF _____)

To: _____

_____

_____

YOU ARE HEREBY NOTIFIED that your tenancy will not be renewed at the end of the present term. You will be expected to vacate the premises on or before _____, _____. In the event that you do not vacate the premises by said date, legal action may be taken in which you may be held liable for double rent, court costs and attorney fees.

Dated this _____ day of _____, _____.

_____
Landlord's Name_____
Address _____
Phone Number _____

AFFIDAVIT OF SERVICE

I, _____, being duly sworn on oath, deposes and says that on the _____ day of _____, _____, (s)he served the foregoing notice on the tenant(s) named herein by delivering a copy hereof to _____ _____.

_____
Signature of person delivering notice

SUBSCRIBED AND SWORN to before me
this _____ day of _____, _____.

_____
NOTARY PUBLIC

DEMAND FOR POSSESSION

(AGAINST HOLD-OVER TENANT)

STATE OF ILLINOIS   )
)   SS.

COUNTY OF   )

To: _____

_____

_____

YOU ARE HEREBY NOTIFIED that your tenancy has been terminated and you are wrongfully holding over in possession of the premises situated in the City of _____, and County of _____, Illinois _____, and described as follows:

The property at _____, Unit Number _____, together with all buildings, sheds, closets, out-buildings, garages, and other structures used in connection with said premises.

DEMAND IS HEREBY MADE that you immediately vacate the premises and deliver possession to the undersigned. In the event that you do not vacate the premises, legal action may be taken in which you may be held liable for double rent, court costs, and attorney fees.

Dated this _____ day of _____, _____.

_____
Landlord's Name_____
Address _____
Phone Number _____

AFFIDAVIT OF SERVICE

I, _____, being duly sworn on oath, deposes and says that on the _____ day of _____, _____, (s)he served the foregoing notice on the tenant(s) named herein by delivering a copy hereof to _____

_____.

_____
Signature of person delivering notice

SUBSCRIBED AND SWORN to before me this _____ day of _____, _____.

_____
NOTARY PUBLIC

IN THE CIRCUIT COURT OF THE _____ JUDICIAL CIRCUIT,

_____COUNTY, ILLINOIS

_____,

Plaintiff(s),

vs.   CASE NO.: _____

_____,

Defendant(s).

STIPULATION

The parties to this action hereby stipulate as follows:

1. The defendant(s) acknowledge(s) the sum of $_____ to be due and owing to the plaintiff(s).

2. In partial payment of the above debt, the defendant(s) agree(s) to immediately pay to the plaintiff(s) the amount of $_____, and the balance of the above debt will be paid as follows:

$_____ due on _____ $_____ due on _____

$_____ due on _____ $_____ due on _____

In addition to the above-stated amounts, the defendant(s), as a further condition hereof, agree(s) to pay to the plaintiff(s) the sum of $_____ on the _____ day of each month, in cash, representing periodic installments payable under the rental agreement between the parties for rent of the subject residential premises.

3. If all of the foregoing sums are paid as set out above, in full, in cash, and when due, this action shall be dismissed with prejudice, and each party does hereby release the other by a general release as if set out here in full.

4. If any of the above sums are not paid as set out above, the plaintiff(s) shall be entitled to an Order of Possession to be executed forthwith upon the filing of an Affidavit of Nonpayment. Defendant(s) hereby waive(s) a hearing on the application of the plaintiff(s) for an Order of Possession in such case.

5. If defendant(s) should default in any of the above payments, and defendant(s) abandon(s) possession of the dwelling or is/are lawfully evicted by reason of such default, it is agreed that plaintiff(s) shall be entitled to a money judgment for any of such payments as are in default at the time of such abandonment or eviction. Defendant(s) waive(s) notice and hearing on the application of plaintiff(s) for such money judgment.

Dated: _____, _____.

_____   _____
Plaintiff   Defendant

_____   _____
Plaintiff   Defendant

IN THE CIRCUIT COURT OF THE _____ JUDICIAL CIRCUIT,
_____COUNTY, ILLINOIS

_____,
Plaintiff(s),

vs.   CASE NO.: _____

_____,
Defendant(s).

Complaint for Eviction

Plaintiff(s), _____,
sue(s) Defendant(s), _____,
and allege(s):

1. This is an action to evict a tenant from real property in _____
_____, County, Illinois.

2. Plaintiff(s) own(s) the following described real property in said county: _____
_____.

3. Defendant(s) has/have possession of the property under a/an (oral/written) agreement to
pay rent of $_____ payable _____.
A copy of the written agreement, if any, is attached as Exhibit "A."

4. Defendant(s) failed to pay the rent due _____, _____.

5. Plaintiff(s) served Defendant(s) with a notice on _____, _____,
to pay the rent or deliver possession but Defendant refuses to do either. A copy of the notice is
attached as Exhibit "B."

WHEREFORE, Plaintiff(s) demand(s) judgment for possession of the property against
Defendant(s).

_____
Signature

_____
Name

_____
Address

_____
City, State, Zip Code

_____
Phone Number

IN THE CIRCUIT COURT OF THE _____ JUDICIAL CIRCUIT,
_____COUNTY, ILLINOIS

_____,
                                         Plaintiff(s),

vs.   CASE NO.: _____

_____,
                                         Defendant(s).

Complaint for Eviction

Plaintiff(s), _____,
sue(s) Defendant(s), _____,
and allege(s):

1. This is an action to evict a tenant from real property in _____
_____, County, Illinois.

2. Plaintiff(s) own(s) the following described real property in said county: _____
_____.

3. Defendant(s) has/have possession of the property under a/an (oral/written) agreement to
pay rent of $_____ payable _____.
A copy of the written agreement, if any, is attached as Exhibit "A."

4. Plaintiff(s) served Defendant(s) with a notice on _____, _____,
giving written notice to the Defendant(s) that the Defendant(s) was/were in violation of this rental
agreement. A copy of the notice, setting forth the violations of the rental agreement, is attached
hereto as Exhibit "B."

5. Defendant has failed to correct or discontinue the conduct set forth in the above-
mentioned notice.

WHEREFORE, Plaintiff demands judgment for possession of the property against
Defendant.

_____

Landlord's Name _____

Address _____

_____

IN THE CIRCUIT COURT OF THE _____ JUDICIAL CIRCUIT,
_____COUNTY, ILLINOIS

_____,
                              Plaintiff(s),

vs.   CASE NO.: _____

_____,
                              Defendant(s).

Complaint for Eviction

Plaintiff(s), _____,
sue(s) Defendant(s), _____,
and allege(s):

COUNT I

1. This is an action to evict a tenant from real property in _____
_____ County, Illinois.

2. Plaintiff(s) own(s) the following described real property in said County: _____
_____.

3. Defendant(s) has/have possession of the property under a/an (oral/written) agreement which terminated on _____, _____. A copy of the written agreement, if any, is attached as Exhibit "A."

4. Defendant(s) failed to vacate the premises at the end of said agreement.

COUNT II

5. This is an action for double rent.

6. Defendant(s) owe(s) Plaintiff(s) the sum of $_____ for each day Defendant(s) remain(s)
in the premises since the termination of the tenancy.

WHEREFORE, Plaintiff(s) demands judgment for possession of the property and rent owed against
Defendant(s).

_____

Landlord's Name _____

Address _____

_____

Telephone Number_____

IN THE CIRCUIT COURT OF THE _____ JUDICIAL CIRCUIT,
_____COUNTY, ILLINOIS

_____,
                                  Plaintiff(s),

vs.   CASE NO.: _____

_____,
                                  Defendant(s).

Complaint for Eviction and Damages

          Plaintiff(s), _____,
sue(s) Defendant(s), _____,
and allege(s):

COUNT I
Tenant Eviction

     1. This is an action to evict a tenant(s) from real property in _____
_____ County, Illinois.

     2. Plaintiff(s) own(s) the following described real property in said County: _____
_____.

     3. Defendant(s) has/have possession of the property under a/an (oral/written) agreement to
pay rent of $_____payable _____.
A copy of the written agreement, if any, is attached as Exhibit "A."

     4. Defendant(s) failed to pay the rent due _____, _____.

     5. Plaintiff(s) served Defendant(s) with a notice on _____, _____,
to pay the rent or deliver possession but Defendant refuses to do either. A copy of the notice is
attached as Exhibit "B."

     WHEREFORE, Plaintiff demands judgment for possession of the property against Defendant.

COUNT II
Damages

6. This is an action for damages that do not exceed $15,000.

7. Plaintiff(s) restate(s) those allegations contained in paragraphs 1 through 5 above.

8. Defendant(s) owe(s) Plaintiff(s) $_____ that is due with interest since _____, _____.

WHEREFORE, Plaintiff demands judgment for damages against Defendant.

_____
Landlord's Name_____
Address _____
_____
Telephone Number:_____

VERIFICATION OF COMPLAINT

STATE OR ILLINOIS   )
)

COUNTY OF _____)

The undersigned, being the Plaintiff in the foregoing complaint, being first duly sworn, deposes and says:

1. That the allegations in the attached Complaint for Eviction are true.

2. That the Defendants are not in the military service of the United States.

_____
Plaintiff

Sworn to and subscribed before me by _____ who is personally known to me or produced _____ as identification on this _____ day of _____, _____

_____
Notary Public
My commission expires:

(Attach a copy of this form to your Complaint.)

IN THE CIRCUIT COURT OF THE _____ JUDICIAL CIRCUIT,
_____COUNTY, ILLINOIS

_____,
                                   Plaintiff(s),

vs.   CASE NO.: _____

_____,
                                   Defendant(s).

SUMMONS

To each defendant:

    You are hereby summoned and required to appear before this court at _____
_____, at _____ o'clock __.M.,
on _____, _____, to answer the complaint in this case, a copy of which is
hereto attached. If you fail to do so, a judgment by default may be entered against you for the relief
asked in the complaint.

To the officer:

    This summons must be returned by the officer or other person to whom it was given for ser-
vice, with indorsement of service and fees, if any, immediately after service and not less than three
days before the day for appearance. If service cannot be made, this summons shall be returned so
indorsed.

    This summons may not be served later than 3 days before the day for appearance.

Witness _____, _____

_____
                                   Clerk of Court

Plaintiff's Attorney (or plaintiff, if he is not represented
by attorney) _____
Address _____
Telephone No._____
Facsimile Telephone No. _____

Date of service _____, _____ (to be inserted by
officer on copy left with defendant or other person).

IN THE CIRCUIT COURT OF THE _____ JUDICIAL CIRCUIT,
_____COUNTY, ILLINOIS

_____,
                                                     Plaintiff(s),

vs.   CASE NO.: _____

_____,
                                                     Defendant(s).

MOTION FOR DEFAULT

    Plaintiff(s) move(s) for entry of a default against _____,
for damages for failing to respond to the complaint in this action as required by law.

_____

Name _____

Address _____

_____

Telephone Number _____

DEFAULT

    A default is entered in this action against the Defendant(s) for failure to respond as required
by law.

DATE:_____

_____

IN THE CIRCUIT COURT OF THE _____ JUDICIAL CIRCUIT,
_____COUNTY, ILLINOIS

_____,

                               Plaintiff(s),

vs.   CASE NO.: _____

_____,

                               Defendant(s).

NOTICE OF HEARING

To: _____

           _____

           _____

      PLEASE TAKE NOTICE that on the _____ day of _____, _____,
at _____ o'clock ____.M. or as soon thereafter as can be heard, the undersigned will bring on to
be heard _____,
before the Honorable _____, judge of the above Court,
at _____,
_____, _____ County, Illinois.

PLEASE GOVERN YOURSELF ACCORDINGLY.

DATED this _____ day of _____, _____.

      I HEREBY CERTIFY that a copy hereof is being furnished by regular U.S. Mail on this date
to the above-mentioned addressee.

                                    _____
                                    Plaintiff

                                    _____
                                    Address

                                    _____

                                    _____
                                    Phone

IN THE CIRCUIT COURT OF THE _____ JUDICIAL CIRCUIT,
_____COUNTY, ILLINOIS

_____,
Plaintiff(s),

vs.   CASE NO.: _____

_____,
Defendant(s).

AFFIDAVIT OF DAMAGES

STATE OF ILLINOIS   )
COUNTY OF   )

BEFORE ME, the undersigned authority, personally appeared _____
_____, who being first duly sworn, says:

1. I am _____ the Plaintiff or ____ the Plaintiff's agent (check appropriate response) in this case and am authorized to make this affidavit.

2. This affidavit is based on my own personal knowledge.

3. Defendant has possession of the property which is the subject of this eviction under an agreement to pay rent of $_____ per _____.

4. Defendant has not paid the rent due since _____.

5. Defendant owes Plaintiff $ _____ as alleged in the complaint plus interest.

6. Defendant owes Plaintiff $_____ as alleged in the complaint plus interest.

_____

Acknowledged before me on the _____ day of _____, _____,
by _____,
who _____is personally known to me/ _____ produced _____
as identification, and who _____ did/ _____ did not   take an oath.

_____
NOTARY PUBLIC
My Commission Expires:

I CERTIFY that, on _____, _____, I __mailed __ hand delivered a copy of this affidavit to the Defendant at _____.

_____

IN THE CIRCUIT COURT OF THE _____ JUDICIAL CIRCUIT,
_____COUNTY, ILLINOIS

_____,
Plaintiff(s),

vs.   CASE NO.: _____

_____,
Defendant(s).

ORDER OF POSSESSION

THIS ACTION came before the Court upon Plaintiff's Complaint for eviction. On the evidence presented, it is

ADJUDGED that Plaintiff(s), _____,
recover from Defendant(s), _____,
possession of the real property described as follows: _____
_____,
and $ _____ as court costs, for which let Writs of Possession and Execution now issue.

ORDERED in _____, _____
COUNTY, ILLINOIS on _____, _____.

_____
Judge

cc: _____
(Insert name of Landlord)

_____
(Insert name of Tenant)

IN THE CIRCUIT COURT OF THE _____ JUDICIAL CIRCUIT,
_____COUNTY, ILLINOIS

_____,
                                          Plaintiff(s),

vs.   CASE NO.: _____

_____,
                                          Defendant(s).

JUDGMENT FOR DAMAGES

THIS ACTION came before the Court upon Plaintiff's Complaint for unpaid rent. On the evidence presented, it is

ADJUDGED that Plaintiff(s), _____,
recover from Defendant(s), _____,
the sum of $_____ with costs in the sum of $ _____, making a total
of $ _____, that shall bear interest at the legal rate allowed by law.

ORDERED in_____, _____
COUNTY, ILLINOIS, on _____, _____.

_____
Judge

cc: _____
    _____
    Landlord(s)

    _____
    _____
    Tenant(s)

IN THE CIRCUIT COURT OF THE _____ JUDICIAL CIRCUIT,
_____COUNTY, ILLINOIS

_____,
Plaintiff(s),

vs.   CASE NO.: _____

_____,
Defendant(s).

SATISFACTION OF JUDGMENT

This document is signed by _____, __individually or __as agent of Plaintiff(s).

Plaintiff(s), acknowledge(s) full payment of the judgment signed by the Judge on _____, _____. Plaintiff(s) agree(s) that Defendant(s) do(es) not owe the Plaintiff(s) any more monies for the judgment.

_____   _____
            (Witness)   (Plaintiff)

_____
            (Witness)

Acknowledged before me on the _____ day of _____, _____, by
_____,
who _____is personally known to me/ _____ produced _____
as identification, and who ____ did/ ____ did not   take an oath.

                                        _____
                                        NOTARY PUBLIC
                                        My Commission Expires:

I CERTIFY that, on _____, _____, I __mailed __ hand delivered a copy of this affidavit to the Defendant at _____.

                                        _____

ADDENDUM TO LEASE/RENTAL AGREEMENT

LANDLORD: _____   TENANT: _____

_____   _____

PROPERTY:_____

The undersigned parties hereby agree that the provisions, terms, conditions, covenants, and agreements herein contained shall be part of the Lease/Rental Agreement, dated _____.

Date: _____   Date: _____

Landlord: Tenant:

_____   _____

_____   _____

IN THE CIRCUIT COURT OF COOK COUNTY, ILLINOIS

NOTICE OF TERMINATION OF TENANCY

To: _____

_____

_____

You are hereby notified that your tenancy of the following premises to wit:

_____

_____

_____

_____

in the County of Cook and State of Illinois, will terminate on the _____ day of _____, _____.

You are hereby required to surrender possession of the said premises to the undersigned on that day.

This notice of termination is issued based on the following: _____

_____

_____

_____

_____

_____

Date: _____, _____

_____
Lessor

_____
Agent or Attorney

PERSON SERVING NOTICE MUST COMPLETE AFFIDAVIT AND PROOF OF SERVICE ON REVERSE SIDE.

DOROTHY BROWN, CLERK OF THE CIRCUIT COURT OF COOK COUNTY, ILLINOIS

State of Illinois
County of Cook } ss:

AFFIDAVIT AND PROOF OF SERVICE

_____ , certifies and says that he/she served the foregoing

NOTICE OF TERMINATION OF TENANCY on this _____ day of _____, _____
as follows:

❑ **By personally delivering a true and correct copy to Tenant.**

❑ **By leaving a true and correct copy with** _____
a person of the age of 13 years or upwards, residing on or in the premises.

❑ **By mailing a true and correct copy to the Tenant by Certified or Registered Mail,
requesting a return receipt signed by Addressee only**

(Certified or Registered Mail Receipt No. _____ **)**

and depositing same in the U. S. Mail located at _____

_____

**Under penalties as provided by law pursuant to Section 1-109 of the Illinois Code of Civil
Procedure, the undersigned certifies that the statements set forth in this Affidavit and Proof
of Service are true and correct in substance and in fact.**

_____

COMPLAINT(JOINT ACTION) FORCIBLE DETAINER-RENT/DAMAGE CLAIMS

form 40

(Rev. 1/11/01) CCM 0020

IN THE CIRCUIT COURT OF COOK COUNTY, ILLINOIS
MUNICIPAL DEPARTMENT/DISTRICT _____

_____

v.

Plaintiff(s)

No. _____

Rent or Damage Claimed $ _____

_____

Defendant(s)

Return Date _____

COMPLAINT

The plaintiff(s) claim as follows.

1.   The plaintiff(s) is/are entitled to the possession of the following described premises in the City or Village of:

_____

_____

_____

_____

_____

_____

2.   The defendant(s) unlawfully withhold possession thereof from the plaintiff(s)_____

_____.

3.   There is due to plaintiff(s) from the defendant(s) for rent or for damages for withholding possession of said premises from _____, _____, to _____, _____ after allowing the defendant(s) all just credits, deductions and set-offs, the sum of $ _____

The plaintiff(s) claim(s) possession of the property and $ _____ as rent or damages.

Atty Code:_____

Name: _____

Attorney for: _____

Address: _____

City/Zip: _____

Telephone: _____

_____

Attorney for plaintiff(s)

I/We, _____, on oath state that I/We am/are the plaintiff(s) in the above entitled action. The allegations in this complaint are true.

_____

[x]   Under penalties as provided by law pursuant to 735 ILCS 5/1-109 the abovesigned certifies that the statements set forth herein are true and correct.

DOROTHY BROWN, CLERK OF THE CIRCUIT COURT OF COOK COUNTY, ILLINOIS

IN THE CIRCUIT COURT OF COOK COUNTY, ILLINOIS
MUNICIPAL DEPARTMENT/DISTRICT_____

_____	No. _____
v. Plaintiff(s)	
	Return Date_____
_____	
Defendant (s)	

COMPLAINT

The plaintiff(s) claim(s) as follows.

1.   The plaintiff (s) is/ are entitled to possession of the following described premises:

_____

_____

_____

2.   Defendant(s) unlawfully withhold possession of the premises from the plaintiff(s) for the following reason:

   a. The defendant(s) failed to pay rent.

   b. The defendant(s) held over after the tenancy ended.

   c. The defendant(s) breached the terms of the lease by _____

_____.

   d. _____.

         (insert specific facts showing how defendant is unlawfully withholding possession)

(Strike "2a", "2b", "2c" or "2d" , as appropriate.)

3.   The plaintiff(s) claim(s) possession of the property.

_____

             Attorney for plaintiff(s) / Plaintiff Pro-Se

I/We _____, on oath state that I/We
am/are the plaintiff(s) in the above entitled action. The allegations in this complaint are true.

Atty No.:_____

Name: _____

Attorney for:_____

Address: _____

City/Zip: _____

Telephone: _____

_____

[x] Under penalties as provided by law pursuant to 735 ILCS 5/1-109 the abovesigned certifies that the statements set forth herein are true and correct.

DOROTHY BROWN, CLERK OF THE CIRCUIT COURT OF COOK COUNTY, ILLINOIS

INDEX

Your #1 Source for Real World Legal Information...

SPHINX® PUBLISHING
An Imprint of Sourcebooks, Inc.®
- Written by lawyers
- Simple English explanation of the law
- Forms and instructions included

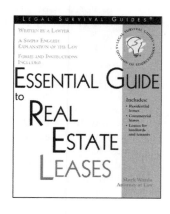

HOW TO START A BUSINESS IN ILLINOIS, 3RD ED.

For anyone starting a business, this book provides essential information on matters to business success.

240 pages; $21.95;
ISBN 1-57248-247-8

HOW TO MAKE AN ILLINOIS WILL, 3RD ED.

This book explains Illinois law regarding wills, inheritance, guardianship of children and joint property. It includes a living will.

136 pages; $16.95;
ISBN 1-57248-170-6

ESSENTIAL GUIDE TO REAL ESTATE LEASES

Do you understand every clause in a real estate contract? A standard form contract can cost you thousands of dollars in unnecessary expenses. This book explains the pitfalls and shows how you can save money.

216 pages; $18.95;
ISBN 1-57248-160-9

See the following order form for books written specifically for California, Florida, Georgia, Illinois, Massachusetts, Michigan, Minnesota, New York, North Carolina, Ohio, Pennsylvania, and Texas!

What our customers say about our books:

"It couldn't be more clear for the lay person." —R.D.

"I want you to know I really appreciate your book. It has saved me a lot of time and money." —L.T.

"Your real estate contracts book has saved me nearly $12,000.00 in closing costs over the past year." —A.B.

"...many of the legal questions that I have had over the years were answered clearly and concisely through your plain English interpretation of the law." —C.E.H.

"If there weren't people out there like you I'd be lost. You have the best books of this type out there." —S.B.

"...your forms and directions are easy to follow." —C.V.M.

Sphinx Publishing's Legal Survival Guides
are directly available from Sourcebooks, Inc., or from your local bookstores.

For credit card orders call 1–800–432–7444, write P.O. Box 4410, Naperville, IL 60567-4410,
or fax 630-961-2168

Find more legal information at: www.SphinxLegal.com

SPHINX® PUBLISHING'S NATIONAL TITLES
Valid in All 50 States

LEGAL SURVIVAL IN BUSINESS

The Complete Book of Corporate Forms	$24.95
How to Form a Limited Liability Company	$22.95
Incorporate in Delaware from Any State	$24.95
Incorporate in Nevada from Any State	$24.95
How to Form a Nonprofit Corporation (2E)	$24.95
How to Form Your Own Corporation (3E)	$24.95
How to Form Your Own Partnership (2E)	$24.95
How to Register Your Own Copyright (4E)	$24.95
How to Register Your Own Trademark (3E)	$21.95
Most Valuable Business Legal Forms You'll Ever Need (3E)	$21.95
The Small Business Owner's Guide to Bankruptcy	$21.95

LEGAL SURVIVAL IN COURT

Crime Victim's Guide to Justice (2E)	$21.95
Grandparents' Rights (3E)	$24.95
Help Your Lawyer Win Your Case (2E)	$14.95
Jurors' Rights (2E)	$12.95
Legal Research Made Easy (3E)	$21.95
Winning Your Personal Injury Claim (2E)	$24.95
Your Rights When You Owe Too Much	$16.95

LEGAL SURVIVAL IN REAL ESTATE

Essential Guide to Real Estate Contracts	$18.95
Essential Guide to Real Estate Leases	$18.95
How to Buy a Condominium or Townhome (2E)	$19.95

LEGAL SURVIVAL IN PERSONAL AFFAIRS

Cómo Hacer su Propio Testamento	$16.95
Cómo Solicitar su Propio Divorcio	$24.95
Cómo Restablecer su propio Crédito y Renegociar sus Deudas	$21.95
Guía de Inmigración a Estados Unidos (3E)	$24.95
Guía de Justicia para Víctimas del Crimen	$21.95
The 529 College Savings Plan	$16.95
How to File Your Own Bankruptcy (5E)	$21.95
How to File Your Own Divorce (4E)	$24.95
How to Make Your Own Simple Will (3E)	$18.95
How to Write Your Own Living Will (3E)	$18.95
How to Write Your Own Premarital Agreement (3E)	$24.95
Living Trusts and Other Ways to Avoid Probate (3E)	$24.95
Manual de Beneficios para el Seguro Social	$18.95
Mastering the MBE	$16.95
Most Valuable Personal Legal Forms You'll Ever Need	$24.95
Neighbor v. Neighbor (2E)	$16.95
The Nanny and Domestic Help Legal Kit	$22.95
The Power of Attorney Handbook (4E)	$19.95
Repair Your Own Credit and Deal with Debt	$18.95
The Social Security Benefits Handbook (3E)	$18.95
Social Security Q&A	$12.95
Sexual Harassment:Your Guide to Legal Action	$18.95
Teen Rights	$22.95
Unmarried Parents' Rights	$19.95
U.S. Immigration Step by Step	$21.95
U.S.A. Immigration Guide (4E)	$24.95
The Visitation Handbook	$18.95
Win Your Unemployment Compensation Claim (2E)	$21.95
Your Right to Child Custody, Visitation and Support (2E)	$24.95

Legal Survival Guides are directly available from Sourcebooks, Inc., or from your local bookstores.
Prices are subject to change without notice.

For credit card orders call 1–800–432–7444, write P.O. Box 4410, Naperville, IL 60567-4410
or fax 630-961-2168

Find more legal information at: **www.SphinxLegal.com**

SPHINX® PUBLISHING ORDER FORM

BILL TO:		SHIP TO:	
Phone #	Terms	F.O.B. Chicago, IL	Ship Date

Charge my: ☐ VISA ☐ MasterCard ☐ American Express

☐ **Money Order or Personal Check**

Credit Card Number

Expiration Date

Qty	ISBN	Title	Retail	Ext.	Qty	ISBN	Title	Retail	Ext.
		SPHINX PUBLISHING NATIONAL TITLES				1-57248-167-6	Most Valuable Bus. Legal Forms You'll Ever Need (3E)	$21.95	
	1-57248-148-X	Cómo Hacer su Propio Testamento	$16.95			1-57248-130-7	Most Valuable Personal Legal Forms You'll Ever Need	$24.95	
	1-57248-226-5	Cómo Restablecer su propio Crédito y Renegociar sus Deudas	$21.95			1-57248-098-X	The Nanny and Domestic Help Legal Kit	$22.95	
	1-57248-147-1	Cómo Solicitar su Propio Divorcio	$24.95			1-57248-089-0	Neighbor v. Neighbor (2E)	$16.95	
	1-57248-238-9	The 529 College Savings Plan	$16.95			1-57248-169-2	The Power of Attorney Handbook (4E)	$19.95	
	1-57248-166-8	The Complete Book of Corporate Forms	$24.95			1-57248-149-8	Repair Your Own Credit and Deal with Debt	$18.95	
	1-57248-163-3	Crime Victim's Guide to Justice (2E)	$21.95			1-57248-217-6	Sexual Harassment: Your Guide to Legal Action	$18.95	
	1-57248-159-5	Essential Guide to Real Estate Contracts	$18.95			1-57248-219-2	The Small Business Owner's Guide to Bankruptcy	$21.95	
	1-57248-160-9	Essential Guide to Real Estate Leases	$18.95			1-57248-168-4	The Social Security Benefits Handbook (3E)	$18.95	
	1-57248-139-0	Grandparents' Rights (3E)	$24.95			1-57248-216-8	Social Security Q&A	$12.95	
	1-57248-188-9	Guía de Inmigración a Estados Unidos (3E)	$24.95			1-57248-221-4	Teen RIghts	$22.95	
	1-57248-187-0	Guía de Justicia para Víctimas del Crimen	$21.95			1-57071-399-5	Unmarried Parents' Rights	$19.95	
	1-57248-103-X	Help Your Lawyer Win Your Case (2E)	$14.95			1-57248-161-7	U.S.A. Immigration Guide (4E)	$24.95	
	1-57248-164-1	How to Buy a Condominium or Townhome (2E)	$19.95			1-57248-192-7	The Visitation Handbook	$18.95	
	1-57248-191-9	How to File Your Own Bankruptcy (5E)	$21.95			1-57248-225-7	Win Your Unemployment Compensation Claim (2E)	$21.95	
	1-57248-132-3	How to File Your Own Divorce (4E)	$24.95			1-57248-138-2	Winning Your Personal Injury Claim (2E)	$24.95	
	1-57248-083-1	How to Form a Limited Liability Company	$22.95			1-57248-162-5	Your Right to Child Custody, Visitation and Support (2E)	$24.95	
	1-57248-231-1	How to Form a Nonprofit Corporation (2E)	$24.95			1-57248-157-9	Your Rights When You Owe Too Much	$16.95	
	1-57248-133-1	How to Form Your Own Corporation (3E)	$24.95				**CALIFORNIA TITLES**		
	1-57248-224-9	How to Form Your Own Partnership (2E)	$24.95			1-57248-150-1	CA Power of Attorney Handbook (2E)	$18.95	
	1-57248-232-X	How to Make Your Own Simple Will (3E)	$18.95			1-57248-151-X	How to File for Divorce in CA (3E)	$26.95	
	1-57248-200-1	How to Register Your Own Copyright (4E)	$24.95			1-57071-356-1	How to Make a CA Will	$16.95	
	1-57248-104-8	How to Register Your Own Trademark (3E)	$21.95			1-57248-145-5	How to Probate and Settle an Estate in California	$26.95	
	1-57248-233-8	How to Write Your Own Living Will (3E)	$18.95			1-57248-146-3	How to Start a Business in CA	$18.95	
	1-57248-156-0	How to Write Your Own Premarital Agreement (3E)	$24.95			1-57248-194-3	How to Win in Small Claims Court in CA (2E)	$18.95	
	1-57248-230-3	Incorporate in Delaware from Any State	$24.95			1-57248-196-X	The Landlord's Legal Guide in CA	$24.95	
	1-57248-158-7	Incorporate in Nevada from Any State	$24.95				**FLORIDA TITLES**		
	1-57071-333-2	Jurors' Rights (2E)	$12.95			1-57071-363-4	Florida Power of Attorney Handbook (2E)	$16.95	
	1-57248-223-0	Legal Research Made Easy (3E)	$21.95			1-57248-176-5	How to File for Divorce in FL (7E)	$26.95	
	1-57248-165-X	Living Trusts and Other Ways to Avoid Probate (3E)	$24.95			1-57248-177-3	How to Form a Corporation in FL (5E)	$24.95	
	1-57248-186-2	Manual de Beneficios para el Seguro Social	$18.95			1-57248-203-6	How to Form a Limited Liability Co. in FL (2E)	$24.95	
	1-57248-220-6	Mastering the MBE	$16.95			1-57071-401-0	How to Form a Partnership in FL	$22.95	
						Form Continued on Following Page		**SUBTOTAL**	

To order, call Sourcebooks at 1-800-432-7444 or FAX (630) 961-2168 (Bookstores, libraries, wholesalers—please call for discount)

Prices are subject to change without notice.

Find more legal information at: www.SphinxLegal.com

SPHINX® PUBLISHING ORDER FORM

Qty	ISBN	Title	Retail	Ext.
___	1-57248-113-7	How to Make a FL Will (6E)	$16.95	___
___	1-57248-088-2	How to Modify Your FL Divorce Judgment (4E)	$24.95	___
___	1-57248-144-7	How to Probate and Settle an Estate in FL (4E)	$26.95	___
___	1-57248-081-5	How to Start a Business in FL (5E)	$16.95	___
___	1-57248-204-4	How to Win in Small Claims Court in FL (7E)	$18.95	___
___	1-57248-202-8	Land Trusts in Florida (6E)	$29.95	___
___	1-57248-123-4	Landlords' Rights and Duties in FL (8E)	$21.95	___

GEORGIA TITLES

Qty	ISBN	Title	Retail	Ext.
___	1-57248-137-4	How to File for Divorce in GA (4E)	$21.95	___
___	1-57248-180-3	How to Make a GA Will (4E)	$21.95	___
___	1-57248-140-4	How to Start a Business in Georgia (2E)	$16.95	___

ILLINOIS TITLES

Qty	ISBN	Title	Retail	Ext.
___	1-57248-206-0	How to File for Divorce in IL (3E)	$24.95	___
___	1-57248-170-6	How to Make an IL Will (3E)	$16.95	___
___	1-57248-247-8	How to Start a Business in IL (3E)	$21.95	___
___	1-57248-252-4	The Landlord's Legal Guide in IL	$24.95	___

MASSACHUSETTS TITLES

Qty	ISBN	Title	Retail	Ext.
___	1-57248-128-5	How to File for Divorce in MA (3E)	$24.95	___
___	1-57248-115-3	How to Form a Corporation in MA	$24.95	___
___	1-57248-108-0	How to Make a MA Will (2E)	$16.95	___
___	1-57248-106-4	How to Start a Business in MA (2E)	$18.95	___
___	1-57248-209-5	The Landlord's Legal Guide in MA	$24.95	___

MICHIGAN TITLES

Qty	ISBN	Title	Retail	Ext.
___	1-57248-215-X	How to File for Divorce in MI (3E)	$24.95	___
___	1-57248-182-X	How to Make a MI Will (3E)	$16.95	___
___	1-57248-183-8	How to Start a Business in MI (3E)	$18.95	___

MINNESOTA TITLES

Qty	ISBN	Title	Retail	Ext.
___	1-57248-142-0	How to File for Divorce in MN	$21.95	___
___	1-57248-179-X	How to Form a Corporation in MN	$24.95	___
___	1-57248-178-1	How to Make a MN Will (2E)	$16.95	___

NEW YORK TITLES

Qty	ISBN	Title	Retail	Ext.
___	1-57248-193-5	Child Custody, Visitation and Support in NY	$26.95	___
___	1-57248-141-2	How to File for Divorce in NY (2E)	$26.95	___
___	1-57248-105-6	How to Form a Corporation in NY	$24.95	___
___	1-57248-095-5	How to Make a NY Will (2E)	$16.95	___
___	1-57248-199-4	How to Start a Business in NY (2E)	$18.95	___
___	1-57248-198-6	How to Win in Small Claims Court in NY (2E)	$18.95	___

Qty	ISBN	Title	Retail	Ext.
___	1-57248-197-8	Landlords' Legal Guide in NY	$24.95	___
___	1-57071-188-7	New York Power of Attorney Handbook	$19.95	___
___	1-57248-122-6	Tenants' Rights in NY	$21.95	___

NORTH CAROLINA TITLES

Qty	ISBN	Title	Retail	Ext.
___	1-57248-185-4	How to File for Divorce in NC (3E)	$22.95	___
___	1-57248-129-3	How to Make a NC Will (3E)	$16.95	___
___	1-57248-184-6	How to Start a Business in NC (3E)	$18.95	___
___	1-57248-091-2	Landlords' Rights & Duties in NC	$21.95	___

OHIO TITLES

Qty	ISBN	Title	Retail	Ext.
___	1-57248-190-0	How to File for Divorce in OH (2E)	$24.95	___
___	1-57248-174-9	How to Form a Corporation in OH	$24.95	___
___	1-57248-173-0	How to Make an OH Will	$16.95	___

PENNSYLVANIA TITLES

Qty	ISBN	Title	Retail	Ext.
___	1-57248-242-7	Child Custody, Visitation and Support in Pennsylvania	$26.95	___
___	1-57248-211-7	How to File for Divorce in PA (3E)	$26.95	___
___	1-57248-094-7	How to Make a PA Will (2E)	$16.95	___
___	1-57248-112-9	How to Start a Business in PA (2E)	$18.95	___
___	1-57071-179-8	Landlords' Rights and Duties in PA	$19.95	___

TEXAS TITLES

Qty	ISBN	Title	Retail	Ext.
___	1-57248-171-4	Child Custody, Visitation, and Support in TX	$22.95	___
___	1-57248-172-2	How to File for Divorce in TX (3E)	$24.95	___
___	1-57248-114-5	How to Form a Corporation in TX (2E)	$24.95	___
___	1-57248-255-9	How to Make a TX Will (3E)	$16.95	___
___	1-57248-214-1	How to Probate and Settle an Estate in TX (3E)	$26.95	___
___	1-57248-228-1	How to Start a Business in TX (3E)	$18.95	___
___	1-57248-111-0	How to Win in Small Claims Court in TX (2E)	$16.95	___
___	1-57248-110-2	Landlords' Rights and Duties in TX (2E)	$21.95	___

SUBTOTAL THIS PAGE ___

SUBTOTAL PREVIOUS PAGE ___

Shipping— $5.00 for 1st book, $1.00 each additional ___

Illinois residents add 6.75% sales tax ___

Connecticut residents add 6.00% sales tax ___

TOTAL ___

To order, call Sourcebooks at 1-800-432-7444 or FAX (630) 961-2168 (Bookstores, libraries, wholesalers—please call for discount)
Prices are subject to change without notice.
Find more legal information at: **www.SphinxLegal.com**